THE TITANIC IN MYTH AI

REPRESENTATIONS IN VISUAL AND L

The Titanic in Myth and Memory

Representations in Visual and Literary Culture

⚓

Edited by

TIM BERGFELDER

and

SARAH STREET

I.B. TAURIS

LONDON · NEW YORK

Published in 2004 by I.B. Tauris & Co Ltd
6 Salem Road, London w2 4bu
175 Fifth Avenue, New York NY 10010
www.ibtauris.com

In the United States of America and Canada distributed by
Palgrave Macmillan, a division of St. Martin's Press
175 Fifth Avenue, New York NY 10010

ISBN Hardback   1 85043 431 x
          Paperback   1 85043 432 8

A full CIP record for this book is available from the British Library
A full CIP record is available from the Library of Congress

Library of Congress Catalog Card Number: available

Designed and set by Pete Russell, Faringdon, Oxon
Printed and bound in Great Britain by TJ International Ltd, Padstow, Cornwall

Contents

Acknowledgements

THIS collection has its origins in the conference *Nights to Remember: Memory, Modernity and the Myth of the Titanic* which took place at the University of Southampton over three days in July 2000, bringing together Titanic scholars from all over the world. As such, our greatest debt is to the conference director Pam Cook, who first came up with the idea of a multidisciplinary academic gathering on the topic of Titanic, and who had the intellectual and creative energy to make it happen. It is to a great extent due to her inspiration, and not least her hard work in preparing the event, that the conference became the stimulating, collegial, and pleasurable experience that it was, as surely everyone who was present will agree. Pam has remained throughout the genesis of this collection an important mentor, and has given her unfaltering support to it in many different ways, for which we are immensely grateful. We thus dedicate this book to Pam.

Further thanks are due to the Conference Administrator Jo Wilcock, and the original Conference Organising Committee, which included Deniz Göktürk, Mike Hammond, and Lucy Mazdon, as well as many other colleagues in the School of Modern Languages and the Faculty of Arts at Southampton who helped with the event. From outside, Simon Brown, Ludo Craddock, Simon Mills, Jeffrey Richards, and Michael Wedel provided invaluable advice and support. Without the generous financial aid and sponsorship of The British Academy, the Faculty of Arts at the University of Southampton, the Goethe Institute London, Southern Arts, and W&G Baird Ltd., Belfast, the conference and the present book, would have been impossible.

In the process of transforming a series of articles into the present collection, our thanks go to Philippa Brewster and Deborah Susman at I. B. Tauris, and to Peter Russell for designing and typesetting the manuscript. For their assistance with illustrations, we are grateful to our contributors, Sarah Hammond, Dimos Glynos, the British Film Institute, the Filmmuseum Berlin—Deutsche Kinemathek, and Marian Stefanowski.

Notes on Contributors

TIM BERGFELDER is Senior Lecturer at the University of Southampton, where he teaches Film Studies. He has published on aspects of German and British cinema, particularly on the impact and influence of European émigrés, and on the practice of European co-productions. He is the author of *International Adventures. Popular German Cinema and European Co-productions in the 1960s* (Berghahn, forthcoming), and co-editor (with Erica Carter and Deniz Gök-türk) of *The German Cinema Book* (BFI, 2002).

PETER BJÖRKFORS has long been interested in the cultural and sociological aspects of the Titanic disaster. He graduated from Åbo Akademi University, Turku, Finland in 2002 with the thesis: *'Be British!' The Titanic Disaster and Projections of British Nationalism, 1912. A Study in National Imagology*.

K. J. DONNELLY is Lecturer in the Department of Theatre, Film and Television at the University of Wales, Aberystwyth. His research is on film and television music, as well as British and Irish cinema. He is author of *Pop Music in British Cinema* (BFI, 2001) and editor of *Film Music* (Edinburgh University Press, 2001).

ALAN FINLAYSON is Lecturer in the Department of Politics and International Relations at the University of Wales, Swansea where he teaches unsuspecting students about the politics of media with much reference to popular cinema. He co-edited *Politics and Poststructuralism: An Introduction* (Edinburgh University Press, 2002) and edited *Contemporary Political Theory: A Reader and Guide* (Edinburgh University Press, 2003). His most recent monograph is *Making Sense of New Labour* (Lawrence and Wishart, 2003).

JOHN WILSON FOSTER was Professor of English at the University of British Columbia until he took early retirement in 2002 to research and write full-time. His recent books include *Titanic* (Penguin, 1999), *The Age of Titanic* (Merlin, 2002) and *Recoveries: Neglected Episodes in Irish Cultural History 1860–1912* (University College Dublin Press, 2002). He is editor of *The Cambridge Companion to the Irish Novel* (forthcoming).

DAVID A. GERSTNER is Assistant Professor and Program Coordinator of Cinema Studies at City University of New York, College of Staten Island. He has published in *Film Quarterly, The Stanford Humanities Review, CineAction, The Velvet Light Trap*, and *Cultural Critique*. He is co-editor with Janet Staiger of *Authorship and Film* (Routledge 2002).

MICHAEL HAMMOND is Lecturer in Film Studies at the University of Southampton. He has published widely on silent British and contemporary

American cinema, and is the author of *The Big Show. British Cinema Culture in the Great War* (forthcoming). He is co-editor of two further forthcoming books, *American Cinema since 1965* (with Linda Williams), and *Previously On: Approaches to the Contemporary Television Serial* (with Lucy Mazdon).

JOHN HILL is Professor of Media Studies at the University of Ulster. He is the author, co-author, or co-editor of a number of books on British and Irish cinema, including *Sex, Class, and Realism: British Cinema 1956–1963* (BFI 1986), *Border Crossing: Film in Ireland, Britain and Europe* (with Martin McLoone and Paul Hainsworth 1994); and *British Cinema in the 1980s: Issues and Themes* (OUP 1999). He is also co-editor, with Pamela Church Gibson, of *The Oxford Guide to Film Studies* (OUP 1998). John Hill is currently completing a book (for the BFI) on the history of the cinema and Northern Ireland.

ALASDAIR KING is Senior Lecturer in German and Film Studies at the University of Portsmouth, UK. His main research interests include German national cinema, contemporary European cinema, and critical theory. He has published articles on National Socialist cinema and its audiences and on space and place in the 1950s Heimatfilm. He is currently completing a book, *Hans Magnus Enzensberger: Writing, Media, Democracy* (Peter Lang, forthcoming).

PETER KRÄMER teaches Film Studies at the University of East Anglia, Norwich. He has published essays on American film and media history, and on the relationship between Hollywood and Europe, in numerous journals and edited collections. Together with Alan Lovell, he co-edited *Screen Acting* (Routledge, 1999). He is currently working on *The Big Picture: Hollywood Cinema from Star Wars to Titanic*, to be published by the BFI, and *The New Hollywood: From Bonnie and Clyde to Star Wars* (for Wallflower Press).

PAUL MALONE is Assistant Professor of German in the Department of Germanic and Slavic Studies at the University of Waterloo, Canada. In addition to his book, *Franz Kafka's The Trial: Four Stage Adaptations* (Peter Lang, 2003), he has published on literature, film, theatre, and virtual reality computer technology, and is currently the editor of *Germano-Slavica: A Canadian Journal of Germanic and Slavic Comparative and Interdisciplinary Studies*.

PETER MIDDLETON is Reader in English at the University of Southamp-ton. He is the author of *The Inward Gaze: Masculinity and Subjectivity in Modern Culture* (Routledge, 1992) and (with Tim Woods) *Literatures of Memory* (Man-chester UP, 2000). A collection of essays on poetics is forthcoming from Alabama UP, and a selection of poems from Salt. He has also published many essays on modern and contemporary literature, and is currently finishing a book on science and poetry in modern America.

ROBERT PECK is Senior Lecturer in Film and Media at the University of

Westminster. He has published articles in *The Historical Journal of Film, Radio and Television*, *Media History*, and *Media, Culture and Society* on aspects of German media history, and is a contributor to the forthcoming *Encyclopaedia of the Documentary Film*.

SEAN REDMOND is Senior Lecturer in Film Studies at Southampton Institute, UK. He is co-editor of *The Cinema of Kathryn Bigelow* (Wallflower Press, 2003) and editor of *Liquid Metal: The Science Fiction Film Reader* (Wallflower Press, forthcoming). His main research interests are in the cultural representations of whiteness and cinematic transgression.

SARAH STREET is Reader in Screen Studies at the University of Bristol. She has written extensively on British cinema, as co-author (with Margaret Dickinson) of *Cinema and State: The Film Industry and the British Government* (1985), and as author of *British National Cinema* (1997), *British Cinema in Documents* (2000) and *Transatlantic Crossings: British Feature Films in the USA* (2002). She has co-edited two collections, (with Linda Fitzsimmons) *Moving Performance: British Stage and Screen* (2000) and (with Jill Forbes) *European Cinema: An Introduction*.

GAYLYN STUDLAR is Rudolf Arnheim Collegiate Professor of Film Studies at the University of Michigan, Ann Arbor, where she has directed the Program in Film and Video Studies since 1995. She is author of *This Mad Masquerade: Stardom and Masculinity in the Jazz Age* (1996) and *In the Realm of Pleasure: Von Sternberg, Dietrich, and the Masochistic Aesthetic* (1988) as well as numerous articles. She is also the co-editor of four volumes, including, most recently, *John Ford Made Westerns: Filming the Legend in the Sound Era* (2001) and *Titanic: Anatomy of a Blockbuster* (1999).

SUSAN SYDNEY-SMITH is Senior Lecturer in Film and Media Studies in the Department of Historical and Critical Studies at the University of Central Lancashire. She is the author of *Beyond Dixon of Dock Green: Early British Police Series* (I. B. Tauris, 2002) and co-editor of *Relocating Britishness* (MUP, forthcoming).

RICHARD TAYLOR is Professor of Politics at the University of Wales, Swansea. He has written numerous books and articles on Russian and Soviet cinema, but this is his first encounter with an iceberg. He edited the five-volume English-language edition of Eisenstein's writings for the BFI (1988–98). His last two books have been studies of Eisenstein's *The Battleship Potemkin* (I.B. Tauris, 2001) and *October* (BFI Film Classics, 2002). He and Alan Finlayson co-teach modules on politics and the media, and especially cinema, at Swansea.

MICHAEL WEDEL teaches in the Department of Media Studies at the Hochschule für Film und Fernsehen 'Konrad Wolf' in Potsdam-Babelsberg, Germany. His articles on early cinema, German film history and contemporary Hollywood have appeared in a number of edited collections and in journals such as *Film History*, *Iris*, and *New German Critique*. He is co-editor (with Thomas Elsaesser) of *A Second Life. German Cinema's First Decades* (Amsterdam University Press, 1996), *The BFI Companion to German Cinema* (BFI, 1999) and *Kino der Kaiserzeit. Zwischen Tradition und Moderne* (edition text + kritik, 2002).

MARK J. P. WOLF is Associate Professor in the Communication Department at Concordia University, Wisconsin. His books as author and editor include *Abstracting Reality: Art, Communication, and Cognition in the Digital Age* (University Press of America, 2000), *The Medium of the Video Game* (University of Texas Press 2002), *Virtual Reality: Morals, Ethics and New Media* (Peter Lang, forthcoming), and *The Video Game Theory Reader* (co-edited with Bernard Perron). He has also published work in several scholarly journals and written a novel.

KENNETH WOMACK is Associate Professor of English and Head of the Division of Arts and Humanities at Penn State University's Altoona College. He serves as editor of *Interdisciplinary Literary Studies: A Journal of Criticism and Theory* and as co-editor (with William Baker) of *Oxford University Press's Year's Work in English Studies*. He is the author of *Postwar Academic Fiction: Satire, Ethics, Community* (Palgrave, 2001), the co-author (with Ruth Robbins and Julian Wolfreys) of *Key Concepts in Literary Theory* (Columbia, 2002), and the co-editor (with Baker) of the Broadview Press edition of Ford Madox Ford's *The Good Soldier* (2003).

AYLISH WOOD is Lecturer in Film Studies at the University of Kent. She is the author of *Technoscience in Contemporary American Film: Beyond Science Fiction* (Manchester University Press, 2002).

TIM WOODS is Head of Department and Senior Lecturer in English and American Studies at the University of Wales, Aberystwyth. His main research interests are in literary theory, American poetry and poetics, twentieth century literatures, and African literature. He has published *Beginning Theory* (1999), *Literatures of Memory* (with Peter Middleton, 2000), *Who's Who of Twentieth-Century Novelists* (2001), *The Poetics of the Limit* (2002), and jointly edited *'I'm telling you stories': Jeanette Winterson and the Politics of Reading* (1998), *Critical Ethics* (1999), and *The Ethics in Literature* (1999). He is the series general editor of *Representing American Events* (Edinburgh University Press) and he is currently writing a book entitled *African Pasts: History and Memory in African Literature* (to be published in 2004).

Introduction

TIM BERGFELDER and SARAH STREET

SINCE its fateful maiden voyage and sinking in April 1912, the Titanic has become a monumental icon of the 20th century, and perhaps more generally of the aspirations and anxieties of modernity. The name of the ship itself has entered vernacular language to become a byword of both human hubris and heroism, and of misguided trust in the securities of modern technology. The Titanic's sinking has been interpreted as signalling the end of the imperial, 19th century world order and as a premonition of World War One. Indeed, apart from the main dates associated with the two World Wars in the first half of the century, and the demise of the Eastern Bloc near the end of it, there have been few other historical caesura in the 20th century that have imposed such a marked distinction between 'before' and 'after' in the collective historical imagination of the West. In this respect the Titanic tragedy and its reception has found an eerie echo at the beginning of the 21st century in the way the attack on the World Trade Centre in 2001 has been seen to mark a historical turning point, seemingly collapsing in a single catastrophic event previously held certainties, boundaries, and values, and raising doubts and anxieties over what may eventually distinguish the world after the catastrophe from what has come before. In the case of Titanic, which might well serve as both precedent and template for future interpretations of '9/11', growing temporal distance has made it difficult to reconnect to the realities of the actual event, and to recapture the traumatic effect it had on the survivors, as well as on countless relatives of perished passengers and crew. Nevertheless, memories of this effect (as well as a diminishing constituency of those personally affected) still persist today, particularly in the cities of Belfast and Southampton, where respectively the Titanic was built and set sail for New York on its maiden voyage. Nearly a century on, the legacy of the Titanic still very much remains part of the psychological fabric, collective self-perception, and external promotion of these communities.

On the other hand, it is precisely the passing of time, the receding of personal involvement, memory and grief, and thus the event's abstraction from private and local histories, that have heightened Titanic's status as a mythical object and as a symbolic event on a more international scale. Titanic has inspired a great wealth of representations across different art forms and media, and across a multitude of different national and cultural contexts. The tragedy has been appropriated to articulate and justify a wide spectrum of ideological positions on issues such as class, gender, national identity, capitalism and

media manipulation, political propaganda, and collective mourning and remembrance. The history of the Titanic is thus a prism which facilitates an
almost infinite range of different stories to be narrativised. Moreover, Titanic
continues to engage and fascinate new generations, witnessed for example by
the phenomenal box office success of James Cameron's Hollywood fictionalisation *Titanic* (1997), the global industry and receptive market for Titanic
memorabilia, which is as thriving as ever and shows no signs of abating, or the
arguably morbid proposals to make the site of the sunken wreck a tourist
destination for international thrill-seekers. Thus, while the Titanic is frequently perceived to relate to a closing door on 19th century values, it is also very
much a symbol of 20th century experience, whose continuing fascination
thrives on heritage tourism and consumerism, but, not least, also on a plethora of cultural meditations and representations which articulate different, and
continuing, meanings of the tragedy.

The aim of *The Titanic in Myth and Memory* is to provide an account of the
variety, in terms of cultural medium, historical chronology, and national context, of perceptions and representations of the Titanic disaster. It is widely
acknowledged that James Cameron's film played a crucial role in re-energising
and multiplying an interest in the Titanic from the late 1990s onwards. This
present anthology, however, aspires to a historically and culturally more in-
clusive perspective, which allows for Cameron's film to be appreciated in its
lineage from, and in comparison with, a variety of other representations. It is
striking how quickly the Titanic became embedded within visual and literary
culture from immediately after the disaster in the form of contemporary
reportage, photographs of anxious relatives waiting for news at the White Star
Line offices, the multitudes of illustrations depicting the ship's collision with
the iceberg, publication of the official inquiries and imaginative, filmic and literary meditations on the ship's sinking. Indeed the Titanic was, as several
authors in this collection demonstrate, in the popular imagination many years
before the actual disaster occurred, in the form of articles and books about ships
colliding with icebergs, providing eerie testament to the many premonitions
people subsequently confessed to have experienced before the event. In this
sense the Titanic is a cultural phenomenon whose many and varied facets can
only be adequately grasped from a multidisciplinary perspective.

With this perspective in mind, *The Titanic in Myth and Memory* draws on the
expertise of scholars from different academic disciplines, including history,
film and cultural studies, and literary studies. We hope that this approach
facilitates the perception of similarities and connections as well as differences
in the way subsequent generations of artists and audiences (which includes
critics and academics as well as Titanic enthusiasts) have made sense of, and
utilised, the Titanic tragedy. In this respect, the book differs in its approach
and methodology from previous publications on the topic, which have fre-

quently concentrated more on historically or culturally focussed or medium-specific aspects.[1] By contrast, this anthology aims to show not only how the Titanic disaster has been represented in a range of different media, but also how it has been adapted and translated in a variety of cultural contexts into nationally specific and meaningful responses.

While, as we have argued above, the Titanic's sinking has reverberated far beyond its immediate local context, it is notable that this impact has not been distributed equally across the globe, nor has the reception of the event been the same in different cultures. First, despite its seemingly universal themes, Titanic is not necessarily a universal myth. It is a myth predominantly created and sustained over the decades by the West, extending beyond its transatlantic associations primarily where countries and individuals from outside have wished to partake in this particular Western heritage by proxy. A recent example of such cultural mimicry have been South African and Japanese initiatives in the 1990s to build replicas of Titanic for themed tourist experiences.[2] Meanwhile, the two countries which have seen the most prolific cultural responses to the disaster, and which continue to produce them, are unsurprisingly those that were originally most affected by it, Great Britain and the United States. The cultural responses from these two countries since 1912, ranging from high literature (Thomas Hardy, Joseph Conrad, H. G. Wells, Virginia Woolf, Beryl Bainbridge, Julian Barnes, among many others) and experimental musical compositions (Gavin Bryars, Ronan Magill) to cartoons and popular songs of America's hit music factory Tin-Pan Alley, have been comprehensively mapped by Steven Biel's *Down with the Old Canoe: A Cultural History of the Titanic Disaster* (largely for the American context), and by John Wilson Foster's *The Titanic Complex* (mainly on the British context).[3] Given the vast number and diversity of cultural expressions and ideological positions charted in these two books (among a plethora of other collections, monographs, and journal articles), it would be too simplistic to define an easily classifiable American or British 'take' on Titanic. Nonetheless, if one wished to indicate at least some broad trends and tendencies, American appropriations and commentaries appear to have interpreted the event more often as an opportunity for the levelling of class boundaries and thus as a lesson in social progress, invariably embodied by the promise of the American dream (in this respect, then, James Cameron's film constitutes only the latest in a long line of similar interpretations), whereas in British responses a more elegiac, commemorative, and melancholy tone has prevailed.

Apart from Britain and America, the countries where Titanic has made a comparably profound cultural impact appear to have been especially those that share all or some of the following characteristics which connect them, or have connected them in the past, to a transatlantic axis – a significant heritage of ship building and maritime trade; a dominantly Protestant culture built on the moral privileging of self-denial and civil duty; a long history of sustained emigration to America; and present or past aspirations towards, or possession of, naval power. These criteria may provide at least a partial explanation for the proliferation of cultural responses to the Titanic in Scandinavia and Germany (which qualifies for all the characteristics above), as opposed to the relative paucity of representations in France or other Southern European countries. France may have competed in the first half of the 20th century with Britain and Germany in the transatlantic shipping trade, yet it could confidently rely on a national maritime counter-symbol to the Titanic, the ocean liner Normandie, which contrasted Titanic's myth of lamentable but honourable class tragedy with an optimistic paean to French craftsmanship.[4]

German culture, by contrast, appears to have been drawn especially to the socially apocalyptic and elementally human dimensions of the Titanic myth, and has, in the process, contributed some of the artistically most ambitious expressions to the Titanic canon. As in Britain and America, the trope of the sinking transatlantic ocean liner as a metaphor of both cataclysmic social change (which would come true for Germany in the radical political overhaul following the end of World War One), and of the shifting cultural hierarchies between Europe and the United States, preceded the actual Titanic disaster by some time. The publication of Gerhart Hauptmann's novel *Atlantis* (1912), in which the main protagonist survives the sinking of an ocean liner on his journey to America, for example, quite spectacularly coincided with the breaking news about Titanic (the book's unexpected topicality led to a film adaptation the following year, by the Danish company Nordisk). In fact, the narrative had first been conceived by the author during a transatlantic passage dating back to 1894, and articulated, as Deniz Göktürk has argued, the author's deep ambivalences about the United States in general, and the prospect of a future dominated by American popular culture in particular.[5] Transatlantic traffic by ship also features in Franz Kafka's novel fragment *Amerika*, the uncharacteristic utopianism of which contrasts markedly with Hauptmann's suspicions about American culture. Although the final text lacks any direct reference to the Titanic, Kafka was an avid reader of travelogues and thus undoubtedly familiar with the details of the tragedy, when he wrote the majority of the text in the year of the disaster, 1912.[6] In the same year, Thomas Mann, whose patrician Hanseatic family history is inextricably bound up with maritime trade, began work on his novel *Der Zauberberg* (*The Magic Mountain*). This novel not only features, as Alan Bance has pointed out, a main protagonist whose background is in ship engineering, but also the societal microcosm of an Alpine sanatorium which is compared with the doomed ocean liner. According to one of the novel's characters, the ship's trajectory charts in Freudian analogy 'the precarious life-journey of the individual ego borne along above the unfathomable depths of the unconscious'.[7]

Arguably the most significant representation of the Titanic in visual art, too, originates in Germany in 1912, with Max Beckmann's *The Sinking of the Titanic*. Beckmann's painting interestingly emphasises not the ship (which sinks, barely noticed, in the distant background), but, in a knowing homage to Géricault's famous *The Raft of the Medusa*, it concentrates on the chaos that emanates from the lifeboats in which the survivors are huddled together. Reviewing a recent retrospective of Beckmann's work, Charles Darwent has pointed not only to some fundamental differences between the two paintings, but also to the debt that Beckmann's representation owes to established traditions in German art. In doing so, Darwent identifies some of the characteristics of German Titanic representations more generally:

> Where the passengers on Géricault's *The Raft of the Medusa* are lent a kind of dignity as actors in a political allegory, Beckmann's are merely wet and scared. Heroism here doesn't lie in power, but in the acceptance of powerlessness: a tendency in German art that can be traced back to medieval depictions of Christ as a Man of Sorrows, bloodied and bowed, in works like Grünewald's Isenheim altarpiece.[8]

As in Britain and the United States, then, German artistic engagements with the Titanic disaster have covered not only a wide spectrum of cultural hierarchies and media (ranging from the distinctly high-brow examples referred to above to popular cartoons, and films), but also of political viewpoints, ranging from the left-wing scepticism of Hans Magnus Enzensberger, via Thomas Mann's bourgeois humanism, to the Nazi propaganda of Herbert Selpin's film version of the disaster in 1943. It is precisely this diversity that this anthology aims to capture and analyse.

The Titanic in Myth and Memory is subdivided into three major sections. Part One covers general historical issues as well as literary adaptations, and opens with two contributions on the local reception of the disaster in Belfast and Southampton, cities inextricably tied up with the ship in terms of labour, respectively shipbuilding, and providing crew. John Hill's discussion of the links between the Titanic and Belfast (dubbed 'Titanic Town') shows how the memory of the ship can be related to specific issues of class, religion and national identification that are pertinent to Northern Ireland. Michael Hammond, meanwhile, not only addresses the impact the disaster had on the city of Southampton, the port of Titanic's departure, but he also analyses the symbolism of memorial imagery (exemplified by the format of the newspaper cartoon, and of memorial sculpture), and memorial rhetoric (as in contemporary news reports), as well as their contribution to local attempts in coming to terms with the tragedy. Hammond frames these responses within and across the contrasting registers of modernism and melodrama. Hill's and Hammond's locally specific analyses are followed by a study by John Wilson Foster on how contemporary discourses on occultism and the supernatural (primarily centred on the British context) were employed in narratives about the disaster. Foster reminds us that the sinking of the Titanic coincided with a decline in Christianity and rise of spiritualism, providing many with an other-worldly imperative to interpret the event as a vector for anti-materialist sentiment. Foster's chapter details in particular how journalist and spiritualist W. T. Stead, author of a story published in 1886 in the *Pall Mall Gazette*, predicted the fate of the Titanic. After Stead drowned when the Titanic sank (ironically *en route* to a spiritualist convention) spiritualists claimed to have communicated with him from beyond the grave.

The remaining contributions in this section engage with a number of literary responses to the Titanic, which amount, as the title of Peter Middleton and Tim Woods' chapter suggests, to an archive of 20th century memory, seen through the prism of historical trauma. In terms of chronology the two popular Scandinavian novels, one Swedish, one Finnish, discussed by Peter Björkfors, constitute some of the earliest entries in this archive, since they were published soon after the tragedy. As Björkfors argues, by making their central protagonists respectively Swedish and Finnish, the novels allowed their nationally targeted readership a greater degree of identification with the disaster, while also channelling nationally distinctive contemporary attitudes and beliefs about issues ranging from national stereotypes and prejudices, emigration, and moral conventions. Peter Middleton and Tim Woods are particularly interested in the accumulative effect of successive literary engagements with the Titanic, and especially those which, as most prominently in Titanic lore Walter Lord's *A Night To Remember* (1955), create and perpetuate in their blurring of fiction and fact what the chapter terms 'textual memory'. As Middleton and Woods argue, a textual memory based on trauma, as in the case of the Titanic, can function both as a therapeutic and, in a negative sense, as a mind-numbing anaesthetic to displace and repress mentally the conditions of (post-)modernity:

Theories of repression and trauma are compelling because they offer solutions to the detemporalisation and anachronisms of modern experiences of spacetime, bypassing or inverting causality in the *Nachträglichkeit* of hindsight, but these solutions also easily collude with or wholly give in to dominant narratives of history.

Kenneth Womack provides a more optimistic approach to the therapeutic use value of the Titanic myth as a kind of post-traumatic *Bildungsroman* (a frame of reference used in a later contribution by Susan Sydney-Smith), and he correlates the literary representation of the Titanic disaster with current diagnostic and therapeutic strategies in the area of 'survival psychology'. Womack's chapter opens with a useful summary of some of the many recent literary adaptations of the Titanic story (ranging from the sublime to the ridiculous), before analysing in greater depth three contemporary fictionalisations by Cynthia Bass, Robert Olen Butler, and Beryl Bainbridge. In all three texts

Womack identifies explicit attempts at ideologically repositioning and re-purposing the Titanic myth for a contemporary readership, attempts which also chart the myth's transfer from being a quintessentially modern(ist) event to becoming a post-modern one.

Alasdair King's contribution discusses one of the formally most unusual literary responses to the Titanic, and moreover a text that looks as much backwards to the heyday of modernist euphoria and hope as forwards to the uncertainties of post-modernity, Hans-Magnus Enzensberger's epic, book-length poem *Der Untergang der Titanic* (*The Sinking of the Titanic*, 1978). As King documents, Enzensberger employs the narrative of the sinking ocean liner as a metaphor for the failing utopian aspirations of the left-leaning West German intelligentsia in the 1970s. Beyond this nationally and historically specific context, however, Enzensberger's understanding of the Titanic disaster, and of the notion of social apocalypse more generally, appears to share the postmodernism of a Jean Baudrillard, when he argues that apocalypse is simultaneously 'omnipresent', yet 'not real'. However, unlike Baudrillard who postulates a break between the past and an apocalyptic future, Enzensberger uses the Titanic disaster to demonstrate that the notion of apocalypse (the 'catastrophe in our heads') is, as King argues, a 'transhistorical' and 'enduring' phenomenon. In this respect, then, Enzensberger's appropriation of the Titanic disaster simultaneously adopts postmodernist literary techniques (most notably the use of falsifications, fragments, and pastiches of historical authenticity), and at the same time provides a critique of postmodern historiography.

Part Two introduces filmic adaptations made before Cameron's landmark film in 1997, including case studies from Britain, Germany, and the United States. As several authors argue in this section, the Titanic's fate was rapidly taken up after the event by the burgeoning film industries in Europe and the United States.[9] Moreover, the disaster and the earliest cinematic Titanic adaptations occurred precisely at the crucial historical moment at which film turned from being a technological novelty and fairground attraction towards becoming the most dominant form of mass entertainment and medium of news dissemination in the 20th century. In this respect, the history of the Titanic myth and the history of cinema, both as a narrative and representational medium, and as a public sphere, are closely intertwined, as Michael Hammond argues elsewhere in this collection. It is this historical conjuncture that is also the central theme of Michael Wedel's discussion of the long believed lost, and only recently rediscovered German film *In Night and Ice* (1912), which, while not being the first ever Titanic film, was shot only months after the actual event. Wedel's chapter thus illustrates how quickly global mythologisation and fictionalisation followed the tragedy.

Subsequent adaptations, too, have coincided with significant moments not only in general, but also in film history. Thus, as discussed by Robert Peck here, the Anglo-German co-production *Atlantic* (1929, based on a well-known stage play and shot in three different language versions) was the first of many such multi-lingual films made after the introduction of sound, with which European film industries hoped to compete with Hollywood. In this economic and cultural dynamic, the Titanic myth provided a suitably spectacular as well as transnationally appealing subject. Paul M. Malone's contribution, by contrast, concerns *Titanic* (1943), a film version produced during World War II by the Nazis as a vehicle for anti-British sentiment. The film's extraordinary production history (which culminated in the director's death in Gestapo custody) and its subsequent exhibition and reception, demonstrates on the one hand the topic's susceptibility to tendentious propaganda, but on the other it documents the Titanic myth's ability to transcend, or even resist, its functionalisation by ideology. Thus, although originally intended to represent and criticise British hubris and arrogance, *Titanic* ultimately reflected back on the hubris and political defeat of the regime that commissioned it.

The 1950s witnessed the release of the two best known film adaptations prior to Cameron, the Hollywood-produced *Titanic* (1953), and the British *A Night To Remember* (1958). Although released in the political climate of the Cold War, and coinciding with the gradual decline of film as a mass medium and the ascendancy of television, these two films reflect their historical context more obliquely, and instead primarily raise issues of gender and class. Sarah Street demonstrates, for example, that the ship's spatial design was used in *A Night to Remember* as a geographic map of the class structures of Edwardian England. A detailed analysis of the film reveals the extent to which it deploys a striking use of realist conventions that are both spectacular and political. In its episodic structure, so typical of contemporary British films, *A Night to Remember* adhered closely to the details in Walter Lord's book, notably resisting the temptation to develop a fictional narrative along the lines of Cameron's focus on Jack and Rose. Yet, as Street's chapter reveals, the film retains a sense of suspense and tragedy that has been difficult to follow. As this and other British films of the period developed themes of class identity and antagonism, Richard Taylor and Alan Finlayson show how the American *Titanic* provided a key register of contemporary discourses on gender, as well as demonstrating, in its antipathy towards Europe, the extent to which isolationist politics persisted in 1950s America. However, one could argue that by assigning the film's most acerbically intelligent, and self-reflective, dialogue to the snobbish pro-European sentiment articulated by the film's most charismatic, if also most effeminate, character, leaves the film with a somewhat conflicting ideological message about both national identity and normative masculinity in the United States of the 1950s.

In sum, this section documents how filmic representations fast appropriated the disaster as entertainment and (not always unambiguous) propaganda, providing Cameron with a wealth of images, narrative conventions, and dramatic constellations, many of which he drew upon for his Hollywood blockbuster. A frame of comparative reference that is striking is filmic claims to 'authenticity', particularly in the use of various technologies to depict the giant ship. While early film representations drew on the scant amount of actual footage of the ship and on illustrations from the popular press, later ones embarked on a quest to depict the event as 'accurately' as possible. Charting the ship's demise through celluloid therefore provides a fascinating register of film styles and technologies that are frequently invited to rise to the 'realist' challenge of depicting the monumental ship in a way that does justice to the popular imagination. This section shows how this mix, also influenced by generic and national traditions, produced intriguing and distinguished precursors to Cameron's film.

Part Three is about the blockbuster *Titanic* (1997), and addresses a number of theoretical issues, such as race, national identity, masculinity, genre, and technology. These essays complement the material produced on Cameron's film in Gaylyn Studlar and Kevin S. Sandler's book *Anatomy of a Blockbuster*, bringing into focus themes relating to ideological context, theoretical insights and the issue of technology which was at the heart of the film's promotion. Above all, this film, with its fictional love-story and use of contemporary film stars, brought the 20th century popular fascination with the Titanic to the surface again. Inspired by Walter Lord's book *A Night to Remember*, and the British film of the same name, as these contributors illustrate, Cameron's film delivered an adaptation of the event in a manner which addressed contem-porary audiences. At the same time, as both Gaylyn Studlar's and Peter Krämer's contributions stress, the film is impossible to understand without acknowledging its deep roots in the conventions of classical Hollywood story-telling and marketing.

Concerns with class, race and 'otherness', as well as with feminism and gender, were key elements of this film's blockbuster status and box-office success. Different critical positions have resulted from analysing this film. For example, while in the accounts of Susan Sydney-Smith and Sean Redmond the character Rose appears as a proto-feminist 'new woman' of the 20th century, for Gerstner she is the result of masculine influence, ingenuity and power. Sydney-Smith and Redmond compare *Titanic* to British 'heritage' films, identifying a similar concern to depict the past in such a way that meets audiences' expectations of a particular period, creating a myth of the past regardless of whether this is accurate or not. As well as via the aesthetic conventions of the heritage film, the *Titanic* phenomenon can also be linked to heritage tourism, with its generation of commodities (posters, the 'Heart of the Ocean' necklace', CDs, key-rings, pens and models of the ship) that are seen, paradoxically, to relate to a by-gone era of safety and security. Cameron's film therefore taps into this trend, resulting in a seductive *mise-en-scène* that has fuelled a desire to possess artefacts that have been created as 'Past Times' commodities. While the film is critical of class structures which are identified with Europe, at the same time it displays the possessions of the rich as desirable, feeding into a materialist culture. This contradictory address makes the film such an apt case-study of how the Titanic myth is 're-written' by different generations.

Another key theme in this section is the impact of new technology on the representation of the disaster, enabling, as Aylish Wood argues, narrative forms that showcase special effects as spectacular interventions in their own right. In their construction, however, Mark J. P. Wolf demonstrates that the special effects nevertheless underscore the film's claims to emotional realism. From different perspectives both K. J. Donnelly and Peter Krämer discuss how the film's musical soundtrack relates to genre, film history and to conceptions of 'otherness' in the film. The consumerist dimensions of the Titanic, in terms of creating an industry of memorabilia which taps into economic aspects of 'heritage', are further highlighted by Donnelly in his discussion of the commodification of 'Irishness'. This process is most apparent in the film's use of Irish music, emphasising an aspect of the disaster (the fate of the Irish passengers) that was not foregrounded in previous film accounts. Indeed, the public's insatiable curiosity about aspects of the disaster that was first evident in 1912 continues to dominate the reception of this film, a trend that is likely to increase in the build-up to the centenary of the disaster in 2012.

We hope that this book will therefore serve several useful purposes. Its stress on multidisciplinary work across visual and literary representations that have spanned more than a century illustrates a range of responses to what can be described, in Hayden White's terms, as a 'modernist event'.[10] From the moment contemporary accounts proliferated, the disaster became mythologised by the numerous representations discussed in this collection, rendering the Titanic 'visible' through a plethora of books, films, illustrations and memories. Yet these accounts are not mere 'fictions', the most elaborate being Cameron's film, with its tension between melodrama and quest for 'realism'. Rather, they are indeed traces of popular fascinations, imaginations and identities, elements that are as much a part of history as more celebrated occurrences. In this sense, the myth and memory of the Titanic remain a strong force in contemporary culture.

Notes

1 For example, Kevin S. Sandler and Gaylyn Studlar (eds.), *Titanic: Anatomy of a Blockbuster* (New Brunswick, New Jersey and London, 1999); Richard Howells, *The Myth of the Titanic* (London, 1999); Werner Köster and Thomas Lischeid (eds.), *Titanic: Ein Medienmythos* (Leipzig, 1999), and Stephen Bottomore, *The Titanic and Silent Cinema* (Hastings, 2000).

2 John Wilson Foster, 'Recent Media Treatments of the Titanic Tragedy', in *Material History Review*, 48 (Fall 1998), p.182.

3 Steven Biel, *Down with the Old Canoe: A Cultural History of the Titanic Disaster* (New York, 1996); John Wilson Foster, *'Titanic Complex': A Cultural Manifest* (Vancouver, 1997). Cf. also Foster's other titles *Titanic* (Harmondsworth, 1999); and *The Age of Titanic* (London, 2002).

4 With grateful thanks to Jackie Clarke who suggested this contrast to us.

5 Deniz Göktürk, *'Atlantis oder: Vom Sinken der Kultur'*, in *Künstler, Cowboys, Ingenieure. Kultur- und mediengeschichtliche Studien zu deutschen Amerika-Texten, 1912–1920* (Munich, 1998), pp. 38–79.

6 According to his biographer Klaus Wagenbach, 1912 was one of the most productive and creative years of Kafka's writing career, see Klaus Wagenbach, *Franz Kafka* (Reinbek, 1979), pp.74–88.

7 Alan Bance, 'Has Thomas run out of steam? Did Hans ever finish reading *Ocean Steamships*', in *Publications of the English Goethe Society*, vol. lxxii (2003)

8 Charles Darwent, 'The Anatomy of Agony, with Balloons', *The Independent on Sunday*, 16 February 2003, ArtsEtc., p. 9.

9 For more information on these, and other Titanic, films, see Bottomore, *The Titanic and Silent Cinema*; and Simon Mills, *The Titanic in Pictures* (Chesham, 1995).

10 Hayden White, 'The Modernist Event' in Vivian Sobchack (ed), *The Persistence of History: Cinema, Television and the Modernist Event'* (New York, 1996), pp. 17–38.

PART I

General Culture, History and Literature

CHAPTER ONE

The Relaunching of Ulster Pride:
The Titanic, Belfast, and Film[1]

JOHN HILL

'Belfast holds the real secret of the Titanic. It was the serial number on the ship, they say that if you held it up to a mirror it read: NO POPE HERE. . . So they were bound to have no luck of the ship. Ill-fated. Like the city itself.'

MARY COSTELLO, *Titanic Town*[2]

'We believe that the vibrancy, optimism and commitment that made Titanic such a majestic ship in her time lives on and is reflected through the resurgence of Belfast today. This is Belfast . . . a Titanic City.'

BELFAST CITY COUNCIL, *Titanic Belfast*[3]

WHILE THE SINKING of the Titanic has assumed the status of a transnational myth, articulating a variety of social and cultural attitudes, the sinking of the ship has also possessed very specific local meanings for the place in which it was built. The Titanic was, of course, made at the Harland and Wolff shipyard in Belfast and, as a result, has held associations for people in Belfast, as well as Ireland more generally, that it has not possessed elsewhere. Thus, while the city from which the ship set sail, Southampton, has figured extensively in public imaginings of the disaster, the role of Belfast has achieved much less prominence.

There are, of course, some obvious reasons for this. Following the completion of the Oceanic in 1871, Harland and Wolff had a close relationship with the White Star Line shipping company and was responsible for the production of virtually all of its vessels. The sinking of the ship was a blow to the prestige of both companies which then had an economic interest in playing down their involvement. The damage to the pride of Harland and Wolff, however, also assumed a more political and ideological aspect within the Irish context. As a number of commentators have noted, the launch of the Titanic coincided with Unionist opposition to Home Rule (involving the repeal of the Act of Union and the establishment of a parliament in Dublin). Indeed, the ship set sail from Southampton only the day before the third Irish Home Rule Bill was introduced into the British House of Commons. Much of the hostility of Unionists to Home Rule derived from the industrial character of the north-east of Ireland and its close economic links with Britain and the British Empire. Along with linen and engineering, shipbuilding was central to the region's prosperity and therefore an emblem of the Unionist cause. Inevitably, the sinking of the Titanic wounded Unionist pride in Belfast's shipbuilding capacity and tempered some of the economic self-confidence associated with it. John Wilson Foster goes so far as to suggest that the loss of the ship became an unconscious symbol of 'the thwarted nationhood of Ulster Protestants'.[4] Given that Unionist opposition to Home Rule was aimed at preserving the union with Britain rather than giving voice to an Ulster nationalism, this is probably an interpretative step too far. However, it does successfully indicate something of the intimate relation that existed between Ulster Unionism and shipbuilding at this politically volatile time.

This link is confirmed by the specific circumstances prevailing within the shipyard during the same period. Although the Harland and Wolff chairman, William James Pirrie, had expressed Home Rule sympathies, the complexion of the company was pre-eminently Unionist. The firm's owners, Edward Harland and Gustav Wolff, had both served as Conservative MPs for Belfast constituencies with Protestant majorities. The workforce, moreover, was overwhelmingly Protestant and, during 1912, there were sectarian assaults on Catholic workers, and expulsions from the shipyard, as a result of the political atmosphere. For many in Ireland, it was the religious and political character of the workforce that came to be held responsible for the fate of the ship. As Mary Costello's semi-autobiographical novel *Titanic Town* suggests, this took the form of popular beliefs about the ship's number enshrining anti-Catholic sentiments or Protestant workers 'cursing the Pope' when the ship was being built.[5] While a conversation amongst workers in James Plunkett's Dublin novel *Strumpet City* (1969) suggests that these sentiments acquired rapid currency, they did not find formal expression in the nationalist press of the time and probably only achieved widespread circulation in the wake of the expulsion of Catholic workers from the shipyard in 1920 and the establishment of a separate Unionist parliament in the North in 1921.[6] For while the sinking of the ship was open to interpretation in terms of Unionist hubris, it was a disaster with consequences that reverberated across the whole of Ireland. This was due to the substantial number of Irish passengers who had boarded the ship at Queenstown (now Cobh) in Co. Cork and the resulting loss of lives amongst the Irish on board. While, in one light, the deaths of so many Irish Catholics could be seen as compounding the offence of Ulster Unionism, the sheer scale of the humanitarian catastrophe weighed against the public articulation of such a view.

Nevertheless, the circumstances surrounding the loss of the ship meant that the memorialisation of the Titanic remained problematic for both Harland

and Wolff, and Ulster Unionism more generally. A memorial statue was unveiled in Belfast in 1920 but, following the partition of Ireland and the foundation of a semi-state in Northern Ireland under Unionist rule, there was little enthusiasm for preserving the memory of Belfast's associations with the Titanic. Two incidents at the BBC in the 1930s and 1940s illustrate well the sensitivities involved. In 1932, the White Star Line (which had been exercised by the negative impact upon British shipping of the 1929 film *Atlantic*) had successfully put pressure on the BBC to abandon plans for a radio play dealing with the disaster. In 1936, when the BBC in London announced plans for a talk on the sinking of the ship by the Titanic survivor, Charles Lightoller, the BBC in Northern Ireland also became involved. BBC NI enjoyed a close relationship with the Unionist establishment and the NI Programme Director, John Sutthery, wrote to the Director of Regional Relations in London, complaining that '[t]he "Titanic", and everything to do with it' was 'an extremely sore point in Belfast history'. '[N]ot only', he continued, 'were some 40 Belfast people drowned—mostly rather important people—but also it was a very grave set-back to civic pride when this much-vaunted ship went out from Harland and Wolff's yard to sink on its maiden voyage'.[7] Although the BBC in London decided to proceed with the broadcast, they assured their Northern Irish colleagues that they were alert to 'the risks involved' and that the resulting talk would be 'quite innocuous'.[8]

A similar incident also occurred in 1947 when the BBC in London planned a programme on the Titanic as part of its 'Sensation' series. As before, Cunard (the owners of White Star since 1934) offered up objections to which the BBC responded by eliminating all 'invented' material and adopting a 'purely documentary style'.[9] Harland and Wolff was also drawn into the controversy and put pressure on both the Northern Ireland government and the BBC in Northern Ireland to cancel the programme. This matter was given added urgency by the fact that the programme was scheduled to be broadcast on the same day as the launch of the first Cunard-White Star liner to be built in Belfast since the war. As a result, the Northern Ireland Prime Minister, Sir Basil Brooke, telegrammed both the British Home Secretary and the Chairman of the BBC to request the programme's cancellation. This led to a postponement of the programme's transmission for a week and an assurance from the Home Office in London, which had also contacted the BBC, that the script was 'quite harmless'.[10] Despite the postponement, the Director of BBC Northern Ireland, George Marshall, remained keen for London to modify the programme. '[I]n Northern Ireland, where a large number of relatives of the drowned are still alive', Marshall wrote, 'the "Titanic" disaster is still a very painful subject and we have always been careful to avoid any reference to it in our local programmes'. 'Moreover', he continued, 'we have felt that a programme dealing with the "Titanic" disaster would undoubtedly damage the prestige of Messrs. Harland & Wolff, one of the main employers of labour in Northern Ireland, and jeopardise the BBC's relationship with this firm'.[11]

The sensitivity of Harland and Wolff towards representations of the Titanic disaster continued into the 1950s as William MacQuitty discovered when he sought the firm's cooperation in the making of *A Night to Remember* (1958). The company's chairman, Sir Frederick Rebbeck, who had previously sought to cancel the BBC's 'Sensation' programme, now refused MacQuitty permission to film in the shipyards or make use of footage of the launch.[12] Despite these obstacles, the film nevertheless constitutes an important milestone in the breaking of the silence towards the Titanic within the Northern Ireland public sphere. MacQuitty's visits to Belfast during the preparations for the film were widely reported by the local press and, in the run-up to the film's opening in Belfast, the *Northern Whig* serialised extracts from Walter Lord's book of the same name (and the main source for the film). The premiere itself became something of a semi-official occasion and was attended by both the Governor of Northern Ireland, Lord Wakehurst, and the Lord Mayor of Belfast, Cecil McKee. The rekindling of civic pride in the ship that this represented was undoubtedly helped by the film's Northern Irish credentials. For while the film may have been an expensive Rank production aimed at an international market, it was also something of a personal project for the film's producer, MacQuitty, who was born in Belfast and had witnessed the ship's launch as a child. As he recalls in his autobiography, this led to 'a great lump' in his throat and a feeling of 'enormous pride in being an Ulsterman'.[13] MacQuitty had begun his filmmaking career with an official production for the Northern Ireland government (*Simple Silage*) and he continued to enjoy cordial relations with senior politicians (providing, for example, the Unionist Prime Minister Sir Basil Brooke with a synopsis for a war effort film entitled 'Ulster Goes To It' in 1943).[14] One of his first collaborators was the actor and singer, Richard Hayward, for whom he found a small part (as a victualler) in *A Night to Remember*. Hayward was himself a key figure in the development of filmmaking in Northern Ireland and had appeared in the first films to be shot there in the 1930s. He too undertook official projects for the NI government and, for all his appreciation of Irish folk culture, was an enthusiastic advocate of the Unionist cause. Like MacQuitty, Hayward had witnessed the launch of the Titanic which he regarded as 'a fabulous creation of Ulster brain and muscle'.[15] Just as he had earlier sought to bring 'Ulster' to the screen, so he now felt 'immense pride' that a Belfast man should have had 'the inspiration and courage' to create 'a Belfast picture, about a Belfast ship, created and fabricated by Belfast men'.[16]

Although Hayward's claims were undoubtedly over-stated, the film does contain elements that support his view. Unlike its precursors, such as *Titanic* (1953) which opens with passengers joining the ship at Cherbourg, the film begins with the launch of the ship at Belfast and shots of the shipyard workers. Although this is not footage of the actual launch, it does succeed in establishing the film's links with Belfast (which is subsequently referred to on a number of occasions). It is worth noting too that despite the promotional claims concerning the film's 'accuracy', the opening sequence also includes an entirely invented christening ceremony. In reality it was the policy of the White Star Line not to bless ships and this omission was later to enter popular mythology in Catholic Ireland as yet another factor contributing to the ship's demise. While this piece of dramatic licence is commonly regarded as no more than a piece of scene-setting, it is also significant for the way in which it introduces Thomas Andrews (Michael Goodliffe) as a character of note. Andrews was both the managing director and chief designer at Harland and Wolff and was generally praised for the calm nobility of his actions once the Titanic had been struck. Despite this reputation, however, he does not appear in either of the earlier German or Hollywood versions of the disaster.

In *A Night to Remember*, however, he becomes one of the film's leading characters, shown providing advice to a variety of passengers and finally going down with the ship while sat at his desk. This emphasis upon Andrews extends well beyond the portrait of him contained in Walter Lord's book and may partly be explained by the film's 'Ulster' connections. For while Andrews symbolised the dignity with which many met their death, he was also a significant figure for Unionist Ulster, the 'most important', indeed, of the 'rather important people' from the North who lost their lives in the disaster (heading, for example, the list on Belfast's memorial statue). Following the disaster, the Unionist writer Shan Bullock was commissioned to write a short biography of Andrews in which he is presented, according to the book's preface, as a 'plain, hard-working Ulster boy, growing into the exemplary and finally the heroic Ulster man that we know'.[17] Unlike his uncle, Lord Pirrie, who had displayed nationalist sympathies, Andrews was a staunch Unionist and opponent of Home Rule (which he believed would be financially ruinous for Ireland). His elder brother, John Miller Andrews, was a Unionist politician, who became Prime Minister of Northern Ireland for a short period during the Second World War. At the time of *A Night to Remember*'s release, his nephew, John Lawson Andrews, had also become the local Minister of Health. The emphasis upon Andrews, and the sympathetic way in which he is portrayed, appears to have been a significant factor in helping to rehabilitate the memory of the Titanic in a way that was palatable to the Northern Ireland establishment. Thus, on the day of the film's opening in Belfast, the local evening paper the *Belfast Telegraph* ran an article on Andrews by the Unionist MP for North Belfast Hugh Montgomery Hyde under the title of 'Gallant shipbuilder who perished in the Titanic'.[18] However, while the film did good business in Belfast and prompted a degree of local interest, this was not sustained. In 1959, when the Titanic memorial statue had to be moved due, ironically, to the number of motor accidents it had caused, there was barely a ripple of interest. Harland and Wolff also persevered with its policy of avoiding publicity and refused to help with the making of a television documentary in the 1960s.[19]

By the time of Cameron's *Titanic*, however, this had all changed. As elsewhere, the film assumed the status of a major cinematic event and encouraged a surge of cinema-going across Northern Ireland.[20] The film, moreover, stirred immense interest in the ship's Belfast connections and decisively ended local reticence concerning its origins. The *Belfast Newsletter* identified Belfast as the Titanic's 'spiritual home' while the *Belfast Telegraph* described the ship as 'the greatest . . . ever built'.[21] This enthusiasm for the ship was accompanied by a concern to divest Belfast of the responsibility for its sinking. In the *Belfast Telegraph* it was argued that Harland and Wolff had little of which 'to be ashamed'; the ship, it was claimed, was 'the engineering triumph of that age' which had fallen victim to 'careless seamanship' rather than flaws of design.[22] Similar views were also in evidence in the local edition of the *Sunday Times* which ran an article under the headline, 'Belfast told to stop feeling guilty and hold Titanic Day'.[23]

However, if the film helped encourage the rediscovery of local pride in the ship, it did so in a different way, and within a different context, from *A Night to Remember*. The film only mentions the city once and, although Andrews (Victor Garber) retains a key role (providing helpful advice and encouragement to the film's leads), there is little sense (even in his accent) of his specifically Ulster origins. Cameron's *Titanic*, in this regard, downplays the specific associations of the ship with Belfast and Northern Unionism in favour of a more generalised sense of 'Irishness'. As previously noted, Irish passengers were among those in third-class or steerage. This was not, however, regarded as particularly significant in early film versions of the disaster. While Nazi cinema had exploited anti-English sentiment in two Irish-themed films, *Der Fuchs von Glenarvon* (*The Fox of Glenarvon*, 1940), and *Mein Leben für Irland* (*My Life for Ireland*, 1941), the German propaganda film *Titanic* (1943) does not refer to the Irish on board the ship. In the Hollywood *Titanic* (1953), the Irish are also absent from the few scenes involving third-class passengers. *A Night to Remember*, therefore, was the first Titanic film to give prominence to the Irish aboard the ship, not only showing Irish villagers setting off for Queenstown but also maintaining an interest in their activities before and after the iceberg is hit. In Cameron's film, this emphasis upon the Irish becomes even more pronounced. According to figures in Molony, the Irish accounted for less than a sixth of passengers in steerage (113 out of 706).[24] In Cameron's *Titanic*, however, it is the Irish characters who are by far the most visible and who are also central to the film's elaboration of class and ethnic divisions. As McLoone argues, the Irish on board the ship, through the communal rituals of music, dancing and the drink-

ing of 'black beer', provide the 'cultural leadership' of a new democratic and
ethnically diverse America that stands in sharp contrast to the old order of
WASP privilege (represented by the first-class passengers).[25] In this respect,
there is a significant departure from the treatment of the Irish in *A Night to
Remember*. For while the earlier film also highlights the apparent proclivity of
the Irish for singing and dancing, the portrait of the Irish characters is
enveloped in more traditional images of Irish 'backwardness'. In this respect,
the scene of the Irish departing their village, under the benign eye of the local
priest, contrasts with the opening sequence at the Belfast shipyards, suggesting
a distinction between the rural 'primitiveness' of the South and the industrial
'modernity' of the North that was still being cultivated by Ulster Unionists
during this period.[26]

What is also of note in the film is how the Titanic's discourse of 'Irishness'
extends to the ship's manufacture as well. In *A Night to Remember*, there is a
scene in a train involving Lightoller (Kenneth More) in which a rather
pompous Englishman proclaims that 'every Britisher is proud of the unsinkable Titanic'. This association of the ship with Britishness is, however, contested in Cameron's film in which an Irish passenger, Tommy Ryan (Jason Barry),
claims that the ship was actually built by the Irish. Such a reclaiming of the
'Irishness' of the Titanic is, nevertheless, problematic. As previously noted, the
workforce that built the Titanic was overwhelmingly Protestant and Unionist
and opposed to Irish Home Rule. The signifiers of 'Irishness' in the film (the
music, the dancing), however, are clearly linked to a Catholic nationalist tradition and, as a result, make improbable markers of Northern Unionist culture.
There is, then, something faintly absurd about Munich and Spiegel's suggestion, following the lead of the film, that the 'Irish wailing tones' of the film's
theme song honours the 'fifteen thousand Irishmen who built this ship'.[27]

From another perspective, however, the film's amnesia concerning the
ship's origins may well have assisted the reception given to the film locally.
What evidence there is suggests that the appeal of the film extended across the
sectarian divide in Northern Ireland. In this respect, the film's postmodern
depthlessness helped to depoliticise the ship's legacy and facilitate its exploita-
tion within local heritage and tourist culture. Thus, while some doubts were
expressed about the promotion of Titanic sites by Belfast City Council, there
has been little resistance to the city's continuing efforts to take advantage of its
links with the ship. This led, in 2002 (the ninetieth anniversary of the ship's
voyage), to the organisation of a Titanic week which now seems set to become
an annual event. The Northern Ireland Tourist Board, which for many years
had avoided reference to Belfast's connections with the ship, also used the
film's success to encourage interest in the area. The ship was also seized upon
as an emblem of Northern Irish enterprise and, as part of the city's bid for economic regeneration, plans were announced for a 105-acre 'Titanic Quarter'

embracing a 'science park, commercial premises, residential units, marina, social and leisure facilities, hotel(s) and a heritage museum' on a site that included the dry dock in which the Titanic was built.[28]

There is, of course, a degree of irony in all of this. The Titanic, which was initially the emblem of a heavily industrialised north of Ireland, has now been mobilised in support of the construction of a new 'post-industrial' Northern Irish economy. This not only reflects the changing economic climate within Northern Ireland but also the change in political circumstances as well. For if the Titanic once suggested the economic and political strength of Ulster Unionism, such symbolism has largely lost its potency as a result of the declin-ing fortunes of both Harland and Wolff and Unionism since the 1960s. Although Northern Ireland shipbuilding may not have been the force it once was at the time of *A Night to Remember*'s release, Harland and Wolff was still one of the largest shipyards in the world. By the 1990s, however, shipbuilding in Belfast was in a state of terminal crisis and the company was on the verge of closure. Far from resisting its association with the disaster, the shipyard was now eager to clutch at straws and obtain whatever commercial advantage it might secure from its historical legacy. Thus, in a striking reversal of previous attitudes, a local headline on *Titanic*'s Oscar nominations reported that 'H&W hope for *Titanic* success'.[29]

The position of Ulster Unionism had also altered dramatically. At the time of *A Night to Remember*'s release, the Unionist government remained firmly in power (despite some advances by the Northern Ireland Labour Party). Following the outbreak of the 'troubles' in the late 1960s, however, the Northern Ireland parliament, dominated by Ulster Unionists for fifty years, was thrown into crisis and eventually suspended by the British government in 1972. Its return, under the Good Friday Agreement of 1998, depended upon a power-sharing agreement whereby both nationalists and republicans would enter government. Under this new political dispensation, for all its ups and downs, it was clear that there could never be a return to single-party Unionist rule. The negotiations leading to this agreement were nearing conclusion at the time of the release of Cameron's *Titanic* in Northern Ireland and repre-sented a clear shift in the political dynamics of the region. Given the film's appearance at this sensitive stage of the 'peace process', it was evident that the old associations which the ship carried would no longer hold sway in the same way as before. Thus, while it is unlikely that the ship will ever become a fully shared part of local Northern Irish culture, there is little doubt that the film contributed to the ending of local reticence regarding the ship's origins and encouraged the proliferation of new local discourses (linked to the economy, heritage and tourism) around the film.

Notes

1 I would like to thank Kelly Davidson for her help with the research for this article as well as John Wilson Foster, Michael McCaughan, Martin McLoone and Simon Mills for their assistance. I am also grateful to Jeff Walden at the BBC Written Archives Centre (BBC WAC) and to staff at the Northern Ireland Public Record Office (PRONI).

2 Mary Costello, *Titanic Town* (London, 1992), pp. 25–26.

3 Belfast City Council, *Titanic Belfast* (Belfast, 2002).

4 John Wilson Foster, 'Imagining the Titanic' in Eve Patten (ed.), *Returning to Ourselves: Second Volume of Papers from the John Hewitt International Summer School* (Belfast, 1995), p. 333.

5 Thus, in Frank McGuinness's play about the Ulster Division at the Battle of the Somme, *Observe the Sons of Ulster Marching Towards the Somme* (London, 1986), one character declares that with '[e]very nail they hammered into the Titanic, they cursed the Pope' (p. 49).

6 James Plunkett, *Strumpet City* (London, 1980 [1969]), pp. 311–2.

7 Memo from NI Programme Director to Director of Regional Relations, 19 August 1936, BBC WAC R51/356/1.

8 Memo from Director of Regional Relations to NI Programme Director, 20 August 1936, BBC WAC R51/356/1.

9 Memo from Director of Features to Norman Collins, 4 January 1947, BBC WAC R19/1936.

10 Letter from J. Chuter Ede to Sir Basil Brooke, 25 February 1947, PRONI CAB /9F/165/1A.

11 Memo from Northern Ireland Director to Senior Controller, 28 February 1947, BBC WAC R19/1936.

12 William MacQuitty, *A Life to Remember* (London, 1991), p. 323.

13 MacQuitty, *A Life to Remember*, p. 6.

14 Letter from William MacQuitty to Sir Basil Brooke, 19 April 1943, PRONI COM/61/661.

15 Richard Hayward, 'A Night to Remember', *Ulster Illustrated*, vol. 6 no. 2, April 1958, p. 14. Ironically, testimonies such as this have tended to acquire their status retrospectively. The launching of the Titanic's sister ship, the Olympic, in the same yards in 1910 was in fact accompanied by much greater public fanfare.

16 Hayward, 'A Night to Remember', p. 15.

17 Horace Plunkett, 'Introduction' in Shan F. Bullock, *Thomas Andrews Shipbuilder*, (Belfast , 1999 [Dublin and London, 1912]), pp. xviii–xix. Given the political climate of the time, this construction of Andrews as an 'Ulster hero' did not go uncontested. In a somewhat sour review of Bullock's book, the nationalist writer F. Sheehy Skeffington complains that the description of Andrews' 'political views' and 'social life' only reveals 'the same deadening of the imagination by his surroundings'. 'Thomas Andrews was Belfast in excelsis', he declares, 'mechanical, unimaginative, soulless' (*The Irish Review*, vol. 2, 1912, p. 614).

18 *Belfast Telegraph*, 27 October 1958, p. 4.

19 Eric Waugh, 'A cautionary marker on humanity's historic march', *Belfast Telegraph*, 21 January 1998, p. 13.

20 'Full house for Ulster cinemas', *Belfast Telegraph*, 24 March 1998, p. 11.

21 'Titanic shown in home town', *Belfast Newsletter*, 20 January 1998, p. 18; *Belfast Telegraph*, 24 January 1998, p. 9.

22 *Belfast Telegraph*, 21 January 1998, p. 13.

23 *Sunday Times*, 18 January 1998 quoted in Michael McCaughan, 'Titanic: Out of the Depths and Into the Culture', in Anthony D. Buckley (ed.), *Symbols: Symbols in Northern Ireland* (Belfast, 1998), p. 147.

24 Senan Molony, *The Irish Aboard Titanic* (Dublin, 2000), pp. 255–6.

25 Martin McLoone, *Irish Film: The Emergence of a Contemporary Cinema* (London, 2000), pp. 45–6.

26 Thus, the year before the release of the film, the Unionist Minister for Home Affairs (and subsequent Prime Minister), Brian Faulkner argued that 'the depressed economic condition of Eire could be a strong propaganda point' for the Northern Ireland government, arguing that an emphasis upon the 'modernity' of 'Ulster' would help buttress a sense of 'Ulster's' distinctiveness from the rest of (economically backward) Ireland (or 'Eire'). Minutes of the Cabinet Publicity Committee, 17 April 1957, PRONI, CAB/9F/123/56.

27 Adrienne Munich and Maura Spiegel, 'Heart of the Ocean: Diamonds and Democratic Desire in *Titanic*', in Kevin S. Sandler and Gaylyn Studlar (eds.) *Titanic: Anatomy of a Blockbuster* (New Brunswick, NJ, 1999), p. 163.

28 Promotional leaflet, Titanic Quarter Ltd. (Belfast, 2002).

29 *Irish News*, 26 March 1998, p. 7.

CHAPTER TWO

'My Poor Brave Men': Time, Space and Gender in Southampton's Memory of the Titanic

MICHAEL HAMMOND

A T THE TOP of Southampton High Street there are two Titanic memorials. The most prominent is the memorial to the engineers who kept the generators running. The other memorial, less prominent, is to the ship's musicians. Both have as their central emblem a female figure. The engineers' monument is grandiose, measuring nineteen feet in height and thirty-two feet in length with a seven-foot figure of 'Angel Glory' holding a laurel wreath in each hand. The engineers are depicted at their posts in bronze bas-relief beneath the angel. The musicians' monument is much smaller, measuring about four feet across and four feet high, and depicts in bas-relief 'a [female] figure symbolising grief' carved from Sicilian marble.[1] The figure is holding the back of the ship as if to attempt to keep it from sinking. Both monuments represent the public memory of the disaster and, in the style of memorial design prevalent at the time, they suspend the moment of tragedy. In their representations of the female figure, however, they suggest quite distinctive interpretations. The angel in the engineers' monument offers absolution, arms spread out to encompass the lost in a heavenly embrace. The moment is eternal and the angel presides over it. By contrast the grief figure in the musicians' monument hints at a kind of hysteria, a desire to break out of the moment, to stretch across the distance between home and shipwreck, and to wrest the ship, and the musicians, from their fate. The engineers' monument elides such an earthbound and secular space in favour of a celestial haven with the undying memory of those who remain the only reference to the world of the living. In their references to time, space and gender, the memorials bear the traces of the origins of the local memory of the Titanic disaster. Those origins can be located in the reportage and the visual depictions of the suffering of Southampton during the week following the disaster, two examples of which I wish to explore in this chapter.

Steven Biel begins his cultural history of the Titanic disaster by noting the importance of the role of technology in relaying a sense of 'synchronicity' to

the event. He draws on Stephen Kern's observation that the disaster 'drama-
tized changing perceptions of time and space'.[2] These perceptual shifts are
associated with the advent of mechanisation, temporal regulation through
timetables of trains, the regulation of work/leisure time brought about by mass
industrialisation, and particularly with technologies such as the wireless telegraph. The wireless enabled the Titanic disaster to be experienced almost
simultaneously across diverse realms from the news-reading public, and the
terrible, helpless waiting of relatives and friends of those on the liner on two
continents, to the victims of the disaster and their potential rescuers on the
Carpathia. This simultaneity provides Biel with a metaphorical platform from
which to launch his cultural study of the event's impact and reception across
the 20th century.

The technologically induced simultaneity of the event highlights aesthetic
continuities that were already apparent in tropes within theatre, cinema, visual and print culture at the time of the disaster. Film audiences of the day were
becoming familiar with narrative codes that centred on the cinema's ability to
cross space and time in rapid succession. D. W. Griffith's development of
increasingly complex editing practices gave full rein to the powers of film to
traverse not only external space and time, but also subjective, psychic, temporal and spatial registers.[3] Theatre audiences were also familiar with the use
of telephones and telegraphs as narrative devices. At one level of its retelling,
the Titanic event does play itself out as a Griffithian rescue, for those who
were saved. Or perhaps more darkly, in the fateful inaction of the Californian,
as a failure in the combination of technology and human error, it resembles
the emplotment of an Andre de Lorde sensation play. Further, the visual representation of thoughts and feelings within and across diverse temporal and
spatial dimensions were central to the photo-postcard industry as well as
theatrical stage mechanics and early cinema. Finally, the press reportage of
the event at the time was the first re-telling of the sinking by virtue of two factors, the temporal gap between the event and its report on the wireless and
then the process of story construction, inflected by varying degrees of hyperbolic suppositions, morally inflected rumours and stories that functioned to fill
the gaps between the sporadic flow of confirmed information.

Biel's entire book effectively illustrates Titanic as an example of what
Hayden White has called a 'modernist event'.[4] The Titanic's circulating interpretations and retellings run a range of narrative possibilities from mythic tales
of individual heroism to the tragic consequences of the irresponsibility of in-
stitutions. According to White, the modernist event is one 'that can be neither
closed and forgotten nor precisely remembered as merely an event of the
past'.[5] White points to the gap between the fact of an event and its meaning:
'What is at issue here is not the facts regarding such events but the different
possible meanings that such facts can be construed as bearing'.[6] The catalysts

for this phenomenon are the modern, technologically reproducible, forms of representation, which characterise the texture of experiencing events in the 20th century. Central to the modernist event, then, is its capacity, through media dissemination, for endless repetitions and re-tellings. This results in a cyclical, even hysterical, repetitiveness of narrative that 'may provide a kind of "intellectual mastery" of the anxiety which memory of their occurrence may incite in an individual or a community . . . but insofar as the story is identifiable as a story, it can provide no lasting "psychic mastery" of such events'.[7] For White psychic mastery requires the kind of anti-narrative strategies developed by literary modernism. Reflexive story telling offers 'the possibility of representing such traumatic events as being produced by the monstrous growth and expansion of technological "modernity" (of which Nazism and the Holocaust are limit case manifestations) in a manner less fetishising than any traditional representation of them could ever be'.[8] In that sense Biel's adoption of a detached speaking position in his use of the stories of the sinking of the Titanic *as stories* works in part to unveil the ideological contradictions they suppress.

In another discussion of the modernist event, Thomas Elsaesser suggests that the modernist aesthetic, one of 'impersonality and understatement' may not be wholly adequate in representing the dislocations and violences of modernity. 'Emotions, one could argue, ought to belong to any engagement with matters of life and death on the part of both those whom history has given the role of spectators and those who are charged with passing on compassion and preserving memory'.[9] Noting the mimetic and affective engagement strategies in the use made of technologies of reproduction (cinema and radio) by the Nazi regime in celebrating 'folk' cultures which in the process hid the 'fanatic ruthlessness with which the regime repressed, destroyed and eradicated other cultures and crafts on an incalculable scale', he points to German filmmaker Rainer Werner Fassbinder's 'black market melodramas' and their use of melodramatic conventions to expose and relate the psychic consequences of these brutalities. Fassbinder's strategy utilised a mimetic medium (film) in tandem with a mode of affective engagement (melodrama) to highlight 'the dislocations caused . . . by capitalism's modernisation as well as by the first society of the spectacle it gave rise to'.[10]

Melodrama's potential in this regard has been theorised and documented to the extent that it stands as a central plank in academic understanding of literary, cinematic and theatre-based cultural production.[11] For my purposes here I draw attention to these two strategies, modernist reflexivity and melodrama, in representing the unrepresentable to examine two contemporary manifestations of narration of the Titanic disaster, a local news report and a cartoon. I have a double purpose in invoking modernist and melodramatic registers here. The first is to underscore, and in the process adopt, a reflexive re-telling of an earlier narration, to contribute to the kaleidoscopic history of the Titanic disaster. Secondly, in adopting that distance I wish to draw attention to the melodramatic mode at play in these retellings, not to unveil their ideological infrastructure, although that will be evident, but more precisely to mark the function of the melodramatic register in its own contribution to either thinly veiling or even exposing the inequities that were transparent to local residents directly affected by the disaster.

My two objects of study here, a news report of the local populace of Southampton waiting for the news of the survivors outside the office of the White Star Line; and a cartoon, which features a woman representing grief, kneeling before a sea-wall with a thought bubble depicting the sinking, are both marked by their distinctive employment of temporality. The news reportage is clearly linear while the cartoon collapses time into an emotionally cyclical reverberation, between the envisioned moment of death and the resolution of grief, and offers a punctuating closure to the news story.

My choice of these two items is prompted by the role Southampton played in the British national imagination soon after the disaster. A significant number of those lost on the Titanic were employed by the White Star Line and were drawn from a community that had grown up in the latter part of the 19th century around the shipping and liner industries. Local residents were employed in various functions on the ship, which represented the social and economic hierarchy that was representative of that of Southampton. Social and gender boundaries played a significant role in the news reportage as Southampton's role in the national imagination gained prominence during the week following the sinking.

Daily reports in the national press featured the story of the relatives waiting outside the offices of the White Star Line. On Tuesday, the day after news of the sinking had been received, the Southampton mayor, Henry Bowyer, set up a relief fund for widows and orphans of those who had perished. Soon after, the Lord Mayor of London, Sir Thomas Crosby, instigated a national relief fund. As early as 17 April the *Southampton Daily Echo* had reported that Bowyer, Crosby and Colonel Ivor Phillips, who represented a third fund being raised by the national newspaper *The Daily Telegraph*, had decided 'that the sums received by the Mayor shall be appropriated to relieving immediate local distress, the balance of the three funds named being invested for the permanent benefit of the widows'.[12] In general the press reports of the disaster during the first week identified Southampton as the centre of suffering relatives of perished Titanic crewmembers.

The first reports of the disaster reached the press offices of the *Southern Daily Echo*, the local daily paper, in time to make the first edition on Monday. Each day until Saturday, there was a running side story concerning the queues outside the White Star Line offices. On 20 April, the Saturday weekly paper, *The*

Hampshire Independent, reprinted a day-by-day account of the unbearable wait-ing and tension in a condensed version, along with the names of the crew who were lost under the heading 'Nearly All Southamptonians'. The account begins with a quotation from 'Dr. [Samuel] Johnson: 'When any calamity has been suffered. The first thing to remember is, how much has been escaped'. This quotation at once places a closure on the event which, as the reader must have known, ushers the event into the realms of memory and also marks out the project of article, and the duty of the reader, to unveil or read into these events a purpose, or what Peter Brooks has called a 'moral occult'.[13] Behind these terrible events a divine hand enacts, and eventually reveals, the power of virtue. The equation of Titanic with Southampton continues as the article compares the size and variety of the crew 'with that of a small town'. This attempt to imagine the disaster in terms of a geographic, land-based space seeks to give perspective to the loss and by implication that loss is measured by what is to follow; the impact of the disaster on the local community of Southampton.

The article then structures the chronological events through its account of the waiting relatives. 'We give full details…' sets out the intent to mark out the significance of an event whose experience is characterised by temporal longuers inflected with the eventless occurrence of the 'no names yet' respons-es of the officials of the White Star Line. However, the retelling is already aware of its ending—a sense of foreboding permeates the sentence 'Early in the morning there were rumours in Southampton that a mishap had occurred, but these were at first set aside as idle talk, but very soon there was a rude awakening, though the first news to hand was in no way the full measure of what really happened'. The balance between rumour and fact has its first articulation along a gendered axis that centres on the heroic sacrifice of the men and the objects of that sacrifice. 'The women and children were reported to be taken off, and this proved to be fact . . . but all the earlier messages [of Titanic limping its way to Halifax or of all aboard rescued] proved to be false'. The 'truth' that women and children had been saved is counterbalanced by the dispelled rumour, which ensures the sacrifice. The 'truth' of the men's sac-rifice continues to inform the article's construction of the objectivity of women and children, and, as the un-eventful time of waiting unfolds, it allows an equation of national mourning simultaneously with Southampton and the per-sonification of the suffering of Southampton's affected population with the feminine. As if to draw from the same lexicon of signs as the signification of female innocence and virtue in melodrama, the paper draws attention to the tradition of suffering from losses at sea; 'Southampton, as has so often been the case with disasters at sea, is a great sufferer by this huge calamity'. The moral order played out along gender lines is confirmed; 'There were hundreds of men in the ship who have wives and families in the port, and in the streets in the humbler parts of the town there is hardly a house which has not to mourn the loss of a breadwinner'. The loss of female employees on the Liner is completely suppressed by this rhetoric. Downplaying the role of women employed on the ship, the story maps the local geography of sorrow through reporting the impact of the disaster on the domestic, and therefore feminine, realm. It does so by listing the number of people lost and the number of affected households. This topography has since become entrenched in the local memory of the disaster—from the publication of photographs of the effected street of Southampton in *The Deathless Story of the Titanic: Complete Narrative with many Illustrations* by Lloyd's Weekly News (1912) to its most recent manifestation in the local reception of James Cameron's *Titanic* (1997).[14]

Following its portentous opening, the news story then reports the events chronologically from Monday to Friday, the days immediately following the disaster. It begins with a flashback to the days leading to the departure of the ship, 'under the bright sunshine the stately vessel moved down the river to the accompaniment of cheers and waving handkerchiefs from ship to shore'. The sinister presence of disaster is invoked by its apparent absence: 'No hint of possible disaster, no premonition of mishap, marred a memorable send-off'. Under the heading 'Reception of the News at Southampton' the story of waiting begins: 'Rarely if ever, in the history of the port have such scenes been witnessed as were seen outside the offices of The White Star Line on Canute Road on Monday'. A message that was put up reads 'names will be posted as soon as received'. Continuing the masculinisation of the victims of the disaster the article refers to the 'anxious crowd', 'grim and silent' as 'nearly entirely composed of men . . . Many of the crew have wives and large families, and almost everyone seemed to have a husband, father, brother, son or sweetheart on board the doomed vessel'.

From a description of the scenes on Monday the account of Tuesday comes under the heading 'Anxiety of the Relatives'. In the evening a cable from New York arrives and 'the crowd pressed forward'. The cable provides information of five saved officers, but none of the crew. This event comes at the end of the account of Tuesday. On Wednesday the heading reads 'More Pathetic Scenes' but recounts a repetition of Tuesday's events, the day being marked only by the erection of the notice board and an address by local councillor O'Dell advising them to go home and wait. 'Thursday's Agony' is the title of the final section, which is divided into morning and afternoon. White Star Line officials announce that the names of the survivors will be posted as soon as they get them and the section and the article ends with the story of a preacher who tries to give a sermon but is met with 'murmurs of dissent'. The end of the article is then followed by a full list of the crew of the Titanic who were 'nearly all Southamptonians'.

The article ends without closure, there is no news to be had, and a chronology of waiting is instead punctuated by stories. This psychic time, or time-lessness, is expressed in melodramatic terms: 'The infinite pathos of the catas-trophe was borne down upon us hourly'. A contrast between light and dark punctuates the prose: 'Another day of suspense dawned on Southampton on Thursday, and though the sun shone brightly from the genial April sky, the shadow of death and disaster hung over the port like a black thundercloud'. The function of the chronology also frames the binaries of public/private, work/domestic space in ways that articulate innocence in the face of loss. The time of day structures each visitor along gendered lines: 'From time to time women with reluctant steps and backward glances detached themselves from the crowd, and went home to get tea for the children who were all too proba-bly orphans'. This culminates in conjoining ideologically diverse spaces under the sign of communal grief:

One o'clock—two o'clock—and still no news. The chimes of the clock of some distant church seemed to fall on the ears of the agonised listeners like a funeral knell. During the dinner hour when the dock gates disgorged their swarms of busy workmen, the waiting crowds swelled considerably, and after this, strangely enough, dwindled to small proportions. It seemed as if the sufferers were stunned, and had melted away to their homes, resigned to accept the worst. For a spell Canute Road was strangely quiet, and the shrill voices of the boys selling the papers with the latest news of the disaster, broke a tragic silence. No one spoke aloud near the fateful board. The looming shad-ow of death awed every body to a whisper. Little knots of men and women united in a community of sorrow still waited—still hoped.

This prose is arguably typical of the journalism of the day, a style that arose with the expansion in Victorian print culture, and mass readership, in the 19th century. A melodramatic language that in its literary reception was charac-terised as feminine fits with the rise of consumer culture, women readers as the assumed audience and consumption of newspapers in the domestic space.[15] However, the attempt to fix the boundaries of gender and ideologies of class becomes occasionally unglued. This is apparent in the reference to 'the sever-al cases of . . . men who had previously been out of employment for some time, rendering the plight of those left behind even more desperate'. The reference here is to a coal strike that had been recently settled, but which had resulted in considerable unemployment among seamen based in Southampton. Many who had gained employment on the Titanic had done so because the vessels, on which they had normally been employed, were docked due to lack of coal. The understated reference may have meant to place blame on the striking coal workers for the deaths of the Titanic, while also drawing attention to the unstable nature of employment in the seafaring trade. Indeed, it became known later that the contracts of the White Star Line's employees had been terminated at the time the ship went down. Resulting hardship was in part ameliorated by the Titanic Relief Fund, however, the attention given to the employment conditions of the seafarers remained one of the elements of pathos with which the Southampton story was inscribed at the time, and which has remained so within local memory.

The article's temporal structure concludes in an open ended, to-be-continued, fashion. The device of light and dark introduces the final paragraph: 'Noon. The midday sun streams down on the waiting crowds that still linger around the fateful black board'. The waiting continues, although the creeping awareness of the fate of many is finally acknowledged, even if their identity is still in doubt: 'The words that may be written on the boards during the coming hours will decide what wives will be widows, what children orphans, and what sweethearts forlorn'. The gender of the bereaved is clearly marked as female, in spite of the crowd being made up of as many men as women. But where women fainted and moaned, men 'unable to bear the tension' paced 'aimlessly up and down the road always with a backward glance to see if anything fresh was being pinned up on the board'.

The article leaves out Friday, the day when most of the names were ascertained. This is not intentional but by necessity of the deadline for the Saturday edition. This lacuna leaves exposed not the narrative or the closure but the affect; hence the introduction of time functions not as a marker of moments but as bearer of fate. Time signals the eventual pathetic conclusion and therefore leaves open the psychic, internal temporalities and introduces their cyclical nature, the capacity for retelling lies in this pathos and it is the narrative locus of the event in local memory.

The second item I wish to explore is from the same newspaper, indeed following on the next page after the report discussed above—the weekly cartoon by Archibald Clements, the regular cartoonist for the *Hampshire Independent*. It depicts a woman kneeling at a sea wall, her head is in her hands and 'Southampton' is written across her dress. At her knees is a copy of the *Daily Press* and the headlines are discernible. They read: 'Terrible Catastrophe— Sinking of 'Titanic'—great loss of life. The column title on the right reads 'Crew Nearly All Southampton Men'. Also at her feet lies a discarded officer's hat. Above her head, superimposed over the sea is an image of the Titanic run aground on to the iceberg and the stern sinking into the water. The caption reads 'My Poor Brave Men'.

As in the news report of the waiting crowds, the emotional effect of the image centres on its gendered structure. The cartoon recalls a tradition of depicting women waiting for the return of their man's ship in 19th century landscape and narrative painting, as well as in other visual forms such as magic lanterns and postcards.[16] The 'vision scene', the superimposed image above the character, was utilised in stage and cinema at this time to express character motivation and interiority. In the case of memorials the trope of woman as grief was well established. Its effect in depicting the emotional terrain and significance of the subject of memorialisation is suggested by Lawrence Weaver, writing in 1914 about two memorials in St. Paul's Cathedral in London. The first was in memory of the fallen of the Coldstream Guards, the second to the war correspondents who died in the South African (Boer) War:

The imaginative note is far more difficult of expression in plastic art than in painting. The sculptor is limited by the definition of his material and must rely on the more subjective power of response in the imagination to which he appeals. He is in difficulties as soon as he ceases to represent facts and sets about the objective presentment of what is unreal physically, however true may be its spiritual message. In St. Paul's Cathedral is a wall tablet in low relief, by Sir Gascombe John, to the Coldstream Guards who fell in South Africa. A soldier supports a wounded comrade, and in the background a group of Coldstreams look down on the scene. They are dressed in various early uniforms of the regiments and symbolise the pride which heroes of old campaigns would have felt in the gallantry of their successors. As sculpture it is successful, as symbolism the effect to me is a little theatrical—but that is merely a personal opinion. In the crypt is the same artist's memorial to the war correspondents who lost their lives in the same campaign. The figure of a woman who sits musing and holding laurel wreaths is seen against a background of hills and conveys the air of contemplative sadness which the subject demands. Less is attempted than in the Coldstream memorial, but I feel that more is achieved.[17]

The fact that the figure of a woman allows emotion to be conveyed more effectively than the masculine pride of men suggests the prevalence of this representational trope at the time. Indeed the Titanic memorials in Southampton utilise this in both the monument to the engineers and to the musicians.

The second order of meaning in the figure of grief in the cartoon however suggests another aspect of the use of the female figure in 19th century visual culture. This is the trope of the fallen woman. In her discussion of the prostitute as social victim Lynda Nead has pointed to the image of the prostitute as outcast, which served as an 'attempt to deflect the power and threat of prostitution'. She suggests that 'prostitution was re-defined through a moral language of temptation, fall and guilt and, in this way, the prostitute could be accommodated within the hegemonic notions of femininity and morality'. The image of the grief-stricken woman at the sea wall not only conjures up the gendered rendering of the emotional state of grief but also hints at the fate that may await the women of Southampton who, having suffered the loss of the breadwinner, will now be thrust into the public realm and the moral dangers that it holds. As Nead argues, 'female deviancy was explained in terms of lost innocence, a result of contact with the public sphere'.[18]

The image's temporal collapse between the sinking and the knowledge of those who are lost exposes the threats to the sanctity of womanhood in morally legible terms. The discourse apparent in the appeal for the relief fund highlights the necessity for benevolence and plugs into the predominant language of public responsibility couched in the language of charity. Local Southampton councillor A. J. Cheverton was quoted in the *Daily Echo* on the Tuesday following the disaster saying: 'The citizens from the highest and the lowest would do all that was possible to support whatever step the mayor might take. The disaster would not only evoke sympathy in Southampton, but also among the wealthy people of London and elsewhere and from these people they would get a great deal of help'.[19] The word destitution was prevalent in the descriptions of the fate awaiting the women without charitable aid. In reference to those seamen who had been affected by the above-mentioned coal strike, one article in the *Southampton Times* on Thursday observed: 'as the majority of [the workers] had been idle for some time they left little money behind them. This is why destitution has so swiftly overtaken those who know only too well that fears of widowhood are correct'.[20]

As well as collapsing time the cartoon also compresses space, achieved through the superimposition of the sinking ship. Here the cartoon most effectively seeks to render the emotional anguish of waiting depicted in the news story, one that works to stretch time out and fill the gaps with renderings of emotional scenes. Through the superimposition, the cartoon traverses the ocean and across the week to produce its effect. In this respect it is emotion that connects the spaces while transforming chronological time into psychic time. Utilising, as I have suggested, visual symbolic codes current in melodramatic theatre, cinema and popular visual forms, this compression vacillates between a rendering of external time and the eternal, cyclical temporality of grief. The superimposition could be interpreted as the depicted woman's dream or fantasy, but the cartoon is in itself a fantasy of femininity, which barely contains the contradictions of social and gender inequities inherent in its use of symbolic space, and the female figure of grief. It seems to respond to the lack of closure of the news reportage about the waiting relatives, by resolving the wait and replacing the 'many men' with the signifying female figure of innocence under threat.

This brief snapshot of the local reportage of the Titanic disaster gives some account of the re-tellings at play at the local level. In the appeals of the Relief Fund and the reports of the queues outside the White Star Line offices in Southampton in the national press, Southampton did in many instances stand in for the mourning of the nation. A year later these representative codes informed the design and construction of the musicians memorial, which seemed to use particularly the Clements cartoon as its inspiration. It was described as: 'a fine piece of work . . . In the centre is a beautifully sculptured panel representing the Titanic, partly submerged, with a figure symbolising grief in the foreground'.[21] The grief figure need not be mentioned as feminine, because by this time the construction of Southampton's memory of the disaster was, in gendered terms, concrete.

Notes

1 These descriptions come from the Titanic file held in the Southampton Public Library.

2 Steven Biel, *Down With The Old Canoe: A Cultural History of the Titanic Disaster* (New York and London, 1996) p. 9. Biel references Stephen Kern, *The Culture of Time and Space: 1880–1918* (Cambridge, 1983) pp. 65–67.

3 Tom Gunning thus describes the narrative of *The Fatal Hour*: 'A woman detective trailing white slavers is captured and subjected to an ingenious revenge. She is tied in front of a gun rigged to fire when a large clock strikes 12. Although such machinery of revenge has a long heritage in stage melodrama, this fatal clock inscribes time itself into the narrative and determines the form of the film's parallel editing climax'. Tom Gunning, *D.W. Griffith and the Origins of American Narrative Film: The Early Years at Biograph* (Urbana and Chicago, 1991), p. 98.

4 Hayden White, 'The Modernist Event', in Vivian Sobchak, ed., *The Persistence of History: Cinema, Television and the Modern Event* (New York and London, 1996) pp. 17–38.

5 White, 'The Modernist Event', p. 37. Cf. footnote 4.

6 White, 'The Modernist Event', p. 21.

7 White, 'The Modernist Event', p. 32.

8 White, 'The Modernist Event'.

9 Thomas Elsaesser, 'Subject Positions, Speaking Positions: From Holocaust, Our Hitler, and Heimat to Shoah and Schindler's List', in Sobchak, *The Persistence of History*, pp. 145–186.

10 Elsaesser, 'Subject Positions', pp. 164–165.

11 The critical work on melodrama is extensive. Significant studies in the last twenty years include Peter Brooks, *The Melodramatic Imagination: Balzac, Henry James, Melodrama and the Mode of Excess* (New York, 1976, reprinted 1985); Christine Gledhill, 'The Melodramatic Field: An Investigation' in Gledhill, ed. *Home is Where the Heart Is: Studies in Melodrama and the Woman's Film* (London, 1988), Ben Singer, *Melodrama and Modernity: Early Sensational Cinema and Its Contexts* (New York, 2001), Linda Williams, *Playing the Race Card: Melodramas of Black and White From Uncle Tom to O.J. Simpson* (Princeton, 2001).

12 'Magnificent Response to Mayor of Southampton's Appeal', *Southern Daily Echo*, Thursday, April 17, 1912, p. 2.

13 Brooks, *The Melodramatic Imagination*, p. 80.

14 'The Deathless Story of the Titanic', Special magazine published by Lloyd's Weekly, May, 1912. For the local reception of James Cameron's *Titanic*, see Anne Massey and Michael Hammond: 'It was True, How can you Laugh?': History and Memory in the Reception of *Titanic* in Britain and Southampton', in Kevin S. Sandler and Gaylyn Studlar (eds.), *Titanic: Anatomy of a Blockbuster*, (New Brunswick N.J. and London, 1999).

15 David Glover and Cora Kaplan, *Genders* (London, 2000), pp. 134–135.

16 The Bamforth Company did issue a number of postcards memorialising the disaster.

17 Sir L. Weaver, *Memorials and Monuments, Old and New: Two Hundred Subjects Chosen from Seven Centuries* (London, 1915), pp. 292 and 297.

18 Lynda Nead, *Myths of Sexuality: Representation of Women in Victorian Britain* (Oxford and Cambridge Mass., 1988), p. 139.

19 'A Relief Fund: Councillor Bowyer to Confer with the Lord Mayor of London', *Southern Daily Echo*, Tuesday, April 16, 1912, p. 3.

20 'From Our Special Correspondent, Tuesday, April 16, 1912', Quoted in Donald Hyslop, Alastair Forsyth and Sheila Jemima, *Titanic Voices: Memories From the Fateful Voyage* (Stroud, 1994), p. 178.

21 'Musicians Memorial', *Southampton Times and Hampshire Express*, April 12, 1913.

CHAPTER THREE

The Titanic Disaster: Stead, Ships and the Supernatural

JOHN WILSON FOSTER

THE MEREST ACCIDENT?

I N THE British House of Commons, the Prime Minister Herbert Asquith referred to the Titanic disaster as 'one of those terrible events in the order of Providence which baffle foresight, which appall the imagination and make us feel the inadequacy of words to do justice to what we feel'.[1] But before long, dozens of people, survivors, relatives of the dead, commentators of one sort or another, claimed to have had *un*baffled foresight, to have foreseen the tragedy, or known someone who did. The air was soon thick with reports of ill-omens allegedly noted as such at the time, of personal premonitions and previsions, of forewarnings from second parties, even of foretellings: fictional stories and historical episodes that anticipated the events of the great ship's destruction.

It is impossible, of course, for any complex event not to repeat or reflect components of previous events and not to have been, in that sense, anticipated. Besides, a maritime disaster involving a large passenger liner had been predicted on quite practical grounds. The famous editor and investigative journalist W. T. Stead had interested himself in merchant and naval shipping for years, particularly Atlantic shipping, and his wide reading and acquaintance with reports of shipping accidents would have informed his story, 'The Sinking of a Modern Liner', published in 1886 in the *Pall Mall Gazette*, of which he had become editor in 1883. (He did not visit the United States until 1893, so in 1886 Stead had no personal experience of transatlantic passage.) Told from the viewpoint of a second-class passenger on a ship that left Liverpool and picked up passengers and mailbags at Queenstown (as did Titanic), this short story is full of circumstances and incidents that anticipate the later, greater calamity. Stead's son, who assumed editorship of the *Review of Reviews* after his father's death on Titanic, thought the story prescient enough to reprint in the June 1912 issue in homage to his late father's grasp of affairs.[2] It was a practical rather than visionary matter, for Stead had appended an editorial footnote in 1886 claiming that 'This is exactly what might take place, and what will take place if the liners are sent to sea short of boats'.[3] The story's narrator counts the lifeboats on the fifth night out and calculates that of the 916 passengers, there are boats for, at most, 390; and indeed, after a collision and a panicky evacuation from the sinking liner, 700 passengers are stranded on board with only one lifeboat remaining. The narrator is washed overboard but manages to clamber into a passing lifeboat, as Archibald Gracie and some other Titanic swimmers were able to do.[4]

Other incidents in Stead's story are also familiar: there is panic around the boats; the captain is forced to brandish and use a revolver; the women are taken off first and some of them resist being separated from their menfolk; men from steerage, many of them Irish, try to storm the boats; some of the boats leave with half their proper complement; and the 'agonised clamour' of the multitude left to fend for themselves when the last boat has gone stuns the narrator. Written without real eloquence, 'The Sinking of a Modern Liner' nevertheless impresses by detail confirmed by what befell Titanic and her passengers which Stead clearly if not specifically foresaw.

Stead's story is a lightly fictionalised version of the warnings the author and others had been issuing about possible mishap at sea because of excessive speed or inadequate safety provisions. When the mishap came in the form of the most disastrous shipwreck in history, it lent to natural cause-and-effect the dimension of prediction and foresight if the warnings were detailed enough.

What happened, however natural and cautioned against, could even seem like inevitability, a kind of fate somehow beyond human control on the night. Observers and commentators then retrospectively saw the collision and sinking as having been scripted before they happened: hence the instant and perpetual use (to this day) of the epithet 'ill-fated' to describe Titanic. (The phrase appeared in print as early as 18 April 1912, when the London *Daily Sketch* used it in a caption to a photograph.) Of course, it is natural to read disaster back into the immediate past through hindsight; in its editions of 17 and 18 April, the *Daily Sketch* reproduced photographs of the ship leaving Southampton and Queenstown and each time referred understandably to the 'doomed Titanic'; in such cases, the past is a re-read as the present laden with the future.[5] But quite soon the spoken or unspoken assumption abroad was that the Titanic tragedy had been waiting to happen, not just in physical but also in metaphysical terms. Everyone knows now, and knew then, of the claims of unsinkability supposedly made on behalf of Titanic; very early, those claims were regarded as amounting to—though the word itself was not known to many—*hubris*, the Greek notion of overweening pride which is an element in the downfall of the Greek tragic hero and in his tragic fate. It suggests the prior existence of some force of cosmic judgment which the hero offends and arouses; his end, if not his beginning, is already written once *hubris* is committed. And so, it was widely believed, it was with Titanic, the fate of which was foregone and deserved.

All of this must have caused a disturbing frisson in those who ought to have travelled on Titanic but for some reason didn't—there were almost fifty fortunate truants we know of, including Lord Pirrie, J. Pierpont Morgan, Alexander Carlisle (co-designer of the ship) and Jack Binns (the celebrated wireless operator).[6] Lawrence Beesley in his 1912 account of the disaster he survived describes a scene he apparently witnessed from over the side of the ship: a knot of stokers running along the quay, their kits over their shoulders, waved back and dismissed by a petty officer when they reached the shore end of the gangway which was dragged back despite their protests. 'Those stokers,' remarks Beesley, 'must be thankful men to-day that some circumstance, whether their own lack of punctuality or some unforeseen delay over which they had no control, prevented their being in time to run up that last gang-way!'[7] In all, at least twenty-six fortunate crewmen signed on but did not sail, while thirteen (!) unlucky crewmen travelled as substitutes.

There were narrow escapes from possible death among passengers who did not embark at Southampton on Titanic. Mr and Mrs George Vanderbilt, of the railway and shipping family, cancelled on 9 April; but their servant, Frederick Wheeler, sailed in second-class with their luggage on 10 April and was lost. Henry Clay Frick, an associate of Andrew Carnegie's, also cancelled his passage. The English novelist Arnold Bennett, recorded in his Paris diary for Saturday, 20 April: 'Yesterday the [Edgar] Selwyns and Calou came to lunch. Only their anxiety to meet us here and hear the rest of my comic novel prevented them from going home with the H. B. Harrises on the Titanic'. Nice to think that literature, in this case Bennett's novel, *The Regent*, saved lives![8] Henry B. Harris was a Broadway producer with whom Bennett had lunched on 23 March ; he said goodbye to his wife on board (she was saved) and he went down with the ship. A fellow theatre manager, Henry C. Jacobs, told a *New York Times* correspondent that it was by 'the merest accident' that he too did not sail from Southampton on Titanic, that a visit to Richard Croker in Ireland had mercifully cost him the maiden voyage and compelled him to book passage on the ship's second east-west passage.[9]

There were those who wished to see these narrow shaves as vaguely providential or the result of extra-volitional forces. Even the hardheaded were unsure. Norman Craig, the Scottish MP and famous King's Counsel, had intended to make the trip 'for a blow of fresh air' and to return on the Cunard liner Mauretania. He was assumed by the *Daily Sketch* of 16 April to have been transferred with other passengers to another liner for safe passage to New York. But, he said later, 'I suddenly decided not to sail. I cannot tell you why; there was simply no reason for it. No; I had no mysterious premonitions, or visions of any kind. Nor did I dream of any disaster. But I do know that at practically the last moment I did not want to go'.[10]

THE JOKER IN THE STACK

Even before she sailed, Titanic had provoked hearsay, rumour and even mild anxiety. In this she differed from other ships only in degree, since sea lore is, or was, widespread and potent. Superstitious belief adhered to maiden voyages especially, as Lawrence Beesley reminded readers. Even the clerk in the White Star office where Beesley bought his ticket admitted that there were those who were disinclined to take maiden voyages. Beesley, like the good science school-master he had been, gave short shrift to the paranormality surrounding Titanic—'I suppose no ship ever left port with so much miserable nonsense showered on her'[11]—yet took care to enliven his narrative by reminding read-ers of the kind of nonsense—entertaining rather than miserable—he was refer-ring to. But most of the 'nonsense' surfaced after the fact of disaster and was by some cultural back-formation activated by disaster in a way that folklorists and psychologists could perhaps identify as a recognizable pattern. Even if there were quantities of humbug generated by the ship, and still are, it is not the possible truth of what was claimed that interests me here but rather the phenomenon of the claims itself, since it tells us much about Anglo-American culture around 1912.

Beesley recorded the 'direst' misgivings he heard expressed by crewmen and passengers around him after the near-collision with New York, though he himself discounted the episode as ominous. With his usual truculent ambiva-lence, Beesley records a second bad omen, this one said to have happened at Queenstown, Titanic's last port of call before heading across the Atlantic: 'As one of the tenders containing passengers and mails neared the Titanic, some of those on board gazed up at the liner towering above them, and saw a stok-er's head, black from his work in the stokehold below, peering out at them from the top of one of the enormous funnels . . . that rose many feet above the highest deck'.[12] Beesley seems to have known at the time that Titanic's fourth stack was a dummy one used for ventilation, but most passengers presumably wouldn't have, and received quite a shock. Even with the knowledge, some passengers thought that the apparition boded ill for the journey. The stoker's joke certainly took place, for a Mr Whyte of Queenstown took a photograph from the tender America that shows the tiny head peering above the rim of the giant funnel.[13]

The joker in the stack had a long life and underwent many metamorphoses. His Queenstown materialisation was not his first. Ellen Williamson was a rich American socialite who wrote a book entitled *When We Went First Class* that relived the era of luxury liners, including the Age of Titanic. Her aunt and uncle boarded the ship in Cherbourg after a buying spree in Europe. Uncle Walter told his wife that he had been talking to some passengers who had embarked at Southampton, where they had seen 'a black-faced stoker peering at them through a hole in a smokestack of an adjacent ship, and had made faces at them'.[14] Several passengers were upset and thought it an ill way to start their crossing.

It is difficult to know how much the alleged foresight was really hindsight; much of it, presumably. And even premonitions that are realised by events might only be notable, and noted, coincidences; after all, premonitions that turn out to be baseless are rarely recorded and indeed cancel themselves out. Even so, omens, premonitions, forewarnings and previsions that reach a high incidence and are vindicated by events achieve a cultural critical mass that is independent of the possibility that they disrupt the time continuum. The answer to the question, 'Why were there so many claims that the Titanic tragedy had been sensed or seen before it happened?' is a cultural one.

Able Seaman Joseph Scarrott crewed Boat No. 14, of which Fifth Officer Harold Lowe was in command, and survived to supply some time later (perhaps with some editorial help, though his testimony to the British inquiry is eloquent enough) a moving account of how he and Lowe eventually manoeuvred their boat among the bodies and wreckage after the liner had gone: 'As we left that awful scene we gave way to tears. It was enough to break the stoutest heart'. Scarrott was stout-hearted, but he afterwards said that he had nevertheless joined the ship 'not with a good heart'. Never in twenty-nine years of seagoing could he recall 'that feeling of hesitation' that accompanied his preparations for the journey. He thought Titanic the finest ship he had ever seen but he bade his sister 'Goodbye' and when asked why, instead of 'So long, see you again soon', he was at a loss to explain. Once on board, he found himself behaving in uncustomary ways, even omitting to don his uniform before fire and boat drill.[15]

Among the embarking passengers, Eva Hart's mother had a famous premonition and as a result refused to sleep in bed but rather sat up each night. Lady Duff Gordon claimed she had a similar unease and that her response was the same: she could not completely undress at night and kept her coat, wrap and jewels ready to hand in case of emergency. 'I have never been a psychic woman,' she later wrote (and one can believe it), 'and in all my life have never been to a séance or dabbled in the occult, so I am even now loath to call this feeling of acute fear which I experienced a premonition, yet the fact remains that though I have crossed the Atlantic many times both before and since I have never had it on any other occasion. Something warned me, some deep instinct, that all was not well'.[16] Mrs J. J. Brown (Unsinkable Molly) later told Gracie that a Mrs Bucknell (whose husband founded Bucknell University) had expressed misgivings about boarding the ship because she had 'evil forebodings'; Mrs Brown laughed at that but of course the anxious Mrs Bucknell was 'proven' right.[17]

In several incidents, the premonition occurred to a second party, who then warned the prospective passenger. Archibald Gracie told the *New York Times* that among the women he last saw on board was a Miss Evans who, he said, virtually refused to be rescued because, in Gracie's words, 'she had been told by a fortune-teller in London that she would meet her death on the water'.[18] He repeated the anecdote in his book, *The Truth about the Titanic* (1912). Young Edith Evans, aged twenty-five, spoke to Gracie during the early stages of evacuation and said that she had been told by a fortune-teller to 'beware of water' and now 'she knew she would be drowned'. Gracie went on: 'My efforts to persuade her to the contrary were futile. Though she gave voice to her story, she presented no evidence whatever of fear, and when I saw and conversed with her an hour later when conditions appeared especially desperate, and the last lifeboat was supposed to have departed, she was perfectly calm and did not revert again to the superstitious tale'.[19] Gracie had been introduced to Edith Evans only during the emergency and it was the husband of one of the women who introduced her, Robert Cornell, a New York magistrate, who relayed to the *New York Times* Mrs Cornell's account of her last view of her niece, Edith Evans. Mrs Cornell, her two sisters (Mrs Appleton and Mrs Brown) and their niece, were travelling together; Mrs Cornell and Mrs Appleton were assigned to boat No. 2 and Mrs Brown and Edith Evans to another boat that left later. When it was found that the second boat had one passenger too many, Miss Evans left the boat, saying that Mrs Brown had children at home and that she, Miss Evans, should forgo her place; she 'left the boat, saying that she would take a chance of getting in a boat later. It seems that this brave girl never got that chance . . . '[20] Mrs J. M. Brown was rescued from Engelhardt boat D which indeed left after Emergency boat No. 2. According to Second Officer Lightoller, D was the last boat to leave the ship and he had difficulty finding women to enter it; 'when that boat went away', Lightoller told the British inquiry, 'there were no women whatever' (that is to say, left on board Titanic as far as he could see).[21] Edith Evans must have deliberately made herself scarce, and the supposition that she was honouring the fortune-teller's warning is tempting.[22]

One of the most interesting letters to arrive at the *Daily Sketch* after the disaster was one from an apparent acquaintance of a psychic, Mrs 'A' (as the newspaper referred to her), who attended a lecture on 3 April in an unnamed British city and was asked by the lecturer afterwards why she was so distracted during it; she had had a vision, she said: she had seen a railway accident, a mansion on fire, a colliery explosion, and a four-funnelled steamship in collision with a mountain of ice. The visionary name of the ship was Tintac and she heard 'Southampton' called out, but of the real ship at the time she was entirely ignorant. The end of the lecture disrupted her vision. According to her acquaintance, the psychic had foreseen other events, including the Hawes Junction railway disaster at Christmas 1911. When asked why she did not make her vision public, she replied that the public was not ready to accept such visions as genuine.[23]

THESE ABSURD DAYS

Yet in 1912 the public in Britain was highly responsive to both spiritualism and superstition of various kinds. Spiritualism itself began a long period of popularity in Britain after 1850 and in 1901, H. G. Wells was provoked to complain about 'these absurd days . . . when we are all trying to be as psychic and silly and superstitious as possible!'[24] Lady Duff Gordon may not have attended a séance before she sailed on Titanic, but many of her contemporaries had. George Bernard Shaw—who would surely have poured contempt on attempts to give the Titanic calamity a supernatural dimension—dismissively remembered the decades before the Great War as those in which people were 'addicted to table-rapping, materialisation séances, clairvoyance, palmistry, crystal-gazing and the like to such an extent that it may be doubted whether ever before in the history of the world did sooth-sayers, astrologists, and unregistered therapeutic specialists of all sorts flourish as they did during this half century of the drift to the abyss'.[25] The fate of Titanic both anticipated and symbolised the surrender to the abyss, while the stories she provoked and inspired betrayed the addiction Shaw lamented in British culture.

Shaw's list of Edwardian paranormalities can be extended to include telepathy or thought-reading, clairaudience and 'phone-voyance' (seeing through a telephone wire) as well as clairvoyance; mesmerism, hypnotism and levitation, automatic writing, astrology and astral voyaging as well as crystal-gazing and palmistry; magic and ritual, theosophy and the occult as well as spiritualism—all flourished during the Age of Titanic. Stead in his *Review of Reviews* regularly surveyed the pages of *Proceedings of the Society for Psychical Research*, *The Occult Review*, *The Theosophist*, *Hindu Spiritual Magazine*, *Annals of Psychical Science*, *Modern Astrology* and *Occult World*. The Society for Psychical Research was founded in 1882 and before long had eminent members, including W. E. Gladstone and Arthur Balfour (Prime Ministers both), Alfred Russel Wallace (the co-formulator of the theory of organic evolution), Alfred Lord Tennyson, John Ruskin, 'Lewis Carroll', and eight Fellows of the Royal Society. The SPR was preceded by the British National Association for Spiritualists (1873) and followed by the London Spiritualist Alliance (1884). Eminent literary figures who at least at some point in their career interested themselves in spiritualism or the occult included Arthur Conan Doyle, W. T. Stead, Rudyard Kipling (all three associated with the Titanic disaster) and W. B. Yeats.

Not surprisingly, many Christian ministers were hostile to spiritualism, but Christianity in the Age of Titanic was faltering, and hostility to spiritualism was something of a rearguard action. Janet Oppenheim argues that spiritualism and psychic research were surrogate religions for refugees from Christianity in the late nineteenth and early twentieth century.[26] She demonstrates, however, that the relationship between spiritualism and Christianity was a complicated one, and this allowed living-room at least for popular, if fugitive, acceptance of the kind of epiphenomena that 'materialised' around Titanic. Spiritualism was an ally of Christianity in opposition to materialism, and it was held to be both a cause and a result of the decline in materialist values: 'materialism has fallen into disrepute,' wrote C. G. Harrison in 1894, 'partly because its foundations have been shaken by the phenomena of the séance room . . . and partly because it is felt to be unsatisfactory as an explanation of the universe'.[27]

At the same time, spiritualists were at pains to distinguish spiritualism from superstition. Spiritualism, insisted Alfred Russel Wallace, is 'a science of human nature . . . an experimental science'.[28] Spiritual phenomena were to be observed, studied and explained in the language, and by the methods, of science. The relations between science and spiritualism were as complicated as those between the Christian churches and spiritualism, and scientists were divided in their attitude to psychical research. But the application of scientific methods by psychical researchers meant that there was a similarity imputed between the material and immaterial worlds. Indeed, some spiritualists rejected the notion of the supernatural, instead viewing it as an extension of the natural.[29] The anti-materialism of spiritualists was in this way a special attitude that permitted some spiritualists, including Stead, to be advocates of applied science and material progress.

We see this bifocal vision in the novel written by a famous casualty of the Titanic disaster, John Jacob Astor. His science fiction work, *A Journey in Other Worlds*, was published in 1894, a year before Wells' *The Time Machine*. In it, as in society, The Machine Age and the Spirit Age comfortably overlap—or rather, the latter is an extension of the former.[30] Conan Doyle too was a champion of psychical research by scientific method, the task of discovering 'the laws which regulate psychic affairs'.[31] Doyle investigated the spirit life from about 1901 and became a wholehearted believer around 1914. Although he did not possess Astor's knowledge of engineering, Doyle too was interested in what the future held for material advance and the progress of nations.

It was the concern with the future that helped to bridge science and spiritualism, and Titanic sailed in the midst of this concern. 'The doctrine of a future state and of the proper preparation for it as here developed, is to be found in the works of all spiritualists', said Russel Wallace.[32] It is not surprising, then, that Titanic as (short-lived) machine triumph should repose in our imaginations as a ship of almost supernatural aura, and that her innumerable commentators should appear as mediums 'transposing down', as electrical engineers would say, her enormous voltage for us.

THE NAPOLEON OF NEWSMEN

Doyle met Stead in London in 1890 and kept in distant touch for the rest of Stead's life, and though Doyle was in collision with Stead, as he was with Shaw, over the Boer War, he thought that Stead was in psychic knowledge a generation ahead of his time. Stead was intensely interested in inventions and scientific innovation and in the future, and until his death was greatly concerned with the threat to British sea supremacy, particularly from Germany. He combined his fervid attention to political realities and scientific developments with an unshakeable faith in the spirit world in all its manifestations. His spiritualism, like his empiricism, was progressive and forward-looking.

For years Stead was the amanuensis for Julia A. Ames, an American woman who had lived in Chicago and who had died ('what we call died'— Stead) in December, 1891, and in 1897 he published a series of her messages communicated to him through automatic writing; in 1909 there was a new and enlarged edition which Stead's daughter Estelle published in 1914 as *After Death: A Personal Narrative*. In her biography, *My Father: Personal & Spiritual Reminiscences* (1913), Estelle Stead reveals that it was 'Julia' who chose the hymn 'Our Blest Redeemer' to be sung at the farewell service of 'Julia's Circle' on 3 April before Stead embarked for New York City on Titanic, bound for the Men and Religions Congress on Universal Peace to be held in Carnegie Hall. In her message of that evening, she failed to foresee Stead's drowning and instead wished him a pleasant journey.

Years before, Stead had published an account of his first visit to the United States in the *Pall Mall Gazette*, of which he had been editor 1883–1890, which the *Irish News and Belfast Morning News* reproduced in its 19 April 1912 issue. It is datelined 'S.S. New York, 10 March 1894' (the vessel which almost put paid to Titanic's maiden voyage before it began) and in it the author marvels at the speed of the liner and the effort put into increasing the speed of these transatlantic ships but complains of the resulting vibrations and wonders if the need for passenger comfort will cap the upward trend of speed. More importantly, he introduces an analogy that he would never abandon. The loneliness of the Atlantic crossing, days going by without another vessel being seen, 'was very like human life. We pass from the cradle to the grave in solitary life, meeting perchance (sic) but two or three in the course of our pilgrimage with whom we can exchange signals of friendly intercourse'. When the fog came down, the ship's foghorn sent its tidings through the darkened air, 'much as the voice from the unseen falls upon the ear of the clairaudient'.

The analogy was developed by Stead in a 1909 article in the *Fortnightly Review*, 'How I know the Dead Return', published in Boston that year as a slim book and reproduced as a Preface to *After Death*. He imagines a modern liner reaching the shores of America, equipped with contemporary wireless, but in this scenario, no ship has reached the New World since Columbus; the crew and passengers discover the Spaniard's innumerable descendants and wish to relay the astounding news to the Old World. Only later is the telegraphy developed sufficiently to communicate clearly by Marconigram the first message, from, in Stead's scenario, one Captain Smith! The message is disbelieved until further messages are sent and received from both sides of the ocean. In an analogous way, Stead believes, communications from 'the other side' have been sent, received and returned. The telegraphy has now been perfected, the ship's passage is now uneventful.

In the light of Stead's analogy (an analogy that connects science with spiritualism), it is a graphic coincidence that Stead should drown on a transatlantic liner, thereby fusing metaphor and literal reality. The fusion grew stronger when it was reported that Stead, like his imagined passengers on his imagined liner, was sending messages by spiritual Marconigrams from the New World of the 'other side'. The *Daily Sketch* of 22 April reported that a Pittsburgh delegate at the Convention of the United States Spiritualists Association had talked to Stead the day before and he was happy and preparing to communicate with the Convention.[33] Perhaps the uneventful perfection of communication between the living and the 'dead' which Stead believed had been achieved by the Edwardian period explains the subdued, not to say disappointing nature of Stead's messages. Or perhaps Stead thought, before and after death, that the manner of death was far less interesting than the provisional destination of the soul. According to the deceased Stead, the destination was as described in the title of the book his daughter published in 1922, *The Blue Island: Experiences of a New Arrival Beyond the Veil, Communicated by W.T. Stead*. Conan Doyle supplied a somewhat wary letter to Estelle as Foreword, welcoming the book but remarking that he had never come across the blue island in the numerous descriptions of the afterlife he had read.

Stead's messages were communicated through Pardoe Woodman, a young man who had met Stead only once and who was a member of Estelle Stead's Shakespeare Company, which was on tour when Titanic sank. Woodman foretold the wreck on the Sunday it happened and Estelle recognised his psychic powers as a result. Through a well-known 'direct voice' medium, Etta Wriedt, Stead appeared to his daughter a fortnight after his death and was in daily touch with her thereafter.[34] When Woodman came to live with Estelle in 1917 he wanted to get in touch with a comrade who had been killed in the war and did so through a medium; later, Woodman discovered his own gift for automatic writing and Stead allegedly exploited this to talk to his daughter.

Unfortunately for those more interested in this life than in the putative afterlife, Stead is parsimonious with his details of his death aboard Titanic. The precise manner of his death had been a matter of speculation in the press, and survivors failed to mention him in their published accounts. Stead himself is not much more forthcoming: 'Of my actual passing from earth to spirit life I do not wish to write more than a few lines'.[35] After he died (but how did he die?) he found himself able to help people (how?) and was already in the company of friends who had passed over years before (who?). The journalist in him regretted not having a telephone at hand: 'I felt I could give the papers some headlines for that evening'.[36] But the journalist's literalism instantly becomes the spiritualist's metaphor: 'Here was I, with my telephone out of working order for the present'; so near to earth and yet so far, the life-and-death communication system not yet set up or mastered. The end came, and the old analogy is put to use again without a tint of irony: 'It was like waiting for a liner to sail; we waited until we were all aboard. I mean we waited until the disaster was complete. The saved—saved; the dead—alive. Then in one whole we moved our scene. It was strange method of travelling for us all, and we were a strange crew, bound for we knew not where'.[37] The picture of the wreck scene is brief and generic—'hundreds of bodies floating in the water—dead—hundreds of souls carried through the air, alive; very much alive, some were. Many, realising their death had come, were enraged at their own powerlessness to save their valuables. They fought to save what they had on earth prized so much. The scene on the boat at the time of striking was not pleasant, but it was as nothing to the scene among the poor souls newly thrust out of their bodies, all unwillingly'.[38] Off they go, then, in something akin to the medieval Irish flying boat that transported souls (or Astor's space capsule), to 'a different land' which turns out to be a blue island.

How one waits for one detail of Stead's experience that would be both realistic and indisputably his, one incidental solution to some Titanic puzzle, but waits in vain! But then 'Stead' like Stead before him is at pains to show just how alike life and the afterlife are: only the body is shed, everything else is retained and, blue island apart, life as it were goes on. In comparison, the sinking of Titanic may have been vulgarly extraordinary and thus to be passed over quickly. But the ship itself he would have relished (and did relish), perhaps at the end regarding its sinking as its last machine triumph, carrying him and others safely to the other side.

Stead was fascinated by shipwrecks, both literal and metaphoric; but because he had imagined them so fully, perhaps 'Stead'—or perhaps we should say his daughter—thought it unnecessary to describe one again, though this one be real and personally fatal. As well as 'The Sinking of a Modern Liner' in 1886 there had been, more oddly, a story his daughter called 'A Dramatic Incident' when in *My Father*, she excerpted it from the 1892 Christmas annual of the *Reviews of Reviews*, an issue entitled 'From the Old World to the New' devoted to the Chicago World's Fair scheduled for 1893 and which Stead visited. The previous annual had been dedicated to the Invisible World, this one to the New World, the modern liner by default becoming a vessel of communication of real and figurative importance. Stead imagines the voyage of a group of English tourists from Liverpool to Chicago, juxtaposing this narrative with a 'dramatic representation of conclusions arrived at after twelve months' experimental study of psychical phenomena; and an exposition of the immense political possibilities that are latent in this World's Fair',[39] the three most important components of Stead's public life thereby conjoined—politics (especially the future role of America), spiritualism, and material improvement (especially in the technologies of shipping and telecommunications).

The dramatic incident is fictitious but the ship and its captain were real— Majestic, the White Star liner, and Captain Smith, with whom Stead had sailed on that liner and who came naturally to Stead's mind in *How I Know the Dead Return*. On Titanic Stead resumed acquaintance with Captain Smith and it seems possible that Stead sought him out after the collision; but how either of them died has never been ascertained. In Stead's story, Majestic with the tourists on board follows another ship that strikes an iceberg in mid-Atlantic. Six men and a boy succeed in reaching the ice alive. The shipwreck had been foretold by one of the Majestic passengers through what the spiritualists called a 'spontaneous' phenomenon: she hears a sudden cry of danger and sees the wreck in vision. She tells another passenger (perhaps Stead in disguise) who happens to be gifted in automatic writing and has already received a message from one of the stricken survivors. In the company of Captain Smith, Compton receives a second message; four survivors have been swept away when the iceberg parted, three remain on a diminished ice-floe. The spiritualist agenda continues. In order for the Captain to be convinced and turn the mighty Majestic off its path to mount a rescue mission, Compton's friend, the Professor, hypnotises the Captain's niece into a clairvoyant state who then 'precedes' the liner and describes what she sees; Smith is still unconvinced; Compton receives more messages: one survivor remains; an ice-warning sounds on Majestic; the ice-fog lifts; the last man alive is at last seen by Captain Smith and is saved.

THE GHOST IN THE MACHINE

Given the increased flow of traffic in the North Atlantic and the increased speed of that traffic, and widespread awareness of icebergs in the region, it is hardly surprising that writers should include in their fictions episodes of collision or that similar episodes should then take place in real life. Nor is it surprising that commentators should predict a catastrophe if conditions in the first decade of the twentieth century were maintained, especially if there continued to be insufficient lifeboats aboard liners. Rider Haggard said that it was curious how often imagination is verified by fact, but that perhaps it is because the lines in which imagination must work are narrow and based on fact.[40] Besides, we know that speed and collision were cultural motifs of the time that would naturally find themselves recruited by story-writers.[41]

Still, writers in their fictions could nevertheless give pause by 'foretelling' elements of the Titanic disaster; they include Mayn Clew Garnett, Morgan Robertson—both well-known to Titanic disaster aficionados—and Rider-Haggard, as well as Stead. But what adds interest to Stead's case is his own conviction of the reality of communication from the Beyond, with the possibility of prophecy it implies. He may have sharply distinguished spiritualism from worthless superstition but he was yet a participant in the mysticism that flourished at the turn of the twentieth century in Great Britain and North America: the fashion for magic, occult societies, exotic religious sects, folklore of the supernatural. It is hardly coincidental that the years from, say, 1880 to the Great War were a golden age in the ghost story, between R. L. Stevenson through Henry James and W. W. Jacobs to M. R. James. Just as interestingly, in W. T. Stead spiritualism and science converge, and do so through the vehicle of the transatlantic liner. The convergence of the twain, science and the supernatural, was a cultural product, like the liner itself. If Titanic—ship and tragedy—magnetically gathered to itself much of the spiritualist energy and superstitious beliefs and practices that were a significant part of Anglo-American culture of the time, that may be because spiritualism and materialism themselves converged. The machinery, including transatlantic liners, that in the late Victorian and Edwardian ages was expanding and improving almost alarmingly had, it could seem, a ghost inside it.

Notes

1 Quoted in 'The March of Events', *The World's Work*, no. 19, vol. 2, May 1912, p. 572.

2 W. T. Stead, 'The Sinking of a Modern Liner', *The Review of Reviews*, no. 45, 1912, pp. 635–637.

3 Stead, 'Sinking', p. 635.

4 It is not known if the famous spiritualist Stead, when the real thing happened to him, lost his life by trying to swim or by choosing instead to go down with the ship, composed in his certainty of an afterlife.

5 A useful compendium of British newspaper responses to the Titanic tragedy is Dave Bryceson, *The Titanic Disaster: As Reported in the British National Press April–July 1912* (Sparkford, 1997).

6 It was Pirrie's 'invariable custom' to sail on the maiden voyages of the mammoth liners

built by Harland & Wolff and only imminent surgery prevented him from boarding Titanic; see the *Daily Mirror*, 17 April, 1912, p. 3.

7 Lawrence Beesley, *The Loss of R,M.S. Titanic: Its Story and Its Lessons* (London, 1912), p. 15.

8 Newman Flower (ed.), *The Journals of Arnold Bennett, 1911–1921* (London, 1932), p. 47. See also Reginald Pound, *Arnold Bennett: A Biography* (London, 1952), p. 243.

9 *New York Times*, 17 April, 1912, p. 8.

10 *Daily Mirror*, 17 April, 1912, p. 3.

11 'The Loss of the S.S. Titanic: Its Story and Its Lessons' in Jack Winocur (ed.), *The Story of the Titanic as Told by Its Survivors* (New York, 1960), p. 108.

12 Beesley, in Winocur, p. 17.

13 E. E. O'Donnell (Society of Jesus), *The Last Days of the Titanic: Photographs and Mementos of the Tragic Maiden Voyage* (Niwot, Colorado, 1997), p. 73.

14 Ellen Williamson, *When We Went First Class* (New York, 1977), p. 112.

15 Donald Hyslop, Alastair Forsyth and Sheila Jemima (eds.), *Titanic Voices: Memories from the Fateful Voyage* (Stroud, 1994), p. 93. It is my understanding, however, that there was no fire or boat drill on board Titanic.

16 Duff Gordon, Lady, *Discretions and Indiscretions* (New York, 1932), pp. 164–65.

17 Gracie, in Winocur, p.177

18 *New York Times*, 19 April, 1912, p. 2.

19 Gracie, in Winocur, p. 128.

20 *New York Times*, 20 April, 1912, p. 4.

21 Quoted by Gracie, in Winocur, p. 212.

22 Incidentally, anyone familiar with T. S. Eliot's modernist epic poem, *The Waste Land* (1922), will find the story of Edith Evans and the clairvoyant intriguing.

23 Bryceson, *The Titanic Disaster*, pp. 129–30.

24 H.G. Wells, 'The New Accelerator' (1901) in Michael Sherborne (ed.), *The Country of the Blind and Other Stories* (New York, 1996), p. 375.

25 Shaw quoted in Janet Oppenheim *The Other World: Spiritualism and Psychical Research in England, 1985–1914* (Cambridge, 1985), p. 28.

26 This is an important thesis in Oppenheim's *The Other World*.

27 C.G. Harrison, *The Transcendental Universe* (1894), quoted in Mike Jay and Michael Neve (eds.), *1900* (London, 1999), p. 121.

28 Charles H. Smith (ed.), *Alfred Russel Wallace: An Anthology of his Shorter Writings* (Oxford, 1991), pp. 93, 94.

29 For example, Wallace's editor writes: 'Wallace regarded spiritualization as a *process continuing the evolutionary progression in a manner rather analogous to the way organic evolution depended on—and itself complemented—inorganic evolution*' in Smith (ed.), *Alfred Russel Wallace*, p. 67.

30 John Jacob Astor, *A Journey in Other Worlds: A Romance of the Future* (London, 1894).

31 Arthur Conan Doyle, *The Edge of the Unknown* (New York, 1930), p. 81.

32 Smith (ed.), *Alfred Russel Wallace*, p. 93.

33 Bryceson, *The Titanic Disaster*, p. 120.

34 It was in a sitting with Wriedt on June 9th that 'Stead' gave most details of his death: he recalled Archibald Butt's threatening to shoot (presumably unruly passengers), his asking Butt and another man to pray and doing so, and simply being passively overwhelmed by the water before being struck on the head: see James Coates (ed.), *Has W. T. Stead Returned? A Symposium* (London, 1913), pp. 64–65.

35 'W. T. Stead', *The Blue Island: Experiences of a New Arrival Beyond the Veil. Communicated by W. T. Stead. Recorded by Pardoe Woodman and Estelle Stead. With Letter from Sir Arthur Conan Doyle* (London, 1922), p. 37.

36 W. T. Stead, *The Blue Island*, p. 38.

37 W. T. Stead, *The Blue Island*, pp. 38–39.

38 W. T. Stead, *The Blue Island*, pp. 39–40.

39 Estelle W. Stead, *My Father: Personal & Spiritual Reminiscences* (New York, 1913), p. 196.

40 Sir H. Rider Haggard, *The Days of My Life: An Autobiography* (London, 1926), p. 95.

41 I explore these and other motifs in *The Age of Titanic* (Dublin, 2002).

FOUR

The Titanic Disaster and Images of National Identity in Scandinavian Literature[1]

PETER BJÖRKFORS

IN MID 1912, an obscure Swedish author named W. A:son Grebst published a novel called *Dödsfärden, en romantiserad skildring af Titanic's undergång* (*The Fatal Voyage, A Romanticised Description of the Sinking of the Titanic*).[2] It was but one among innumerable books, pamphlets, sermons and poems that were written soon after the disaster, and that prompted the editor of the *New York Times* to write: 'To write about the Titanic . . . takes more than paper, pen and a feeling that the disaster was a terrible one'.[3] Within the course of the same year, an equally obscure Finnish author named Esko Waltala plagiarised Grebst's novel as *Titanicin perikato, Romantillinen kuvaus Titanic-laivan haaksirikosta yöllä vasten 15 päivää huhtikuuta 1912* (which also translates as *The Fatal Voyage, A Romanticised Description of the Sinking of the Titanic*).[4] It is almost a word for word translation, but the Swedish settings, characters, and patriotic references have been substituted with Finnish ones. To the best of my knowledge, these two Scandinavian publications were the first Titanic novels ever to be written.

As stated above, relatively little is known about the authors. Daniel William August Simon Andersson Grebst (1875–1920) wrote several popular travel books, as well as an account of the Messina earthquake in 1908. From 1913 onwards, he was editor-in-chief of the anti-Semitic, pro-German periodical *VIDI*. Hardly any biographical or other literary information appears to exist on Esko Waltala, and the name might have been a pseudonym.

The contemporary reception of *Dödsfärden* and *Titanicin Perikato* appears to have been quite enthusiastic. The novels responded to great public curiosity in Sweden and Finland in the first months after the Titanic had sunk. One particular incident pertaining to Grebst's book has been documented: a Carl Eriksson from Gothenburg reacted strongly to the novel's vicious treatment of Bruce Ismay in the book. Eriksson notified Grebst that he had sent Ismay a translation of certain condemning passages from *Dödsfärden*, and that, with Ismay's consent, a lawsuit for slander would be filed against Grebst.[5] In all likelihood, this remained an empty threat, since nothing more was heard about the case.

In this chapter I will explore how the concept of national identity is invoked and used in the two novels. Although there are of course a great number of theoretical conceptions of national identity, I will be drawing in particular on the work and terminology of Menno Spiering. In his book *Englishness, Foreigners and Images of National Identity*, he writes: 'National identity is what people feel it to be. National identity is an image, it carries meaning in the sense that it abides in feelings and convictions; often it is part and parcel of an ideology'.[6] Expanding on this idea, Spiering goes on to define what he refers to as auto-images and hetero-images.[7] An auto-image, or a self-image, is the image that a group of people has of itself. A hetero-image, or a counter-image, is the image of 'otherness' or foreignness against which the auto-image is projected. In all, the auto-image of national identity is seldom defined without an attendant hetero-image. Within the scope of national identity, the hetero-image can be highlighted, exaggerated, and magnified in order to create a contrast to the 'sameness'; a phenomenon he calls silhouetting. In many ways, literature, and fiction in particular, is the primary vessel of the imagology of national identity: 'as national identity is an image shaped by emotions, rather than an objective verity, works of fiction might prove a particularly suitable vehicle for its creation and expression'.[8]

In the following pages I will demonstrate how Waltala's and Grebst's novels are heavily laden with nationalist and patriotic sentiment, and how images of national identity are projected onto the voyage and sinking of the Titanic. The novels' national imagery is boldly presented without further explanation or justification, since it is explicitly aimed at a nationally defined readership (Finns and Swedes) that is assumed to recognise and agree with it. In order to even partly understand where these constructions of national identity emanate from, one would have to go into the historical, sociological and cultural background of Scandinavian nationalism, which is beyond the scope of the present chapter. Here, I will take the national references offered at face value, and restrict myself to analysing the *notion* of national identity—a form of cultural production—as it appears in the work of two dramatic and emotional writers who have depicted it and projected it onto the Titanic. The texts I study echo Swedish and Finnish reflections upon foreign and domestic space:

[These novels] are the self-effacing literary transmutations of an intercultural confrontation; and in that respect they belong alongside other literary articulations of national identity and alterity phenomena such as the use of regional of exotic settings, of ethnically stereotyped stock characters or of historical material from the national heritage.[9]

Both *Dödsfärden* and *Titanicin perikato* are nationalistic to the core. Even though they are practically identical, they differ, as I have already noted, in the sense that one invokes Swedish national identity, and the other a Finnish national identity. However, in both novels, the issue of 'sameness' is silhouetted in a similar manner against 'otherness'. 'Sameness' here alludes to Finnish/Swedish national identity, while 'otherness' entails all the other nationalities encountered in the novels. In many instances, this 'otherness' is openly defamed in order to accentuate the basics of Swedishness/Finnishness. Waltala and Grebst, in other words, introduce, in fictionalised form, antagonistic characters and, indeed, antagonistic nationalities into the story of the voyage and the sinking of the Titanic. These hetero-images are not always derogatory, but they invariably carry some evidence of the silhouetting of 'sameness'. Let us turn, then, to determine how 'sameness', i.e. Swedishness and the Finnishness, is depicted in the two novels.[10]

In *Dödsfärden*, Gustav Larsson, a Swedish engineer, decides to go to America in early 1912 to try his luck and broaden his horizons. He travels first-class on the Titanic. On board he meets the daughter of an American multimillionaire, Alice McDean. While Gustav Larsson is the embodiment of modesty and decorum, Alice is depicted as spoiled, extravagant and vain, and she is referred to as 'a typical American'. Larsson falls secretly in love with her, but she is more interested in the Italian Count Uffiezi; in fact, the couple become en-gaged on board the Titanic. During the voyage, Gustav mingles with various real and fictional first-class passengers, and he also goes down to steerage to visit some fellow passengers from Sweden.

During the four days leading up to the disaster, the author creates a stereotypical picture of the voyage of the Titanic. We have the alleged speed breaking record, the domineering behaviour of the company owner, Mr Ismay, class distinctions, and the exaggerated luxuries of first-class, to cite but a few examples. When the collision occurs, Gustav is offered a seat in the same lifeboat as Alice, only to give it up to Count Uffiezi when Alice pleads for his safety. When the Titanic sinks, Gustav swims for his life, and happens upon Alice who has been swept into the water. He helps her back on a lifeboat and loses consciousness, only to wake up later in a lifeboat when the Carpathia has already arrived on the scene. In the aftermath of the disaster Alice realises that the Count is a coward, that her money and power mean nothing, and that she is actually in love with Gustav Larsson. The novel ends with the two married, visiting the Halifax graveyard where the victims of the Titanic are buried.

With regard to some of the characteristics that constituted Swedish national identity in 1912, Grebst offers a vivid remark at the very beginning of the novel when Gustav Larsson's father bids goodbye to his son: 'never forget that you are a Swede, and that all around the world that stands for honour and capability, loyalty and manliness'.[11] Honour, capability, loyalty and manliness, then, are the four cornerstones of a good Swede, and constitute what is expected of Gustav Larsson as well. The novel moreover implicitly addresses a number of other virtues which are relevant in relation to Swedish national identity: modesty, morality, faith in God, hard work and—surprisingly in this context—a sense of adventure. The novel rather boldly proclaims that mass emigration from Sweden to America is not so much due to poverty, but rather an expression of national pride, and of a hereditary desire that harks back to the memory of a time when Sweden was a great conquering empire of Vikings and warriors. In the same way the new emigrants are seen to conquer America.

The Finnish version, *Titanicin perikato*, is nearly identical to its Swedish counterpart, with the following exceptions. Here, the main, Finnish, character leaves for America without his father's consent, and there is the implication that he and his fellow emigrants are, in a sense, betraying their country. In *Titanicin perikato*, it is not the main character who falls in love with and eventually marries Alice, but his Finnish friend and fellow passenger; a character who has no counterpart in Grebst's version. The main hero returns to Finland, is reconciled with his father and marries his childhood sweetheart. One of the more notable differences between Waltala's and Grebst's versions is how in the former the characters experience premonitions and fear that the Titanic will sink, long before the ship hits the iceberg.

In *Titanicin perikato* issues of national identity are magnified, and made even more apparent, than in *Dödsfärden*. Finns, according to Waltala, are a tough and hardened people; formerly occupied by Sweden and in 1912 by Russia. As noted previously, the novel suggests that young men emigrating to America are in a sense abandoning their home country, and at the end of the novel the main character returns to Finland in a fashion resembling the return of the prodigal son. In this novel, there is also a notion of poverty as a part of Finnish national identity. In view of this, it is interesting to note that the author nevertheless puts his main characters in first-class on the Titanic. Waltala apparently still wants to depict the opulence of first-class in his novel and have his characters mingling with real and famous people, and yet glorify the virtues of modesty in the third-class. A similar rhetoric is evident throughout Titanic lore; all the way up to James Cameron's *Titanic* (1997). Waltala gets away with this by letting his main character scorn the very opulence he is travelling in, and pronounce that he would rather travel third-class with the emigrants. Moreover, in accordance with the inherent modesty, morality and faith in God of every true Finn, Olli Laurila (the Finnish version of Gustav Larsson) is immune to the praise of the Titanic's unsinkability and all that that stands for in terms of human vanity and hubris.

All this relates to Spiering's suggestion that national identity functions as a 'second hand' image abiding in feelings and convictions.[12] But Spiering raises another interesting point when he argues that '[a war] is apocalyptic; it destroys, it brings the end of an era. The period that follows is a period of *Bildung*.[13] Literature about a war in progress, and about the time following a war, offers explorations of both individual and national identity. I would suggest that the same theory could be applied to the Titanic. From a historian's point of view, the Titanic disaster was a relatively insignificant incident with little historical impact, aside from the changes in safety regulations on passenger liners.[14] Still, the Titanic disaster can be compared to the apocalyptic effects of a war in the sense that here, too, thousands were caught up in a freak circumstance which few would survive. Similar to the situation during a war, the disaster channelled the sympathy and imagination, horror and outrage of an entire world. The Titanic was, indeed, an apocalypse, and the time that followed it was, indeed, a period of *Bildung*.

The characteristic and stereotypical images of Swedish and Finnish national identity are not only explored and defined against the apocalyptic setting of the Titanic disaster; they are also put to the test. Gustav Larsson (representing both Sweden and Swedishness) is measured against the code of behaviour seen as appropriate in the sphere of public opinion in the first, passionate months after the Titanic sank, and against the stark oppositions available—glorification or vilification, heroism or cowardice, gentlemanly behaviour or barbarity. While the world was screaming for scapegoats, the surviving men often found that the mere fact that they were alive gave rise to doubts as to their honour and conduct on the Titanic. Since the main male protagonists in both novels survive, their survival has to be justified. They cannot simply escape in a lifeboat alongside women and children. Instead, they are required to perform heroic deeds before swimming for hours in icy water and finally being rescued. Otherwise, their 'honour and capability, loyalty and manliness' might be called into question.

As I have noted earlier, a national auto-image is seldom found without an attendant counter-image. There are several different nationalities presented in the two novels. Some of them are only mentioned briefly, while others actively contribute to the plot, and function as 'other' to the images of Swedish or Finnish national identity. In many early reports of the Titanic disaster commentators were eager to attribute negative incidents to certain nationalities: most particularly the Italians, Irish and Chinese. This is no different in *Dödsfärden* and *Titanicin perikato*. The nationalities that are only mentioned briefly are usually dealt with in a derogatory manner. Thus, there are six Chinese stowaways, a German hiding in a lifeboat, and a set of Russian Jews, smelling of onions, to name only a handful of such racist stereotypes.

Of all the various nationalities (apart from the Swedes/Finns) depicted in the two novels, only three are given enough space to really develop into the hetero-images that I have discussed previously. These are the English (exemplified by the Titanic's crew), the Americans (represented by Alice) and the

Italians (in the figure of Count Uffiezi). None of these three are directly compared to Finns and Swedes by the authors or the main characters. However, the descriptions of Alice as a typical representative of America and Count Uffiezi as a typical Italian implicitly articulate a silent comparison with Finland and Sweden. As for the depiction of the English crewmembers, there is one particularly potent section in Grebst—promptly plagiarised by Waltala—when a number of panicking firemen try to rush to a lifeboat:

Hard though their lives were, they still loved life. They wanted to live, live! To the boats, to the boats! But the officers and the seamen stood in front of the excited men and shoved them aside. 'Show that you are Englishmen', shouted the captain through the megaphone. This had a strange effect. The firemen drew back and rejoined the lines. Englishmen will remain Englishmen. If you appeal to their sense of chivalry, the result is seldom negative . . . However, this had a bad effect on the Italians and the Irish. Some of them had been kneeling and in mortal fear calling out the names of the Madonna and St Patrick. Now they rose and tried to rush to one of the lifeboats . . . The officers drove them away. Their shouts and screams did not abate, but they were subdued. The Englishmen had them under control, and the rescue work could continue.[15]

This passage clearly conveys a sense of admiration on the part of the authors towards what they perceive to be typical Englishness. The English sense of 'chivalry', in fact, closely corresponds to Grebst and Waltala's views on Swedishness/Finnishness, thus rendering, at least in this instance, 'Englishness' more of an auto-image than a hetero-image. In the case of 'the Americans', their depiction in both novels corresponds closely to the prevalent Scandinavian perception of America at that time. The Titanic disaster occurred at the very peak of Scandinavian emigration to North America, and America was stereotypically seen as the place where dreams could be realised. By Scandinavian standards of the time America meant fast and easy money.[16] Indeed, Grebst himself had already promoted an utopian view of America in a previous book.[17] In *Dödsfärden*, Alice McDean represents this idealised perception of America. In accordance with Grebst and Waltala's code of Swedish/ Finnish nationalism and sense of morality, she needs to be brought down and humbled by the disaster. Alice realises her own shortcomings and sees all the virtues of 'that brave, unmistakably knightly young Swede'.[18] She also realises the cowardice of Count Uffiezi, who 'in *the unmanly way of his people* [my emphasis] had been crying out the names of the saints and the Madonna'[19] from the deck of the sinking Titanic. This is the third and final hetero-image to be dealt with here, and the one most openly articulated. The English (the crew) are chivalric by nature, the Americans (Alice) are opportunistic but can be brought to their senses, while the Italians (embodied in Count Uffiezi) are the token villains.

It is evident that Grebst and Waltala made extensive and uncritical use of Swedish and Finnish newspaper clippings that were direct translations of British and American newspaper reports. These more often than not contained accounts of Anglo-American heroism and stoicism versus Italian cowardice and culpability. While the first-class, English-speaking men developed their heroism individually or (sometimes) formed clusters or coteries of heroes, the third-class Italians or 'immigrants belonging to the Latin races' were 'throngs', 'sets', 'bands' and 'masses'.[20] The only times a third-class 'foreigner' was individually pointed out was when he had done something particularly cowardly, such as 'entering a lifeboat dressed as a woman'.[21] Grebst and Waltala have gone a step further in placing their embodiment of Italian cowardice–Count Uffiezi–in first-class. While the novels' depiction of Uffiezi does not reflect any official Scandinavian relations with Italy at the time, differences in language, culture and religion rendered Italy a stronger hetero-image than, for instance, Britain. However I would suspect that the main reason for the novels' inclusion of negative Italian stereotypes is that, as outlined above, Grebst and Waltala simply adopted from translated newspaper reports the same national prejudices which were already contained in the British and American originals.

With regard to the authors' choice of placement for their main characters on the social scale on the Titanic, I have already mentioned the paradoxical phenomenon that the main characters travel first-class even though it contravenes their virtues. The authors make Gustav Larsson and his Finnish counterpart transcend themselves and travel first-class. In the case of falling in love with–and eventually marrying—Alice McDean, the situation is much the same. Even though Alice is humbled by the disaster, she inherits her father's money and remains an American dollar princess. She does not descend to Gustav Larsson's social level. Instead we get the age-old story of how a brave and worthy commoner gets the princess. This tale of social mobility, though, is only evident in the Swedish version, as pointed out earlier, and appears to be related to the differing views in Sweden/Finland about emigration at the time.

The question of what prompted Grebst and Waltala to fictionalise the Titanic disaster and infuse it with images of Swedish/Finnish national identity only a few months after the Titanic went down raises endless possibilities for speculation. In one sense, they were but two among thousands of amateur writers all over the world with 'a feeling that the disaster was a terrible one'. The disaster resulted in an urge in many people to share their thoughts and sentiments on the disaster in print. These people saw that there was a moral lesson to be told, and that they were the ones to tell it. The recurring theme was outrage: outrage over the shortage of lifeboats, the alleged speed record being set by the Titanic, the behaviour of Mr Ismay, the 'vaingloriousness' referred to by Thomas Hardy in 'The Convergence of the Twain'.[22] Yet amidst all this outrage was a sense of pride: pride over the heroic conduct of the Titanic's victims and survivors, and pride over the entire glorified notion of 'women and children first'. Soon after the disaster, George Bernard Shaw invented the term 'romantic lying' to describe the mechanism of turning devastation into triumph.[23] In many ways, these romantic 'lies' were part of an individual and a group mechanism of self-defence against pain, and the disaster happened to occur at a time in history when this mechanism perhaps developed particularly bombastic and hyperbolic undertones.

Dödsfärden and *Titanicin perikato* spring both from this outrage and pride, and they are clearly a link in the chain of romantic imaginings attached to the Titanic. They have all the passion and melodrama that signifies the literature and media reports of the first few months after the Titanic had gone down. However, beyond wanting to illustrate their outrage over the Titanic disaster, Grebst and Waltala use the background of the sinking in order to articulate aspects of Swedish/Finnish national pride. In constructing this national pride, the authors set their superhuman examples of 'sameness'—Gustav Larsson and his Finnish counterpart—against the myriad 'otherness' of the outer world. In dealing with this contrast, their nationalistic and utopian characters intermingle with foreign characters that are made up from series of stereotypes, misconceptions and preconceived ideas. In summary one could argue that on one hand, *Dödsfärden* and *Titanicin perikato* are merely two among the thousands of documents of moral outrage and national pride in 1912 alone. On the other hand, these novels are unique in the way they have fictionalised the disaster a mere few months after the Titanic went down, and by translating it into a particularly Scandinavian national context.

Notes

1 This chapter forms part of the foundation work for my Master's thesis in English Philology at Åbo Akademi University, Finland, in 2002. My critical approach is indebted to the concept of 'imagology', which is taken here to refer to an interpretation of literary images according to social, cultural, geographical and temporal factors. Prominent contemporary scholars to have defined the concept of imagology are Hugo Dyserinck, Joep Leerssen and Menno Spiering. Imagological readings of texts involve focussing on the intersection between the texts' formal (poetical) and historical (political) properties; to make the distinction between the text as a literary tissue and the text as a social act. This allows for an integrated textual, historical and social study of cultural, political or, in my case, nationalistic imagery.

2 W. A:son Grebst, *Dödsfärden, Romantiserad skildring af 'Titanic's' undergång* (Göteborg, 1912).

3 Steven Biel, *Down with the Old Canoe, A Cultural History of the Titanic Disaster* (New York, 1996), p. 31.

4 Esko Waltala, *Titanicin perikato, Romantillinen kuvaus 'Titanic'-laivan haaksirikosta yöllä vasten 15 päivää huhtikuuta 1912* (Helsinki, 1912).

5 Claes Göran Wetterholm, *Titanic* (Stockholm, 1988), pp. 128–129.

6 Menno Spiering, *Englishness: Foreigners and Images of National Identity in Postwar Literature* (Amsterdam, 1992), p. 8.

7 Spiering, *Englishness*, pp. 18–19.

8 Spiering, *Englishness*, p. 12.

9 Joep Leerssen, 'Reflections upon Foreign Space', in R. Corbey & J. Leerssen (eds), *Alterity, Identity, Image. Selves and Others in Society and Scholarship* (Amsterdam, 1991), p. 12.

10 In the synopsis, I will name the characters according to the Swedish version. The Finnish names are entirely different, but that is of no importance here.

11 Grebst, *Dödsfärden*, p. 9. My translation.

12 Spiering, Menno, *Englishness*, p. 8

13 Spiering, *Englishness*, p. 3.

14 Biel, *Down With the Old Canoe*, p. 7.

15 Grebst, *Dödsfärden*, pp. 126–127 and Waltala, *Titanicin Perikato*, pp. 104–106. My translation.

16 One Finnish Titanic victim, Jakob Johansson, had been to America earlier and participated in the Alaskan gold rush. Upon his return to Finland, he was described as 'a fancily dressed man with lots of gold teeth who came home and bought a piece of land "just like that"'; Interview with Jakob Johansson's son, Anders Nordström, in 1994.

17 W. A:son Grebst, *Ett år på min farm. Öden och missöden i Vilda Västern* (trans. *A Year on My Farm. Fortunes and Misfortunes in the Wild West*) (Göteborg, 1912).

18 Grebst, *Dödsfärden*, p. 156. My translation.

19 Grebst, *Dödsfärden*, p. 155. My translation.

20 See e.g. Archibald Gracie, *The Truth About the Titanic* (New York, 1913) p. 47, p. 156; Everett Marshall, *The Story of the Wreck of the Titanic* (London, 1912, 1998) p. 47.

21 Gracie, *The Truth About the Titanic*, pp. 156–157.

22 Reprinted in John Wilson Foster, *Titanic* (London, 1999) pp. 269–270.

23 Reprinted in Foster, *Titanic*, pp. 214–223.

CHAPTER FIVE

Textual Memory: The Making of the Titanic's Archive

PETER MIDDLETON and TIM WOODS

HERE IS THE PAST as it was once in all its witnessable importance, an unfolding present moment, sinking in front of our eyes down into the depths of history.[1] In James Cameron's movie *Titanic*, the great 'unsinkable' liner upends itself in the air and people dressed in the signifiers of a past just out of reach of individual memory fall through the air, while all our hopes for the future are focussed on the survival of the young lovers clinging to the deck rail. During the editing of the movie, Cameron told an interviewer that one of his main goals was 'to *put you there*—'There! You're on the Titanic', although he had subsequently realised that a 'completely realistic, subjective experience of being on Titanic while it sinks' was not enough, and was now busy editing out some of the shots whose only rationale was verisimilitude, so that the 'emotional reality' of the past event was there as well as 'the one that was perfectly detailed, minute by minute, historically'.[2] Cameron's problem was to create an aura of 'pastness' so persuasive that viewers would experience not only the liner, they would experience the past itself, and he thought he achieved this by providing a tangible location, a 'there' in time and space, and transporting (the pun is particularly relevant) his viewers to it. Re-enactment and affective stimulation were, however, not on their own sufficient algorithms of historicism. Firstly, the discovery of a ruin was needed. Long before the liner sinks we have seen (thanks to footage of the actual wreck, still a novelty since its recent discovery by Robert Ballard in 1985) the rusticle-like organic growths on the metal structure of the actual sunken ship dimly visible through the intervening layers of the thick glass porthole of a submersible and the murky ocean bottom, as if temporal distance were a visual distortion that would need better cinematic technology to make the lost world of the ship's history perceptible again.

Even the application of eidetic technologies and their special textualities to the ruin turn out not to be enough; other more obviously cultural, and gendered, practices of memory, especially oral recall, keepsakes, and photographs, will also be needed. The treasure-hunters fly in an old woman to help them locate a fabulously valuable jewel on the ship, but for her this shipwreck under the ocean is a site of memory, not loot, and it is her recollections, kept alive by photos and treasured possessions, which cue the historical scenes on the ship. Only the force of Rose's memories of the voyage that she survived without her lover, and the consequent absorptive power of her narrative of the voyage and the doomed love affair, which binds the otherwise tough, sceptical, technology-loving men of the crew to her every word, is capable of carrying them and us back in time to see the past re-enacted. The collaboration of the search technology and the survivor's memory, focussed on this site of memory, at last makes it possible to travel back in time with the camera and witness the whole of the final voyage and its immediate aftermath. In this image of the past as a wreck at the bottom of the ocean which can be raised through the power of these combined technologies of memory, the movie displays Foucault's idea that contemporary ideology of the past relies on oceanic depth metaphors: 'history, as we know, is certainly the most erudite, the most aware, the most conscious, and possibly the most cluttered area of our memory; but it is equally the depths from which all beings emerge into their precarious, glittering existence'.[3] As Margaret Atwood's narrator (a highly articulate spokesperson for contemporary ideologies of time and memory), says in her novel *Cat's Eye*: 'You don't look back along time but down through it, like water'.[4] At the end of the film, Rose walks out on the deck of the treasure ship watched only by the audience and produces the diamond for which the crew have been searching, only to cast it down into the ocean as a tribute to this site of memory; and her ethical sacrifice is rewarded by a gaze so powerful that she is able to look down through the miles of water and years of time and then re-enter and reconstruct the ruined ship, taking her cinematic audience with her.[5] As she enters the wreck, the past re-emerges glitteringly redeemed as the special effects transform green and decayed watery corridors into brightly lit halls leading to the central staircase where all the lost passengers and crew cheer as she embraces Jack again, undoing the unalterability of the past, climactically recovering it from both time and history.

Cameron's film conflates text, memory and history to produce what we have called 'textual memory' in our study of history in contemporary writing, *Literatures of Memory*,[6] but it is not alone in doing so. The Titanic's literary archive registers the transformation of social memory by emergent fantasies, narratives and images of the past shaped by two converging forces: a growing acknowledgement of the aftershocks and responsibilities of historical traumas, and the adjustments made necessary by new landscapes of space and time in late modernity. The final fantasy of Cameron's film *Titanic* encapsulates several dominant features of contemporary cultural belief about the past: it is hidden; it can be recovered through memories graven by the force of trauma whose reversal requires an ethics of emotional sacrifice, as well as catharsis

and the lifting of repression; and when recovered, the past will appear as a witnessable event in a specific space and time.

Everyone is talking about memory today, whilst what is less noticed is that
this discourse of memory is a response to the degree to which the relation to
the past has been disembedded, fractalised, and repackaged by new practices
of time and space emerging in scientific theory, new technology, new relations
of production, and shifting discourses of political and social legitimation,
which together have transformed and disoriented our understanding of experiences of both chronology and place, and therefore of history as knowledge of
the past. As we argue in *Literatures of Memory*, theories of repression and trauma
are compelling because they offer solutions to the detemporalisation and
anachronisms of modern experiences of spacetime, bypassing or inverting
causality in the *Nachträglichkeit* of hindsight, but these solutions also easily collude with or wholly give in to dominant narratives of history. We argue that
there is a need for a more articulate ethics of history to develop out of this
increasing preoccupation with memory that would acknowledge the democratic and ideological contests over the making of pasts, as well as ceaseless
constructions of identity and difference at work. Paul Ricoeur sees this happening only in the novel (sometimes too readily perhaps); he says that fiction
'permits historiography to live up to the task of memory' by revealing 'possibilities buried in the actual past'.[7] Even Cameron superficially acknowledges
the relevance of an interest in the past for his film. He concluded his preface to
a newly edited version of the U.S. Senate hearings from 1912 on the sinking of
the ship, by saying: 'While remaining respectful of the work of the good and
thorough historians who have gone before us, each of us must function as his
or her own historian, sceptical of everything'.[8] This book was all part of the
marketing of the film, whose success amongst older viewers less likely to be
drawn in by the romantic plot and the cult of DiCaprio, would depend on
appealing to widespread curiosity about history in general and the Titanic in
particular. Such an appeal can be interpreted as pure aggrandisement: one
critic, Alexandra Keller, describes a transitive relation between the director
who wants to 'own' history, and 'a desire by some of the viewing public to own
history as well,' which is why, she argues, that films like *Titanic* 'take the place
of historical events' and the audience 'aspire to become history not by doing
anything, but by appearing, or passing, as history'.[9] The problem with this
hypothesis that history is commodified spectacle, however, is that it doesn't go
nearly far enough. We need to know much more about the workings of this
economy, of the process of simulated perception, and the spatio-temporal and
mnemonic structures at work in passing as history. Otherwise this critique will
amount to no more than an updated version of the old complaint about historical fictions, that they encourage false, daydream experiences of the past
which risk supplanting the objectivities of rigorous history.

Despite Cameron's assertion about the Titanic archive that 'it was as if history wrote a great novel for us, and it was all right there', the history of fictionalised narratives does not really bear this out.[10] After all, the enquiry reports, the memoirs, and the interviews accumulated in significant quantity at the start of this history of reception, so why did it take so long for novelists to see the literary potential of the shipwreck (poets were quicker)? Virginia Woolf, for example, had attended Lord Mersey's inquiry into the loss of the ship on May 3, 1912, and was fascinated by the stories that were emerging. She wrote in a letter: 'Do you know it's a fact that ships don't sink at that depth, but remain poised half-way down, and become perfectly flat, so that Mrs Stead is now like a pancake, and her eyes like copper coins'[11] (both W. T. Stead and his wife died on the ship, although Stead continued to communicate with his daughter from the afterlife).[12] Despite her near first-hand exposure to the story, the nearest Woolf came to using the material was a passing reference to shipwrecks in her first novel, *The Voyage Out*.

Neither direct encounter with the emerging archive of testimony, nor the mourning of local and national memory, were enough to create conditions for a popular fiction of the sunken liner. Changes in the culture of memory, time and history were also needed, and their effects were first felt in the publication of Walter Lord's *A Night to Remember* (1955) and then backed up by the accompanying film (1958). Once this documentary 'faction' was widely available others could follow, but even then there was a considerable time-lag, which was due to the absence of one more remaining element, a site of memory for the time-travelling of historical realism to work. This was eventually provided by the finding of the site by Robert Ballard and others, and the looting of artefacts that then went on display all over the world finally set off the current wave of interest amongst writers and film makers. Even some cultural historians and theorists have found this fruitful ground for discussing the 20th century, notably Stephen Kern, Jeremy Hawthorn, and Slavoj Zizek.[13]

Why was Lord's book so important? Even its very title signalled the possibilities for writers, because it was carefully chosen to foreground the importance of memory not least because Lord thought of his text as a collage of memories: 'There are no reconstructed conversations in this book. The words quoted are given exactly as people remembered them being spoken'.[14] The idiom of the title carries with it a syntactic ambiguity which Lord plays upon— this is both a night that should be memorialised, and a night which offers special conditions for remembrance. It is this second meaning, the site of memory, that has been potent for writers and film-makers since, although it ought to strike us as odd that Lord needed to make this point at all, since from the start of the news coverage and the inquiries in 1912, the event depended to an unusual degree on painstaking acts of memory, as survivors and investigators attempted to reconstruct what had gone wrong, to ascertain error and apportion blame, and were often then denounced as having failed to do so (the British Board of Trade inquiry has often been called a 'whitewash').

More tangible evidence of a change in memory practices can be found by looking at the memoir of the Lawrence Beesley who appears in Julian Barnes's novel, *A History of the World in 10 1/2 Chapters* (1989). Beesley concluded the hastily written account of his ordeal with a quotation from Shelley's elegy for Keats, 'Adonais', apparently assuming that this disaster could be accommodated by the familiar protocols of mourning.[15] Beesley argued that it was not the memory of the event itself that was painful (and we might notice that the pop-Freudian term 'traumatic' was not yet current). The moment by moment experience of the sinking was not in itself shocking, and most people rose to the occasion in a non-heroic yet responsible manner; it was the deferred action of hindsight gained when they arrived on the Carpathia in New York that was unbearable. Only then did they learn that the ship had disregarded ice warnings, and it was this extension of their historical knowledge, rather than personal memory, which overpowered the survivors with the belated dissociation and hysterical symptoms we might expect to appear as symptoms of trauma today. 'It is no exaggeration to say that men who went through all the experiences of the collision and the rescue and the subsequent scenes on the quay at New York with hardly a tremor, were quite overcome by this knowledge and turned away, unable to speak; I for one did so, and I know others who told me they were similarly affected'.[16] History, not memory, was traumatic.

By the time that Lord was writing about the event in a book whose very title now took for granted that this was history as social memory, more than forty years more history had passed, and so the conversations and actions recalled by his informants were memories of history as well as subjectivity and affect. Both Lord and his informants were, however, now influenced by the growing importance of new models of memory, especially popular psychological ones. At intervals in his text he notes the lasting effects of the incident as hysterical symptoms in his informants: 'Mr. Silverthorne still sits up with a jolt'[17] when he recalls the 'grinding jar' of the collision, for example. Now memory *is* traumatic. Yet despite recurrent mention of such lasting hysterical symptoms of memory, Lord has little to say about the social and psychological mechanisms of memory, its implications in desire, fantasy and identity, nor its imbrication in national myths and history. It was this new space for considering the subjectivity of cultural memory that would prove so enticing to recent novelists, uniting otherwise utterly dissimilar writers like Julian Barnes and Danielle Steel, once the site of memory was locatable.

New ideas and experiences of memory, time and space were synthesised by Lord into an overarching synthesis without acknowledging that he was able to do so because the history had been pre-interpreted from a postwar standpoint. Lord's use of time depends on the unusual degree to which *A Night to Remember* is constructed from a large network of simultaneous, although consecutively narrated, incidents taking places in different, but related locations. This spatialises time strongly, emphasising the degree to which the past has a very precise location. This is supported by the clever way Lord shows that a ship is an entirely constructed space which organises everyday life totally, and represents social hierarchy and tradition through its structure and décor; at the same time the ship itself is traversing a wide and featureless void. Lord shows how the ship had been carefully designed to keep its three categories of passengers (first, second, and third, or steerage) apart, in social spaces whose built environment reflected the social status implied by the cost of their respective tickets. One reason for the extensive loss of life was the difficulty that passengers in the third class had in finding their way to the lifeboat decks through this maze of passages and gateways. It was so hard to find a way past the gates set up to fulfil the demanding U.S. immigration regulations that they had to be ingenious:

Like a stream of ants, a thin line of them curled their way up a crane in the after well deck, crawled along the boom to the first-class quarters, then over the railing and on up to the boat deck. . . . Others somehow reached the second-class promenade space on B deck, then couldn't find their way any further. In desperation they turned to an emergency ladder meant for the crew's use. This ladder was near the brightly lit windows of the first-class *à la carte* restaurant, and as Anna Sjoblom prepared to climb up with another girl, they looked in. They marvelled at the tables beautifully set with silver and china for the following day. The other girl had an impulse to kick the window out and go inside, but Anna persuaded her that the company might make them pay for the damage.[18]

Part of the power of this passage is the way that these young third-class passengers enact the metaphor of social climbing as they puzzle their way through an internal topography that is an architecture of social class, and look like ants from the exalted perspective of those at the top of the hierarchy. Lord's narrative recognises the point that underlies much of Henri Lefebvre's research on social space: 'If space is produced, if there is a productive process, then we are dealing with *history*'.[19] What the shipwreck does in Lord's narrative is to make the produced character of the social space of the ship as a microcosm of an earlier, highly stratified society, suddenly evident in its failure.

Lord not only produced a synthesis of memory, time and space, he offered a world-historical reading of it too (which is probably why Kern uses it in the first place), a historical assessment of the entire century based on the sinking of this one ocean liner. At the moment the ship disappears from view and from history, the action is suddenly halted while Lord outlines the consequences, which range from new shipping regulations to the inauguration of a new, more egalitarian era: 'A new age was dawning, and never since that night have third-class passengers been so philosophical'.[20] Why does Lord offer the following historically unfounded claim?

> Overriding everything else, the Titanic also marked the end of a general feeling of confidence. Until then men felt they had found the answer to a steady, orderly, civilized life. For 100 years the Western world had been at peace. . . . The Titanic woke them up. . . . Before the Titanic all was quiet. Afterwards, all was tumult. That is why, to anybody who lived at the time, the Titanic more than any other single event marks the end of the old days, and the beginning of a new, uneasy era.[21]

This, we might note, implies that the celebrated style of the narrative, its rapid cuts from point to point across the field of the action, is an inevitable consequence of the sinking of the ship, as if modernist techniques of montage and fragmentation were mourning the loss of a central authority represented by the great liner. The halting of the narrative of time unfolding towards catastrophe implies an epistemic break, a fault between two tectonic plates of history, and encourages the reader to infer that the sinking was not just co-incidental with it, but somehow causative. The Real has fallen into the past.

Although these lines were crucial to Lord's success, they were not his own invention, for it was not only the conversations in his documentary that were authentic. Even these words about the 20th century's wake-up call were actually taken from the memories of a survivor, from a privately published memoir by John B. Thayer, which Lord does not mention at this point in his narrative, although it is listed in the acknowledgements. Thayer's own account merges self and world in a metaphorical manner which might have pleased Heidegger: 'It seems to me that the disaster about to occur was the event, which not only made the world rub its eyes and awake, but woke it with a start, keeping it moving at a rapidly accelerating pace ever since, with less and less peace, satisfaction, and happiness'.[22] Disaster made him aware that the self is a 'Being-towards-the-end' as Heidegger describes it, a self whose awareness of its own inevitable mortal ending helps constitute its sense of the world.[23] Existential self-comprehension is largely erased when the phrases are relocated from 1940s memoir to 1950s documentary text, because the reflexivity of Thayer's assertion—our opportunity to read his judgement on the 20th century as his own post-disaster sensibility—is lost, and the displacement of the individual affects of grief into collective historical nostalgia enables the authorial voice to make a conclusive judgement on the passing of an entire age. But Lord knew what he was doing; the memory of modernity was beginning to be the memory of trauma, and it would be the historicism of eras riven by shock and catastrophe, modernism as shipwreck, that would appeal to subsequent generations of writers.[24]

Trauma and spacetime have become essential to our cultural images of the past. The Titanic archive shows how we redeem the past in contemporary culture, prompted by senses of irreversible loss, and competing ideologies of time. If you can just work the temporal magic, make the 'textual memory' active, then the past will be there in front of you, unfolding in all its detail. Yet there is more to this touching and pervasive contemporary social fantasy than the wish to raise the Titanic unscathed, and thus recover lost pasts and elide historical distance, and that is the wish to find submerged possibilities in the time and space of the past that are not yet in history, and therefore not yet ready to be remembered. The willingness of readers and viewers to go on being there as the Titanic sails and sinks again and again suggests that history is as much what sinks late modernity's representation of the past, as the outcome of such representational projects, and it is within this paradox that radical possibilities of textual memory remain active.

Notes

1 A longer and slightly different version of this article appears in *Textual Practice*, 15:3, November 2001, pp. 507–526.

2 James Cameron interview with Ken Marshall, *The Titanic Commutator*, 1997, supplement, p. 17.

3 Michel Foucault, *The Order of Things: An Archeology of the Human Sciences* (London, [1966] 1970), p. 219.

4 Margaret Atwood *Cat's Eye* (London, 1990), p. 3.

5 Tag Gronberg suggests that Rose's gift of the jewel to the site of the wreck is a 'symbolic re-enactment of current debates about Titanic. What is the most fitting memorial to the Titanic: its undisturbed presence on the seabed or a museum exhibiting salvaged artefacts? The very notion of a memorial, however, is problematised by the ways in which the Titanic's complex relationship to memory has been affected by modern technology'. Cf. Tag Gronberg, 'The Titanic: An Object Manufactured for Exhibition at the Bottom of the Sea,' in M. Kwint, C. Breward and J. Aynsley eds, *Material Memories* (Oxford, 1999), pp. 237–251, p. 250. The words of the title are, Gronberg explains, Marcel Duchamp's, which he once applied in jest to a picture of another ship, Normandie. Duchamp had a keen grasp of the strange vicissitudes of modern representation.

6 Peter Middleton and Tim Woods, *Literatures of Memory: History, Time and Space in Postwar Writing* (Manchester, 2000).

7 Paul Ricoeur, *Time and Narrative*, Vol. 3, trans. Kathleen Blamey and David Pellauer (Chicago, 1985), pp. 189, 192.

8 James Cameron, Preface, in Tom Kuntz ed. *The Titanic Disaster Hearings: The Official Transcripts of the 1912 Senate Investigation* (New York, 1998), p. xiv.

9 Alexandra Keller, '"Size Does Matter": Notes on *Titanic* and James Cameron as Blockbuster *Auteur*', in Kevin S. Sandler and Gaylyn Studlar, eds, *Titanic: Anatomy of a Blockbuster* (New Brunswick, New Jersey, and London, 1999), pp. 132–154, p. 151. According to Richard Howells this process of replacing history with representations of desire began much earlier, as soon as the newspapers got hold of the story, so that 'the

sinking of the Titanic is an event whose mythical significance has eclipsed its historical importance', and for this reason, a study of the first stages of the development of that myth, as Howells does, can offer a better understanding 'of the relationship between popular culture and modern myth'. Cf. Richard Howells, *The Myth of the Titanic* (London, 1999), p.1, p. 159.

10 Cameron interview, p. 2.

11 Hermione Lee, *Virginia Woolf* (London, 1996), p. 309.

12 See *The Blue Island: Experiences of a New Arrival Beyond the Veil through the hand of Estelle Stead*, (London, 1922), excerpted in John Wilson Foster, *Titanic* (London, 1999), pp. 281–282. See also Foster's chapter in this volume.

13 According to Slavoj Zizek, looking at images of the wreck, we see not the symbolism but something beyond the symbolic, something that exceeds all representation, 'the material leftover . . . the forbidden domain . . . a space that should be left unseen . . . a kind of petrified forest of enjoyment', and he concludes that 'perhaps all the effort to articulate the metaphorical meaning of the Titanic is nothing but an attempt to escape this terrifying impact of the Thing, an attempt to domesticate the Thing by reducing it to its symbolic status, by providing it with a meaning'. Although he glosses 'the Thing' as the Lacanian symptom of the Real, it is effectively the pastness of the ship as a material, 'coagulated remnant' to which he is referring in a discussion which relies almost entirely on Lord's version of events. Cf. Slavoj Zizek, *The Sublime Object of Ideology* (London, 1989), p. 71. Jeremy Hawthorn argues that the ship 'bequeaths an unending stream of textual relics to posterity' in an extended somewhat teleological discussion of the poetry of the disaster, which treats Enzensberger as the culmination of the history, and dismisses Pratt, because 'as with much popular realism the reader is left uninvolved'. Jeremy Hawthorn, *Cunning Passages: New Historicism, Cultural Materialism and Marxism in the Contemporary Literary Debate* (London, 1996), p. 148, p. 133. Stephen Kern uses the shipwreck to introduce a chapter on 'the present' in the new culture of time in the early 20th century, because he is able to talk about the new consciousness of simultaneity that was evident in accounts of the disaster. Cf. Stephen Kern, *The Culture of Time and Space: 1880–1918* (Cambridge, Mass., 1983).

14 Walter Lord, *A Night To Remember* (Harmondsworth, [1955] 1981), p. 153.

15 Lawrence Beesley *The Loss of the S.S. Titanic: Its story and its lessons* (Riverside, Conn. [Boston, 1912] 1987), p. 302.

16 Beesley *The Loss of the S.S. Titanic*, pp. 148–149.

17 Lord, *A Night To Remember*, p. 17.

18 Lord, *A Night To Remember*, p. 65.

19 Henri Lefebvre, *The Production of Space*, trans. Donald Nicholson-Smith (Oxford, 1991), p. 46.

20 Lord, *A Night To Remember*, p. 96.

21 Lord, *A Night To Remember*, pp. 100–101.

22 John B. Thayer, *The Sinking of the S.S. Titanic* [with Colonel Archibald Gracie, *Titanic, A Survivor's Story*] (Chicago [1940] 1998), p. 330.

23 Martin Heidegger, *Being and Time*, trans. John Macquarrie and Edward Robinson (Oxford, 1962), p. 288.

24 From the beginning, attempts to narrativise the Titanic disaster were construed in terms derived from a long tradition going back through Montaigne, Lucretius and Aristippus, of treating shipwrecks as metaphors of the contingency of human affairs, which Walter Lord borrows for his own construction of the shipwreck of modernity. For an account of the tradition see Hans Blumenberg, *Shipwreck with Spectator: Paradigm of a Metaphor for Existence*, trans. Steven Rendall (Cambridge, Mass., 1997), p. 29 and *passim*.

CHAPTER SIX

Enzensberger's *Titanic*: The Sinking of the German Left and the Aesthetics of Survival

ALASDAIR KING

HANS MAGNUS ENZENSBERGER's book-length poem *Der Untergang der Titanic. Eine Komödie* (*The Sinking of the Titanic. A Poem*) on the sinking of the Titanic appeared in the Federal Republic of Germany in autumn, 1978.[1] A complex, multi-layered work, it juxtaposes three distinct temporalities, 1912, 1969 and 1977, and three separate locations, the ship, Cuba and West Berlin. The verse epic draws on a wide range of documents and literary and popular cultural texts, as well as on semi-autobiographical episodes. Its aim, as indicated in flyers accompanying its initial publication, is both to reconstruct the disaster and simultaneously to reflect on enduring public fascination with narratives of the Titanic, to explore the contemporary resonance of myths of catastrophe in the popular imagination, the 'Untergang im Kopf' (the 'catastrophe in our heads'), in the author's terms.

Titanic became an immediate literary bestseller and, at the same time, a highly problematic text for literary critics and cultural commentators on account of its aesthetic complexity and also because of what many perceived as its pessimistic stance towards the possibilities for radical social change. Whilst some critics relished the mammoth challenge of tracing Enzensberger's sources, quotations and allusions, others accused the author of formalism, cynicism, inconsistency and political resignation. For the previous fifteen years Enzensberger had occupied a prominent position in West Germany's political culture, becoming one of the brightest stars associated with the New Left and the extra-parliamentary opposition. He had shot to fame in the late 1950s as an 'angry young man', a brilliant and bitter socially critical poet seen by many as the successor to Brecht. By the mid-1960s his energies were concentrated less and less frequently on poetry as he devoted himself to political journalism and publishing. He set up the hugely influential political journal *Kursbuch*, advocated the politicisation of the German public through the use of reportage and documentary literature, published the much-anthologised 'Constituents of a Theory of the Media' and fostered links with theorists and radicals beyond

Germany, not least Cuba, where he spent a year in 1969. In the context of the general exhaustion of the student movement in the 1970s, and the turn to political violence by groups such as the Rote Armee Fraktion, Enzensberger was accused on the publication of *Titanic* of finding the right moment in the intellectual season to jump from the train which he himself had set in motion.[2]

In view of his subsequent publications in the 1980s, which saw him again cause controversy by praising the everyday life practices of the *Kleinbürger* or petit-bourgeois and by celebrating West Germany's political 'mediocrity', Enzensberger's *Titanic* increasingly appears to document not only an ending of sorts, but also the transition to a cultural-political perspective which has been of enduring importance in his own writing. As such, it is a pivotal text in his prolific career. In this context, Enzensberger's *Titanic* acts as a large-scale textual project of an unusual kind. It is, quite deliberately, a confusing poetic labyrinth concerned not least with the production, circulation and consumption of representations of catastrophe and also an understated manifesto for a modest role for the critical intellectual in Germany. It explores the *personal* implications of the loss of faith in utopian projects and the *political* implications of the pleasures of aesthetic representation and of the everyday life practices of the ordinary citizen.

The *Titanic* project is born out of concerns with historiography and facticity. Moreover, the sinking of the 'unsinkable' ship has come to represent the foundering of modernity, the liner figuring as a microcosm of society's precarious commitment to technological advance, and thus its sinking is fully part of Enzensberger's critique of technological 'progress'. His *Titanic* juxtaposes textual material from a diverse range of sources, both to narrate the events leading up to the 1912 catastrophe and at the same time to call into question the 'authenticity' of that, and all other, narrations. Enzensberger provides no bibliography of sources consulted and used, so the reader is cast adrift into a textual ocean, something which has led at least one critic to suggest that the text itself acts as the iceberg in rupturing reader expectations. And in fact the cover of the book depicts not the ship but an iceberg. The actual catastrophe in 1912 is examined then using what may well be eye-witness reports, passenger details, documents relating to the ship's technical specifications, a menu, all of which appear to be taken from Walter Lord's celebrated book, *A Night to Remember*.[3] Significantly, some details are occasionally quite deliberately changed, such as the inaccurate length of the ship given by Enzensberger. This complex intertextual borrowing is supplemented with a variety of related archival material, including quotations from German, English and American popular song and descriptions of the narrator in Cuba watching the 1953 Twentieth Century Fox film, *Titanic*, directed by Jean Negulesco and starring Barbara Stanwyck and Clifton Webb. However, Enzensberger's textual borrowings are highly unpredictable. Although there are references to Lord's book, and to a variety of news wires sent on April 15, 1912, he ignores a whole tradition of German cultural representations of the Titanic, including a number of well-known German films on the catastrophe. Instead, he includes quotations purporting to belong to an earlier, lost, poem by Enzensberger himself.[4]

Enzensberger's refusal to tell the reader 'what really happened', at least according to Lord's account, ties in with an overriding concern of the volume, namely to focus more on the creative process of writing about the Titanic and on the Titanic's status as catastrophic myth in the popular imagination.[5] The 33 cantos and 16 supplementary poems which comprise Enzensberger's *Titanic* explore the way the sinking of the Titanic and related fears of apocalypse have an enduring hold on the 'social imaginary' in an age saturated with media information, with documentation, with fact.[6] Enzensberger draws attention to the multiplicity of meanings the catastrophe has for us in his 16th Canto, positioned almost exactly halfway through the volume:

> The sinking of the Titanic proceeds according to plan.
> It is copyrighted.
> It is 100% tax-deductible.
> It is a lucky bag for poets.
> It is further proof that the teachings of Vladimir I. Lenin are correct.
> It will run next Sunday on Channel One as a spectator sport
> . . .
> It is better than nothing.
> It closes down in July for holidays.
> It is ecologically sound.
> It shows the way to a better future.
> It is Art.
> It creates new jobs.
> It is beginning to get on our nerves.
> . . .
> It isn't anymore what it used to be.[7]

The continual presence of the Titanic in the 'social imaginary', surfacing at regular intervals in popular culture particularly, can be seen as the other side of the eternal faith in progress, namely the enduring faith in impending apocalypse and the related pleasure in the catastrophe as spectacle. In an essay published in *Kursbuch* again in 1978, Enzensberger argued that the idea of the apocalyptic catastrophe is essentially a negative utopia.[8] In his 'Two marginal comments on the End of the World', Enzensberger suggested that, despite the impetus given to it in contemporary society by, among others, the emerging ecology movement in the Federal Republic, apocalyptic thinking is a transhistorical, enduring phenomenon, typified by the continuing resonance of the Titanic disaster. Importantly, apocalyptic thinking is not dismissed by Enzensberger as irrational, an attitude which he equates with an unreflexive commitment to reason, history and progress exemplified by what he calls vaguely 'the-oreticians on the left'. He notes instead how the apocalypse belongs to and is produced by a range of different discourses, how it is overdetermined with meaning given its multitude of social positions and functions:

> The apocalypse belongs to our ideological hand-luggage. It is an aphrodisiac. It is a nightmare. It is a commodity like any other. It is, if you like, a metaphor for the col-lapse of capitalism, which, as is well known, has been imminent for over a hundred years. It confronts us in all possible figures and disguises, as a finger raised in warning, and as a scientific prognosis, as a collective fiction and as a sectarian wake-up call, as a product of the entertainment industry, as a superstition, as a trivial myth, as a picture puzzle, as a kick, a joke, a projection. It is omnipresent, but not real: a second reality, an image we fashion for ourselves, a never-ending production of our imagination, the catastrophe in our heads.[9]

Enzensberger argues that although the idea of the apocalypse has always been part of the social unconscious, in contemporary society it has lost its previous, theological, nature and today has more secular names: 'police state, paranoia, bureaucracy, terror, economic crisis, arms race, destruction of the environ-ment'.[10] Having established that apocalyptic thinking is itself a constant, a nec-essary myth, rather than a forerunner to any actual catastrophe, he moves to a consideration of its connection to utopian politics in general.

Part of the strength and attraction of the body of utopian theory, running, according to Enzensberger, from Babeuf to Bloch, was its claim to be able to understand the course of history and to anticipate a more humane future.[11] Enzensberger's rejection of this teleological movement of history is a conscious and deliberate rejection of cultural-political positions based on Marxist theory:

> . . . our theorists, bound to the philosophical tradition of German Idealism, even now refuse to admit what every passerby has long since understood: that there is no 'world spirit'; that we don't know the laws of history; that even class conflict is an 'organic' process which no avant-garde can consciously plan and lead; that social, like natural, evolution has no subject and that therefore it is unforeseeable; that when we act politi-cally, we therefore never achieve what we set out to, but rather something very differ-ent, something which we couldn't even imagine, and that this is the reason underlying the crisis of all positive utopias.[12]

As his statement suggests, and the autobiographical elements in *The Sinking of the Titanic* confirm, political action never turns out as hoped: one never achieves exactly what one sets out to. This could lead to apocalyptic thinking, but for Enzensberger, given the unknowability of the future, the terms 'optim-ism' and 'pessimism' are inadequate, merely 'sticking plasters for leader writ-ers and fortune-tellers'.[13] What is needed is clear thinking and modesty, rather than fear and confusion, in the face of uncertainty. This is a provisional but nonetheless cheerful politics, a point from which the present can be survived and the future negotiated, summed up in his final phrase, 'then we will see what happens'.[14]

Strategies for surviving the loss of utopias are a major element in *The Sinking of the Titanic*. There is a semi-autobiographical thread in many cantos which parallels the events in Enzensberger's life between his long stay in Cuba and his subsequent return to Berlin. In several early cantos, the narrator, writing from Berlin in 1977, the moment of the gloomy *deutscher Herbst* ('German Autumn') when the state and its antagonists in the Rote Armee Fraktion seemed locked in a hopeless political struggle, attempts to piece together recollections of his time in Cuba in 1969 and fragments of a poem about the Titanic, which he had begun there. The reader is led to believe that in this early version of the *Titanic* poem, written in the middle of revolutionary euphoria, the old capitalist class-based society (symbolised by the liner) is about to hit the revolutionary socialist iceberg. However, this utopian version of the poem never appeared. The later *Komödie* (comedy) written in Berlin claims in its text to be a reconstruction of the earlier version, which itself went missing (or sank!) in a mailbag en route to Paris.[15] What does surface, though, is the Berlin model of *The Sinking of the Titanic*, written in 1977, which, with the benefit of hindsight, is able to look back at a revolutionary experience just before it would turn sour. The narrator notes how, although no one was thinking at the time of any kind of *Untergang* (sinking or demise), the hopes for a utopian future were in vain:

> It seemed to us
> as if something were close at hand,
> something for us to invent. We did not know
> that the party had finished long ago,
> and that all that was left was a matter
> to be dealt with by the man from the World Bank
> and the comrade from State Security,
> exactly like back home and in any other place.[16]

Striking about the actual text of *The Sinking of the Titanic* is the way in which the conventional symbolic properties of the iceberg and the liner are here reversed.[17] The euphoric conversations in Cuba about revolution mirror the self-absorption of the passengers on the Titanic, heading blindly towards the iceberg which will puncture their vanities. The iceberg here figures as a symbol for the jagged forces of experience on which all utopian plans, as Enzensberger argues, run aground. The loss of faith in utopias, triggered by the narrator's experiences in Cuba and Berlin, is not necessarily the end of the narrator's world but a perspective from which he can explore the various ways that that loss is survived.[18] One way of coming to terms with the process of inevitable, routine loss is to pin one's faith on the apocalypse, the spectacular ending. Enzensberger describes a figure who predicts the coming Day of Reckoning while all around him people get on with the day-to-day business of living:

> And thus even now he feels,
> perched on the top of his barn and crowing away,
> that Doom, however unpunctual, will always be
> a tranquilliser of sorts, a sweet consolation
> for dull prospects, loss of hair, and wet feet.[19]

The theme of loss is connected to Enzensberger's focus on what endures. The sinking of the Titanic does not mean the historical cessation of class conflict. In several places, *The Sinking of the Titanic* suggests that what survives the disaster in 1912 is the enduring economic and political inequality across different sections of society. The poor and powerless are always the first to suffer:

> We are in the same boat, all of us.
> But he who is poor is the first to drown.[20]

What survives the misguided revolutionary zeal in Cuba is the persistence of an unequal economic and political order. This fact is recognised in the 29th Canto, which suggests that there are no absolute endings 'as if anything/ever were to founder for good'.[21] There are always traces which endure, no matter what epochal changes seem to be taking place:

> We believed in some sort of end then
> (What do you mean by "then"? 1912? 1917? '45? '68?)
> and hence in some sort of beginning.
> By now we have come to realize
> that the dinner is going on.[22]

In the face of the loss of faith in utopias, and in the persistence of inequalities, Enzensberger explores not resignation but different ways of coming to terms with this condition. Two tactics of survival, of making do in the aftermath of loss, deserve particular attention, namely a rejection of grand theory in several cantos in favour of a celebration of ordinary ways of living, and also a series of supplementary poems which reflect on the processes and pleasures of aesthetic production.

The French theorist, Michel de Certeau, makes a distinction between *strategy* and *tactics* which is useful for understanding Enzensberger's position here. Drawing on von Bülow's formulation that 'strategy is the science of military movements outside of the enemy's field of vision; tactics within it',[23] (and that phrase 'field of vision' is pertinent given Enzensberger's comments below on state surveillance in the 1970s) de Certeau's suggestive essays explore a range of *tactics* used by ordinary people in everyday situations which both

recognise the constraints imposed by the existing social conditions and yet find
momentary means of acting autonomously, of temporarily subverting the
established order. The aspect of *The Sinking of the Titanic* which irritated many
of Enzensberger's contemporaries was its disavowal of the usefulness of an
oppositional political *strategy* able to challenge directly and with finality the
existing social order. As the poem maintains, 'the dinner is going on', there is
no prospect of radical change. It is easy to see in the absence of *strategy* a form
of political resignation, but that would be to ignore the way that the poem sal-
vages and celebrates the actions, the *tactics*, of the marginalised, not least with
the inclusion of a Titanic Toast about the fictional black subversive survivor,
Shine.[24] These marginal figures are significant, not because they are the locus
for lasting revolutionary change, but because occasionally, in different ways,
they are able to act in their own interests within the existing order. Enzensberger repeatedly contrasts political theorists and prophets, apocalyptic strate-
gists if you will, with ordinary people. In the supplementary poem, 'Keeping
Cool', Enzensberger juxtaposes a prophet and his followers, who warn the
public about the approaching apocalypse, with the rest of the population who
carry on with their ordinary business:

> . . . We, of course, go on bothering
> about our humdrum business, supposing the deluge
> to be something antediluvian, or else
> an elaborate practical joke—while they, perched
> on their respective lookouts, know exactly the moment
> When. They have returned their hire cars in good time,
> emptied their Frigidaires and prepared their souls.[25]

The passing of time proves them wrong about the end of the world and those
whom they had admonished watch as

> [f]irst one, then another will slowly come down
> and join us in the nether regions of routine,
> meeting the mockery of the commonplace . . ..[26]

The distance even in the period in Havana between ordinary people and misguided political theorists, who still believed in the emancipatory power of critical theory, is noted in the 9th Canto:

> In the entrails of Havana, you see, the ancient misery
> went on rotting regardless, . . . "The People" were queuing up
> patiently for a pizza . . . at the Nacional,
> on the hotel terrace facing the sea, now just a few
> forlorn old Trotskyites lingered, exiles from Paris,
> feeling "sweetly subversive", tossing breadballs
> at each other, and stale quotations from Engels and Freud.[27]

In complete contrast is the positive portrayal of everyday pragmatism in the face of real emergency. Enzensberger describes watching a news broadcast of an impending volcanic disaster off Iceland, where the television spectacle came to a premature end after an old man simply trained his hosepipe on the cascading lava:

> . . . thus postponing,
> not forever perhaps, but for the time being at least,
> the Decline of Western Civilization, which is why
> the people of Heimaey, unless they have died since,
> continue to dwell unmolested by cameras
> in their dapper white wooden houses,
> calmly watering in the afternoon
> the lettuce in their gardens, which, thanks to the blackened soil,
> has grown simply enormous, and for the time being at least,
> fails to show any signs of impending disaster.[28]

The question arises of how Enzensberger, as a cultural producer and critical intellectual, is going to 'survive' the sinking of utopian projects without a strategy. Several cantos question the possibility of art's usefulness as a strategic means of critical enlightenment. Just as critical theory seems undermined by popular needs and concerns, art, too, can offer no guarantees that it communicates the truth.[29] Several poems contribute to a debate about the legitimacy of the artist's activity,[30] not least four supplementary pieces on painters attempting to represent catastrophe. There is a consistent equation of the activity of aesthetic creation with the notions of forgery, falsification, concealment and play, rather than with public enlightenment. The painter of 'Last Supper. Venetian. Sixteenth Century' is adamant that pleasure is the principle upon which all art is based[31] and pleads for his representation to be accepted with a certain ludic licence instead of being forced to conform to what the critics consider 'authentic/verisimilar'.[32] His paintings turn into games of hide-and-seek with his interpreters—in one he paints a turtle into a picture only to cover it up before the critics can see it, an important example of the way that aesthetic production can recover something for the private sphere by hiding what is important from the regulators.[33] Concealment becomes for Enzensberger the *tactic* of the artist forced to reveal, to clarify, to enlighten and to display. In a little-known paper also presented in 1978, Enzensberger was unusually clear on a theory of writing as a means, not of enlightenment or revelation, but as a process of hiding, of resisting assimilation. In his speech on the subject of 'Writing as a Disguise', he considered the different ways that literature could be an activity of *concealment*:

The one I liked best, because it corresponds to what is, and has been, a favourite notion of mine ever since I started writing, asked if literature could not perhaps be considered as a hiding-place.[34]

In a subsequent speech, he explained how he found talk about literature disturbing:

I shut the door behind me, I hide away. Yes, my friends, my poem is my hiding-place.[35]

The activities of hiding and concealment, and the ability of the writer to adopt disguises, are all means to thwart social attempts to classify, order, control and assimilate:

Writing is an attempt to escape from social control, and this is precisely what makes it irresistible to some of us.[36]

Irresistible too, to many readers—there is a legitimate and welcome role for those readers who try to engage in the pleasures of reading through a process of 'productive anarchy',[37] rather than attempting to categorise and furnish official interpretations.[38] Literature as concealment becomes tactically significant, moreover, in the context of Enzensberger's analysis of the sorry state of democracy in the Federal Republic at this time, given the government's allocation of massive resources to support politically motivated surveillance and the introduction of a massive new police database system.[39] In fact, he argues that the obsession of the government and the police with 'security considerations',[40] with leaving no aspect of contemporary life beyond the technologies of surveillance and with eliminating all possible disruptive elements, is the only current utopian project.[41]

As the artist in 'Apocalypse. Umbrian Master, about 1490' discovers, there is even pleasure to be had in trying to represent doom, to paint the end of the world. Despite fears of ageing and the growing awareness of his own mortality, he finds rich satisfaction in his ability to surmount the technical difficulties of composition and in the final completion of his masterpiece.[42] The parallels between the act of aesthetic creation as pleasurable, even life-enhancing, to the old artist here and also to the narrator of the whole *Komödie* of *The Sinking of the Titanic*, are unmistakable. The narrator, having constructed a multi-layered work from the detritus of personal and political loss, from a range of texts concerning the apocalypse, and drawing on art, popular culture, and factual material relating to the demise of the Titanic, is the last figure in the book. He is alive in the water, swimming on, making do, surviving.[43]

Notes

1 Hans Magnus Enzensberger, *Der Untergang der Titanic. Eine Komödie* (Frankfurt am Main, 1978). All references in this chapter are to Hans Magnus Enzensberger, *The Sinking of the Titanic: A Poem* (translated by the author, Manchester 1981). Further references are cited in the text by page number.

2 See Karl Heinz Bohrer, 'Getarnte Anarchie. Zu Hans Magnus Enzensbergers *Untergang der Titanic*', *Merkur*, 12, 1978, p. 1276.

3 Walter Lord, *A Night to Remember* (New York, 1955). This book was reprinted on numerous occasions, with several later editions carrying photographs and illustrations. It has a strong claim to have influenced much of the subsequent popular cultural interest in the sinking of the Titanic.

4 A useful account of Enzensberger's sources can be found in Christian Bachler, 'Der Untergang der Titanic. Eine Komödie von Hans Magnus Enzensberger. Eine Motiv- und Strukturanalyse', Karl-Franzens-Universität Graz, 1992, (unpublished dissertation).

5 See Richard Howells, 'And the band played on ...', *The Higher*, April 24, 1992, p. 17.

6 See 'The Titanic as symptom', in Slavoj Zizek, *The Sublime Object of Ideology* (London, 1992), pp. 69–71. Zizek notes how the impact of the sinking was immense because it was somehow *expected* and had been foretold in popular literary tales. Zizek argues that the *Zeitgeist* proposed that a certain age was coming to an end and the sinking of the Titanic was seized upon as symbolic proof.

7 Enzensberger, *The Sinking of the Titanic*, p.44.

8 Enzensberger, 'Zwei Randbemerkungen zum Weltuntergang', *Politische Brosamen* (Frankfurt am Main, 1985), p. 225. First printed in *Kursbuch*, 52, 1978, pp. 1–18. All translations my own (AK).

9 Enzensberger, 'Zwei Randbemerkungen', p. 225.

10 Enzensberger, 'Zwei Randbemerkungen', p. 226.

11 Enzensberger, 'Zwei Randbemerkungen', p. 229.

12 Enzensberger, 'Zwei Randbemerkungen', pp. 234–35.

13 Enzensberger, 'Zwei Randbemerkungen', pp. 235–36.

14 Enzensberger, 'Zwei Randbemerkungen', p. 236.

15 Given the complexities of this poem and the recurring theme of art as concealment and falsification, it would be no surprise if the references to an earlier *verschollenes* (lost) manuscript were another deliberate ruse by the author. See Bachler, 'Der Untergang der Titanic', pp. 90–92.

16 Enzensberger, *The Sinking of the Titanic*, p. 9.

17 See Moray MacGowan, '"Das Dinner geht weiter": Some reflections on Enzensberger and cultural pessimism', in Hinrich Siefkin and J. H. Reid (eds.), *Lektüre—ein anarchischer Akt* (Nottingham, 1990), p. 14.

18 See the supplementary poem, 'Notice of Loss', *The Sinking of the Titanic*, p. 11.

19 Enzensberger, *The Sinking of the Titanic*, p. 58. Even here, Enzensberger permits a certain ambivalence about what is actually lost. According to the rationalist philosophy of the engineer on board, for example, popular attempts to equate personal loss with the end of the world are misplaced.

20 Enzensberger, *The Sinking of the Titanic*, p. 59.

21 Enzensberger, *The Sinking of the Titanic*, p. 81.

22 Enzensberger, *The Sinking of the Titanic*, p. 81.

23 Michel de Certeau, *The Practice of Everyday Life* (Berkeley, 1988), p. 37, fn. 14.

24 Enzensberger, *The Sinking of the Titanic*, pp. 54–55.

25 Enzensberger, *The Sinking of the Titanic*, p. 57.

26 Enzensberger, *The Sinking of the Titanic*, p. 57.

27 Enzensberger, *The Sinking of the Titanic*, p. 28.

28 Enzensberger, *The Sinking of the Titanic*, p. 34.

29 This point is made explicit in 'Further Reasons Why Poets Do Not Tell the Truth', in Enzensberger, *The Sinking of the Titanic*, p. 50.

30 See Philip Brady, 'Watermarks on the Titanic: Hans Magnus Enzensberger's Defence of Poesy', in *Publications of the English Goethe Society 58*, 1987/88, p. 12.

31 Enzensberger, *The Sinking of the Titanic*, p. 24.

32 Enzensberger, *The Sinking of the Titanic*, p. 23.

33 Enzensberger, *The Sinking of the Titanic*, pp. 24–25.

34 Enzensberger, 'A Game of Hide and Seek', unpublished paper read to the International P.E.N. Club, in Stockholm, 1978. A copy was submitted by Enzensberger to the editor of the British literary magazine, *Rialto*, and extracts were used to accompany several of his poems. See *Rialto*, 3, Summer 1985, p. 19. I am grateful to the editor for the opportunity to read through the complete manuscript.

35 Enzensberger, 'Eine Rede über die Rede', unpublished speech delivered at the 'Nights of Poetry' event in Yugoslavia in 1980 and quoted in Karla Lydia Schultz, 'Writing as Disappearing: Enzensberger's Negative Utopian Move', *Monatshefte*, 1986, 78 (2), p. 201.

36 Enzensberger, 'A Game of Hide and Seek'.

37 Enzensberger, 'A Game of Hide and Seek'.

38 Enzensberger, 'A Game of Hide and Seek'..

39 See Enzensberger, 'Traktat vom Trampeln', *Der Spiegel*, 1976, 25, p. 141.

40 The title of a supplementary poem in Enzensberger, *The Sinking of the Titanic*, p. 30.

41 See Enzensberger, 'Unentwegter Versuch, einem New Yorker Publikum die Geheimnisse der deutschen Demokratie zu erklären', *Kursbuch* 56, 1979, p.13. In a late essay, Foucault also discusses just this dialectic of social control as part of the history of policing. See Foucault, 'The Political Technology of Individuals', in Luther H. Martin, Huck Gutman, Patrick H. Hutton (eds.), *Technologies of the Self* (London, 1988), pp. 145–62.

42 Enzensberger, *The Sinking of the Titanic*, p. 13.

43 Enzensberger, *The Sinking of the Titanic*, p. 98.

CHAPTER SEVEN

Reading the Titanic: Contemporary Literary Representations of the Ship of Dreams

KENNETH WOMACK

T HE TITANIC's disaster narrative has been an enduring literary subject, particularly since the discovery of the shipwreck in 1985 by Dr. Robert Ballard and an international team of oceanographers. Nearly a dozen fictive accounts involving the steamship appeared in the 1990s alone, including Danielle Steel's *No Greater Love*, Jack Finney's *From Time to Time*, France Huser and Bernard Géniès's *La nuit de l'iceberg*, Barbara Williams's *Titanic Crossing*, Erik Fosnes Hansen's *Psalm at Journey's End*, and Jim Walker's *Murder on the Titanic*, among a host of others. The decade also saw the publication of a novel written for children, Daisy Corning Stone Spedden's *Polar the Titanic Bear*, as well as Carolyn M. Keene's *Operation Titanic*, a Hardy Boys/Nancy Drew mystery for young adults. The literary attention that the disaster received has bordered on the ridiculous at times, as witnessed by the publication of William Seil's *Sherlock Holmes and the Titanic Tragedy: A Case to Remember*, in which Holmes and Dr. Watson come out of retirement in order to travel to America on board the Titanic as secret agents for the British government.[1] Quite obviously, much of the attention devoted to the disaster in recent years can be attributed to the considerable swell of interest generated by the staggering global success of James Cameron's 1997 film.

Clearly, the magnificent, doomed liner provides storytellers with a dramatic backdrop for spinning their tales of adventure, courage, and romance. The mere mention of Titanic's disaster narrative, moreover, is enough to conjure up a powerful form of shared nostalgia for an era that most of us scarcely even knew. 'There seems to be no limit to the public's fascination' with the ship and its tragic story, Walter Lord writes in *The Night Lives On*. 'The Titanic has come to stand for a world of tranquillity and civility that we have somehow lost', Lord continues.[2] 'Today, life is hectic, prices are climbing, quality is falling, violence is everywhere. In contrast, 1912 looks awfully good'.[3] For the few authors who have impinged upon the ship's disaster narrative with more

serious literary intentions—and there are scant few—the Titanic's tragic
maiden voyage affords them with the opportunity for evaluating Edwardian
notions of gender, class, and identity in relation to the simultaneously more
socially liberated and more fragmented value systems that mark the present.

   In such novels as Beryl Bainbridge's *Every Man for Himself* (1996) and Cynthia
Bass's *Maiden Voyage* (1996), as well as in selected stories from Robert Olen
Butler's *Tabloid Dreams* (1996), each author underscores the modernity—and in
the latter instance, postmodernity perhaps—inherent in their textual representations of the Titanic through their self-conscious and ironic appropriations of
the ship, the various myths that surround its demise, and its symbolic place as a
20th century icon of human fallibility.[4] While each writer carefully establishes
a sense of verisimilitude through his or her depictions of the various historical
and mythological *accoutrements* associated with the ship—from the unheeded ice
warnings and the infamous missing binoculars in the crow's nest to the luxurious appointments of the Turkish baths and the elusive Californian anchored
nearby—Bainbridge, Bass, and Butler distinguish their textual forays into the
fateful events of April 1912 by drawing upon the Titanic's considerable power
as a cultural icon, rather than simply adopting it as an extravagant plot device.
By re-imagining the ship and its tragic maiden voyage for a contemporary
audience, Bainbridge, Bass, and Butler offer intriguing commentaries on gender politics and equality, the vexed notions of courage and heroism, and the
psychological, social, and ethical implications of survival.

   In *Every Man for Himself*, Bainbridge critiques early 20th century notions
of class and gender through her depiction of the shipboard experiences of
Morgan, the novel's 22-year-old narrator. Bainbridge devotes particular attention to the sexual double standards that Morgan both encounters and perpetu-
ates in *Every Man for Himself*. The Titanic's tragic narrative also provides
Bainbridge with a fictional mechanism for representing Morgan's personal
voyage of self-discovery, as well as for highlighting the complex social inequalities with which we continue to struggle. As with the narratives by Bass and
Butler, Bainbridge's novel functions as a *de facto* survivor's account that not
only memorialises the ship's sudden and cataclysmic loss, but also encounters
the foreboding modernity and subsequent disruption of innocence that will
ultimately manifest itself in two world wars and countless instances of social,
cultural, and artistic transformation. The liner itself, of course, was already
fated to experience its own unforgettable clash with modernity. Consider, for
example, Captain E. J. Smith's well-known and prophetic words during a 1907
interview with *The New York Times* after directing the Adriatic's maiden voyage
to America: 'When anyone asks how I can best describe my experiences of
nearly 40 years at sea, I merely say "uneventful". I have never been in an accident of any sort worth speaking about. I never saw a wreck and have never
been wrecked, nor was I ever in any predicament that threatened to end in dis-

aster of any sort'.[5] Smith's complacency exemplifies the kind of self-assurance that characterises a culture that could actually believe in its own infallibility and capacity for producing an 'unsinkable' ship.[6]

As a member of the liner's elite coterie of first-class passengers—the narrator's uncle is J. P. Morgan, the American financier and the ship's principal investor—Morgan enjoys an exclusive entrée into the coveted and insular circles of the rich. In addition to socialising with, among others, John Jacob Astor and Sir Cosmo and Lady Duff Gordon (who were travelling, rather ironically, under the alias of 'Morgan'), Bainbridge's youthful narrator struggles between a life of privilege in which 'nothing could go wrong with the world'[7] and an upper-class existence wherein the rich dabbled in rampant infidelity and led lives that, all too frequently and ominously in the novel, ended in suicide. In many ways, the ship's demise functions as a form of spectacular cultural suicide in which an entire economic stratum crashes into an unyielding future, ignorant not merely of the multitudinous ice warnings of the moment, but the larger social ramifications of their own fallibility. 'We had spent our lives in splendid houses and grand hotels', Morgan observes, 'and for us there was nothing new under the sun, nothing that is, in the way of opulence; it was the sublime thermodynamics of the Titanic's marine engineering that took us by the throat. Dazzled', he continues, 'I was thinking that if the fate of man was connected to the order of the universe, and if one could equate the scientific workings of the engines with just such a reciprocal universe, why then, nothing could go wrong with my world'.[8] Significantly, Morgan's most important moment of personal crisis does not occur because of the ship's collision with the iceberg or because of the disaster's tragic aftermath—in the novel, Morgan survives the early morning hours of 15 April 1912 by clinging desperately to one of the collapsible lifeboats—but rather, via his experiences with the mysterious Scurra, a fellow passenger of vague origins who betrays Morgan and teaches him yet another meaning of 'every man for himself', as well as through his relationship with Wallis, a beautiful socialite with whom he becomes enamoured during the voyage.

After composing a love letter to Wallis strewn with romantic passages from *Romeo and Juliet*, Morgan covertly witnesses a sexual encounter between Scurra, with whom he had developed a casual friendship, and his beloved. Shocked by Scurra's easy betrayal of him, Morgan seems even more confused by the seemingly prim and proper Wallis's sudden transformation into an animalistic, sexualised being. After escaping the scene of Scurra and Wallis's tryst, an angry and confused Morgan scrawls the word 'fuck' on Wallis's bathroom mirror with a bar of soap. Scurra and Wallis's self-serving behaviour—and in particular, Wallis's unbounded eroticism—clearly throws Morgan's previous notions of identity, friendship, and gender into a state of flux. The sinking of the ship itself, punctuated for Morgan by Scurra caressing himself under his plum-coloured robe on the boat deck and telling his young companion that 'there is nothing, absolutely nothing, that a man cannot forget—but not himself',[9] pales in destructive comparison to his recognition that 'now that I knew I was going to live there was something dishonourable in survival'.[10]

Morgan's painful words, delivered as his travelogue comes to a close, underscore the complicated nature of his own survivorship, for he does not merely survive the Titanic's foundering, but also the crumbling foundations of the early 20th century Anglo-American aristocracy and an entire way of life, the permanent alteration of his gender expectations, and the very fact of his existence, of course, when so many others (indeed, so many other men, women, and children) perished. This aspect of *Every Man for Himself* demonstrates the novel's intriguing multiple layers of meaning. Bainbridge's narratives often possess a 'problematising function', according to Elisabeth Wennö, 'which relates the dichotomy of subjective consciousness and the material world to the problem of mediating between conception and experience, expectation and fulfilment, truth and falsity'.[11] As a survivor, Morgan must necessarily confront the realities of his existence on a multiplicity of levels; his understandable inability to cope, at times, with the radical redefinition of his world results in an interesting form of post-traumatic stress disorder that manifests itself via a number of textual *lacunae* throughout the text. These moments of ellipses—instances for which Morgan has no memory and can only struggle to recollect his activities—are followed by guilty emotions and relative unease. Morgan's dissociative condition, hastened no doubt by the psychological power of his various transformative experiences, impairs his ability to recall the past as he begins to assume a new, heightened sense of identity. [12]

Surviving a disaster or other traumatic event clearly offers the possibility for intense feelings of shock and denial, as well as the straining or sudden alteration of existing interpersonal relationships.[13] As with Morgan in *Every Man for Himself*, the narrator in Bass's novel discovers his life transfixed by the Titanic's watery demise. Bass's *Maiden Voyage* traces the late-adolescent experiences of Sumner Jordan, the 12-year-old son of a leading Boston suffragist, as he returns to America during the Titanic's ill-fated inaugural crossing. Bass's feminist reading of the ship's disaster narrative—especially during the loading of the lifeboats as the ship's officers plea for 'women and children first'—offers a penetrating account of 20th century gender discrepancies. Bass's novel also contextualises the loss of the Titanic in terms of a relatively mysterious yet steadily approaching modernity. In *Maiden Voyage*, Sumner literally encounters modernism in the personages of James Joyce and Ezra Pound at a poetry reading. Bass's narrative explores the ways in which Sumner's discoveries about his sexuality, his incipient young adulthood, and the ethical and cultural power of his mother's suffragism on land become enmeshed with his confused emotions regarding his conceptions of heroism and manhood after the disaster at sea. As with Morgan's narrative, Sumner devotes much of his quasi-travelogue to his discourse on the burden of survivorship: 'My personal story', Sumner writes, 'relates how I cringed. I flinched, I faltered, I ran. The truth is, I *survived*'.[14]

Sumner's own maiden voyage embarks well before the Titanic steams away from Southampton. During an annual visit with his father in London, Bass's narrator develops a new sense of sexual identity when he begins masturbating, for the first time, after witnessing an erotic encounter between his father and his English girlfriend. His notions of selfhood and sexuality seem even more bewildering after he observes the heroic behaviour of Ivy Amanda Earnshaw, a 21-year-old American suffragist, at a London feminist rally. Bass allows Sumner's infatuation with Ivy to blossom when they both opt to travel back to America, rather coincidentally, on the Titanic's own ill-fated Atlantic crossing. He also travels in the company of Pierce Andrews, a cynical aviator in his twenties with whom Sumner develops a casual shipboard acquaintance: 'Never had I heard someone zip through so many moods and modes of expression in so little time', Sumner remarks after meeting Pierce. 'His monologues; his talk about air and sex and energy; his cruel, surprising rejection and his mind-reading reassurance'.[15] Thunderstruck by Ivy's beauty and ideological steadfastness, Sumner seems equally dazzled by Pierce's robust and unapologetic masculinity. Much later, during the loading of the lifeboats, Sumner experiences an epiphany: he would stand on the boat deck and wait 'for the women and helpless children to be lowered away in anticipation of the moment when I could come forth, to be saved along with the rest of my sex'. He would wait 'for adulthood, with its attendant responsibilities, sacrifices, and instructive heroism', and 'for manhood', he reasons, 'to arrive at last'.[16]

Sumner's own night to remember assumes even greater levels of complexity when Ivy, whom he had theorised would never allow herself to adhere to a masculinist ideology of 'women and children first', pleads with him to join her on one of the lifeboats. Sumner becomes even more distressed when an officer on the boat deck dutifully informs him that his youth qualifies him for admittance to one of the ship's paucity of lifeboats: 'I'm not going to be a child anymore', he tells his distraught companions. Yet after considering the possibility of drowning at sea or freezing to death in the frigid North Atlantic, Sumner allows himself to be saved. 'I could not believe how I had acted', Sumner later reflects. 'What had I done? Taken the first excuse, the most obvious, transparent, falsely forgiving excuse imaginable. I am a child. Somebody save me'.[17] For Sumner, survivorship becomes decidedly more conflicted when his suffragist mother praises the very dictum of 'women and children first' that succeeded in sparing her son's life: 'She had made me feel worse than ever. For she might be able to thank those poor dead heroes for choosing to die and leave it at that, but I couldn't; I knew exactly what it had taken for each of them to have made his choice, because I had faced it myself and had failed to make the correct one'.[18] Sumner only comes to terms with survival after glimpsing a statue in the Boston Common memorialising the tragedy and emblazoned with the now ubiquitous phrase, 'women and children first'. When he realises that survivors such as Ivy will live to impact the lives of others—as perhaps he will do himself—he understands that heroism is 'not always lifeboats and icebergs and statues. It's little things too. It's kindness. It's goodness. It's everyday effort and everyday sweat'.[19]

While emerging triumphantly from his own dissociative trauma provides Sumner, finally, with the capacity for once again 'speaking, gratefully, of everyday things',[20] the characters in Butler's narrative musings on the Titanic and survivorship seem to enjoy no such relief. In *Tabloid Dreams*, Butler features a selection of stories about the doomed ocean liner and its passengers—including the quirky but deeply moving 'Titanic Victim Speaks through Waterbed' and 'Titanic Survivors Found in Bermuda Triangle'—in which his male and female characters must contend eternally with the ramifications of their quasi-survival. Adopting actual tabloid headlines as the bizarre inspiration for his imaginative tales about two participants in the disaster narrative, Butler confronts both his characters and his readers with the possibility that coming to terms with one's grief and the attendant dilemmas of survivorship may indeed require an eternity of consolation. In 'Titanic Victim Speaks through Waterbed', a gentleman passenger drifts in an air bubble throughout the water cycle, from the icy waters of the North Atlantic, through the rain, rivers, and streams, into a cup of Darjeeling tea, and finally, into the interior of a waterbed, where two shadowy figures thrash above him in mysterious ecstasy and human connection.

Much of the watery survivor's travelogue concerns his nearly wordless encounter with a female passenger, a suffragist, on the boat deck prior to the ship's demise. Suddenly unlikely partners in the night's awful tragedy, the couple stroll along the listing deck and quietly contemplate their predicament. Resolving to carry out his duty and accompany her to the lifeboat that will save her life—and *only* her life; he, of course, will not be spared—the narrator listens as she recounts an ominous premonition that she experienced during the ship's collision with the iceberg: 'It's a thing in the air. I can smell it. A thing that I smelled once before, when I was a little girl. A coal mine collapsed in my hometown', she continues. 'Many men were trapped and would die within a few hours. I smell that again'.[21] Later, when the water rushes in upon him during the ship's final moments, the narrator remarks that 'it made no difference whatsoever. I was already dead. I'd long been dead'.[22] His spiritual death—and perhaps more importantly, the disintegration of his way of life as the ship foundered—leaves the narrator with a vast emptiness that pursues him throughout his eternity in the water cycle.

The latter tale, 'Titanic Survivors Found in Bermuda Triangle', provides readers with the point of view of the female passenger, who survives the ship-wreck only to be captured by an alien spaceship and deposited, years later and without having aged, in a much warmer clime in the South Atlantic. As she recalls her experience with the gentleman on the boat deck, she longs to touch him, to thank him for persuading her to enter the lifeboat despite her ideolog-ical misgivings regarding a world that elevates 'women and children first', while denying women the right to vote. As her narrative comes to a close, the woman exists in the 'terrible silence' of grief and survivorship. Standing naked in her purgatorial hotel room in Bermuda, she fills a bathtub and slides quietly into its watery depths. 'He is nearby', she remarks. 'I will find him and we will touch'.[23]

The narrator's words indeed seem to offer a hopeful conclusion to each character's eternity of sadness and anguish regarding their vague and myster-ious forms of survivorship. Metaphorically reunited across the ostensibly unbridgeable vastness of space and time, Butler's lost souls finally traverse the textual and cultural *lacunae* that irrevocably trouble Morgan's soul and that briefly derail Sumner's search for identity and selfhood among the mysterious and infinitely perplexing world of adults. During such a period of 'post-trauma' that inevitably follows any disaster, John Leach writes in *Survival Psychology*, the survivor quickly realises that 'the very act of surviving may itself be a thankless and joyless task'.[24] The fortunate, long-term survivor, Leach remarks, 'seeks to establish new behavioural fitness between [her-] or himself and [a] new envi-ronment' during what psychologists usefully refer to as the 'period of consolid-ation'.[25] In the vast array of fictionalised accounts devoted to the Titanic—a literary genre where so many narratives memorialise yet again the liner's dead *glitterati*—Bainbridge, Bass, and Butler refreshingly highlight the travails of sur-vivorship, the powerful rewards made possible by psychological self-consolid-ation, and the simple interpersonal values inherent in living.

Notes

1 Finney, Jack, *From Time to Time* (New York, 1995); Erik Fosnes Hansen, *Psalm at Journey's End*, trans. Joan Tate (New York, 1996); France Huser and Bernard Géniès, *La nuit de l'iceberg* (Paris, 1995); Carolyn M. Keene, *Operation Titanic* (New York, 1998); William Seil, *Sherlock Holmes and the Titanic Tragedy: A Case to Remember* (London, 1999); Daisy Corning Stone Spedden, *Polar the Titanic Bear* (Boston, 1994); Danielle Steel, *No Greater Love* (New York, 1991); Jim Walker, *Murder on the Titanic* (Nashville, 1998); Barbara Williams, *Titanic Crossing* (New York, 1995).

2 Walter Lord, *The Night Lives On* (New York, 1986), p. 14.

3 Lord, *The Night Lives On*, p. 18.

4 Cynthia Bass, *Maiden Voyage* (New York, 1996); Beryl Bainbridge, *Every Man for Himself* (New York, 1996), Robert Olen Butler, *Tabloid Dreams* (New York, 1996).

5   Lord, *The Night Lives On*, p.39. Captain Smith's remarks seem amazing when considered in light of his actual safety record at sea. Prior to the final disaster that would claim his life in 1912, Smith's ships suffered no less than three groundings, a number of serious onboard fires, and a variety of other mishaps that threatened the safety of passengers and crew. For a virtual catalogue of Smith's problematic safety record, see Robin Gardiner and Dan van der Vat, *The Titanic Conspiracy: Cover-Ups and Mysteries of the World's Most Famous Sea Disaster* (New York, 1995), pp. 48–52.

6   Gardiner and van der Vat problematise contemporary reflections on the Edwardian era as a kind of early 20th century 'Golden Age of peace, prosperity, and progress'. The period was 'anything but golden to all but the privileged minority presiding over a class-ridden society in what was still very much the richest country in the world', they write. The myth of the Golden Age 'was invented after the First World War', when England longed for the heady days of technological expansion and economic growth (cf. *The Titanic Conspiracy* , p. 28). The popular notion that the Titanic was unsinkable, moreover, finds its origins in a 1911 special issue of the *Shipbuilder* magazine, which claimed that the ship's watertight bulkheads and doors would 'make the vessel practically unsinkable' (qtd. in *The Titanic Conspiracy*, p. 4).

7   Bainbridge, *Every Man For Himself*, p. 36.

8   Bainbridge, *Every Man For Himself*, p. 36

9   Bainbridge, *Every Man For Himself*, p. 220.

10 Bainbridge, *Every Man For Himself*, p. 224.

11 Elisabeth Wennö, *Ironic Formula in the Novels of Beryl Bainbridge* (Göteborg, 1993), p. 19.

12 BehaveNet, an online clinical reference and diagnostic source, describes such moments as fugue states in which patients experience an impaired recall of their past. Having become confused about their former, pre-disaster identities—via what clinicians refer to as a process of depersonalisation—patients emerge from such states with the potential for assuming new identities. Cf. BehaveNet, 'Dissociative Disorders', 1997–2000, www.behavenet.com/capsules.

13 The American Psychological Association defines a variety of patient responses to disasters and other traumatic events. While reactions may vary among patients, normal responses to traumatic events include unpredictable and often intense emotions; irregular thoughts and behaviour patterns; recurring, uncontrollable emotional reactions; conflict within close, interpersonal relationships; and a number of physical symptoms, including headaches, nausea, and chest pains. Cf. American Psychological Association, 'Managing Traumatic Stress', 1998, www.apa.org/practice/traumaticstress.html.

14 Bass, *Maiden Voyage*, p. xi.

15 Bass, *Maiden Voyage*, p. 118.

16 Bass, *Maiden Voyage*, p. 154.

17 Bass, *Maiden Voyage*, p. 186.

18 Bass, *Maiden Voyage*, p. 207. Sumner's attempt at imbuing his experiences with deep, personal senses of meaning typifies patient responses to traumatic events. As clinical psychologist David V. Baldwin notes, 'We create meaning out of the context in which events occur. Consequently, there is always a strong subjective component in people's responses to traumatic events' (David V. Baldwin, 'About Trauma', 1995–2000, www.

trauma-pages.com). Hence, Sumner responds to the devastating aftermath of the Titanic disaster by contextualising himself within the disaster narrative and its various, tragic outcomes.

19 Bass, *Maiden Voyage*, p. 217. Despite the novel's ethical conclusion and its attempt to read the Titanic's disaster narrative in terms of survivorship, Lynn Karpen derides Bass's novel for depicting 'a very familiar set of conflicts' (*New York Times Book Review*, 14 July 1996, p. 16.) 'The novel turns out, in the end, to resemble a *Lord Jim* for young adults—not exactly an original premise', she writes. Yet Karpen fails to account for *Maiden Voyage*'s significant place within the annals of Titanic fiction because of the simple fact that it explores the psychological terrain of survivorship previously neglected by the vast majority of literary works devoted to the disaster.

20 Bass, *Maiden Voyage*, p. 218.

21 Butler, *Tabloid Dreams*, pp. 8–9.

22 Butler, *Tabloid Dreams*, p. 20.

23 Butler, *Tabloid Dreams*, pp. 202–203.

24 John Leach, *Survival Psychology* (New York, 1994), p. 177.

25 Leach, *Survival Psychology*, p. 149. Leach notes that the 'underlying foundations of long-term survival are adaptation and consolidation. Physically, physiologically, and psychologically the survivor changes to fit his [or her] new environment or he [or she] remains a victim and goes under'. According to Leach, survivors typically emerge from their grief and desolation when they re-establish a purpose for their existence when so many others have perished needlessly. Cf. Leach, *Survival Psychology*, pp. 169–70.

1. Titanic Musicians Memorial, Southampton (Photo: Sarah Hammond)

2. Detail of the Titanic Musicians Memorial, Southampton (Photo: Sarah Hammond)

3. (*top left*) W. T. Stead

4. (*top right*) Bram Stoker

5. (*right*) Arthur Conan Doyle

THE LATE W. T. STEAD

Writing in the "*Review of Reviews*," October 1911, said:

"The Waterman Pen does not scratch, sulk, stain your fingers, or strike work just when you want it most. I have used fountain pens which require to be jerked vigorously before they can be roused to action, with the result that around my office chair the floor is a variegated pattern of ink-stains. If you have got the right nib it is a positive pleasure to write with it.

"Of Waterman Pens there are endless varieties. That which I am now using, which has written the whole of this article from start to finish without requiring refilling, is a safety pen, which can be carried in any pocket in any position, whereas the ordinary fountain pens should never be stood on their heads. It has also the great advantage that you never need to unscrew it to refill. You unscrew the cap, fix it on the end of the pen, give it a few turns, and the pen slowly emerges from the barrel and is ready for use. When you cease using it you screw it the other way, the pen sinks into the barrel, you screw on the top, and the pen can be put in your breeches pocket either end up without danger of losing a drop."

"MY POOR BRAVE MEN!"

6. (*above*) Stead was everywhere—even in death

7. (*left*) 'My Poor Brave Men' cartoon by Archibald Clements, *Hampshire Independant*, 21 April 1912

8. *In Night and Ice* (1912)
(Courtesy of Filmmuseum Berlin—Deutsche Kinemathek; and Marian Stefanowski)

9. *In Night and Ice* (1912)
(Courtesy of Filmmuseum Berlin—Deutsche Kinemathek; and Marian Stefanowski)

E. 30·4·4·

10. *Atlantic* (1929) (Courtesy of BFI)

Titanic

11. (*above left*) *Titanic* (1943) (Courtesy of BFI)

12. (*below left*) *Titanic* (1953) (Courtesy of BFI)

13. (*above*) *A Night to Remember* (1958)
(Courtesy of BFI)

14. (*above and below*) *Titanic* (1997) (Courtesy of BFI)

PART II

Cinematic Titanic Adaptations
1912–1958

CHAPTER EIGHT

Early German Cinema and the Modern Media Event

Mime Misu's
Titanic—In Night and Ice (1912)

MICHAEL WEDEL

MAPPING THE IMPACT OF A MEDIA EVENT: TITANIC AND THE CINEMATIC PUBLIC SPHERE

LESS than two weeks after the ocean giant of the White Star Line sank in the early hours of 15 April 1912, the German film company Continental-Kunstfilm announced the May release of a filmic dramatisation of the tragedy.[1] Under the title *The Sinking of the Titanic*, a 'sea drama' was to be produced, 'encompassing the whole disaster, including the collision with the iceberg and highly dramatic scenes on board'.[2] In May the release date was put back to 22 June and it was announced—'in order to avoid possible misunderstandings'—that the film, directed by Mime Misu, 'is a longish drama, absolutely faultless with respect to dramatic values and technical implementation. It is therefore neither an arbitrary series of scenes (partly taken from older footage) nor is it blatant sensation-seeking'.[3]

The different versions of the Titanic disaster that had already reached German cinemas did indeed partially consist of existing footage only superficially adapted to the requirements of the current media event. The first German newsreel, *Der Tag im Film* offered for the week of 23–29 April 1912, under the title *The Floating Icebergs*, an item whose topicality and therefore its attraction value rested entirely on a written commentary, added to the images via intertitle, indicating that 'floating icebergs are extremely dangerous even for giant ocean cruisers. The Titanic collided with such an iceberg and sank, with approximately 1,500 people losing their lives'.[4]

But it was the 130-metre Gaumont newsreel item *Titanic Disaster* that gained the widest distribution in Germany (and internationally[5]). Released on 11 May, its sequence of shots was necessarily disparate in nature given that there

existed hardly any original footage of the Titanic.[6] Less the content of the
Gaumont newsreel than the way it was exhibited gave rise to controversy
among German film critics and theatre owners. In early June a trade journal
reported on the presentation of the Gaumont newsreel in Katowice. This
'actuality footage' had, it was said, already by this time 'done the rounds of all
top-class picture palaces in all big towns. . . . They must use every such event
to fill their coffers, every dreadful, terrifying and even hideous event. . . . The
public everywhere wants "to have been there". They are like the fairytale
character who never learns the meaning of fear. They see the Titanic leave
port. Then they see an "iceberg". Finally they see the Carpathia entering New
York harbour carrying the Titanic survivors'.[7]

At the showing of Gaumont's *Disaster of the Titanic* in Katowice, the audience
was asked to sing 'Nearer My God to Thee', which—according to the Titanic
legend already established—the ship's orchestra had played as the ship was
going down. 'Every member of the audience gets a free copy of the words'.[8]
For cinema owner Fred Berger the cathartic effect of the audience's collective
intonation of the hymn was the central argument in his defence against accu-
sations of emotive sensationalism raised by the German press.

Similar attempts to bring emotional charge to the newsreel footage at hand,
by means of dramatising intertitles, accompanying commentaries and above
all musical colouring are also known from exhibitors in other countries.[9] The
shot of drifting icebergs—inserted into the Gaumont newsreel between old
footage of Captain Smith on the bridge (filmed the previous year on the
Olympic, the Titanic's sister ship) and images of the throng of people outside
the White Star Line office in New York after the announcement of the disaster—along with its emotive final shot of waves on the open sea backlit by the
setting sun, did however also serve to add a strong notion of causality to the
succession of individual scenes, a structuring process which clearly removes
the film from the simulation of a continuing present characteristic for the
'mimesis of the act of observing' exercised in so many early non-fiction films.[10]
Within a processual logic of 'before and after', the iceberg image evokes a
spatio-temporal proximity to the absent event, while the last shot of the film,
accompanied by the audience's singing, links the imaginary place of the event
with the time and place of the film's reception.[11]

The first completely dramatised film version, the American Standard production *Saved from the Titanic*, was released in Germany in early July 1912 under
the German distribution title of *Was die Titanic sie lehrte* ('What the Titanic
Taught Her').[12] The lead performer, and heroine of the film, was actress and
Titanic survivor Dorothy Gibson, who is also thought to have collaborated on
the script. Within a framing story showing the anxiety of her relatives on hearing news of the accident and the return of the heroine to her home, the film
used a long flashback to depict the events as recounted by Dorothy to her

parents and fiancé. According to written sources the film (now lost) used in its inner story original documentary footage of the Titanic. In another scene within the flashback the collision with the iceberg was reconstructed.[13] The nested narrative technique of the flashback lent this first filmic fictionalisation of the disaster a complex structure in which the diegetic narration of the main character to her relatives doubles the filmic narration of the event to a cinema audience. In its emphasis on the act of narration itself, *Saved from the Titanic* signalled on the one hand the freedoms of a *cinematically* dramatised representation of the event. On the other hand the fact that the experiences of a survivor were being visually re-created here was meant to lend the filmic representation authenticity and credibility, expressed also by the use of documentary footage within the subjective flashback. By integrating newsreel footage, *Saved from the Titanic* 'quoted' from its cinematic predecessors only to underscore, it seems, the break with the existing, non-fiction Titanic films: here, for the first time, was one of the many 'silent' survivors from the newsreels given a 'voice', brought before a camera and appear on the screen not as an object 'on show' but as the narrator of 'her story'.

The market presence of (externally dramatised) non-fictional footage and a first dramatic film about the sinking of the Titanic only increased the time pressure on Misu and his collaborators. While the shooting of Misu's film was in full flow, there were already opinions voiced in the German trade journals to the effect that public interest in cinematic representations of the disaster was largely exhausted: 'And can it [the audience, M.W.] imagine finally that it has "been there too", has shared that fearful experience? No, for the audience must see, unless it is completely stupid, that it has been taken for a ride. And that's why "icebergs" have disappeared from films too. There was no horror in them; they don't attract audiences any more'.[14]

Against this background Continental's repeated announcements postponing the release of Misu's film must have read like very bad news for cinema owners. The deck scenes were shot in May 1912 in Hamburg and Cuxhaven, 'with a real ship and the kind collaboration of the totally real sea', as Misu informed interested journalists.[15] The shoot probably took place on the Auguste-Viktoria, a ship of the Hamburg-Amerika Line, which along with the two sister-ships of the White Star Line was one of the few ocean cruisers with four funnels. In return for permission to shoot, the Auguste-Viktoria is named in the film, which was good publicity, and also shown—supposedly from the point of view of the Titanic. The long shots of the collision with the iceberg and the sinking of the Titanic were done using a miniature model on the Grüpelsee, a lake near Berlin. According to Emil Schünemann, one of the film's cinematographers, Max Rittberger, the head of Continental and not only a famous figure skater, but also an engineer by profession, himself made the single-sided, eight-metre long model ship.[16]

The shooting of other parts of the film was also turned to good promotional use. This took place in the first week of June in Berlin in the backyard of the Continental head office. Numerous journalists were invited and reported in detail. Although a comparison of Misu's surviving photographs with the extant film prints does not permit certain identification, the press reports suggest that Misu himself played the role of Captain Smith.[17] The future film director Otto Rippert, also equipped with a stick-on beard, can be identified with certainty as the actor playing the millionaire Isador Strauss. Other main roles were taken by Anton Ernst Rückert (as J. J. Astor) and another Continental director, Waldemar Hecker. Siegfried Wroblensky handled costumes, props and sets and Willy Hameister shot the scenes in Hamburg and Cuxhaven while in Berlin and surrounding area two cameras were sometimes used, manned by Emil Schünemann and Viktor Zimmermann.

A press screening took place in Berlin in the first week of July. Schünemann reports that most of the critics present left before the end, disappointed.[18] The *Lichtbild-Bühne* correspondent, however, reported: 'We must admit that the "Continental-Kunstfilm" has treated this very difficult matter, which due to its tragic character could have led to a sensation-seeking mode of representation, with laudable delicacy'.[19]

The film's official première finally took place on 17 August, the beginning of the new season. But it was not until mid-October that Continental was able to report the sale of 148 prints (certainly a remarkable figure), mostly abroad.[20] While the film seems to have had a successful international career its success at home was probably rather limited. As early as the beginning of November German distribution companies put *Titanic—In Night and Ice* out on the home market as part of a 2000-metre long compilation of hits 'at the lowest rates'.[21] Also striking is the minimal amount of press coverage the film's premiere received in Germany. The only detailed appreciation of Misu's film still verifiable today was written by the critic Walter Thielemann and published in an Austrian journal under the title 'Education in Entertainment Form? Critical Observations on Some Recent Hits'. Thielemann took the film to task for 'giving the audience an entirely false impression of the events on board and creating unrest among the German people'. He expressed regret for the fact that the film speculated on the sensation-seeking taste of the masses and qualified its representation of the disaster as tasteless 'kitsch'.[22] This verdict, intended to expose Continental's rhetoric of enlightenment, defines sharply the cultural battleground on which Misu's project took its place. It may also explain some of the reservations the German press held against this film.

LOOKING BACK TO THE FUTURE: MEDIA MODERNITY
AND THE PARADOXES OF TIME

Already the first intertitle of the film gives an indication of the potential for cultural conflict that characterises the film's entire conception. The words 'In Night and Ice. Sea drama. True to life and based on authentic reports' are meant to authenticate the following representation of a 'true' event, but they also signal the 'structuring absence' of the event itself, a constituting lack of representation at the centre of the media discourse. When adapting the disaster to the screen, Misu only had recourse to reports in the press and cinema. In this sense, the sinking of the Titanic qualifies as one of the archetypal 'modernist events' of the 20th century in which, as Hayden White has argued, the *opposition* between fact and fiction is radically undermined: The 'historical' event dissolves as an object of verifiable knowledge and becomes identical, as if of the same ontological order, with the meanings assigned to it. No longer the point of departure from which the historical significance of the event— its 'myth', 'legend' or 'moral'—can be deduced, the 'facts' disseminated about a historical event appear in the media as a function of the meanings ascribed to it.[23]

According to Stephen Kern the new communication technology of wireless telegraphy, with which the Titanic was sending out its SOS calls, together with the modern mass media, helped create an impression of 'simultaneity' between the event and its mediatised dissemination and interpretation.[24] Historians of the Titanic disaster have documented and described how the myth-making potential of the last telegraphically-transmitted message ('Sinking by the head—Have cleared boats and filled them with women and children') was picked up by journalists and worked into dramatic headline stories even before the first witnesses on the Carpathia had reached New York. 'By the time the survivors reached shore,' Steven Biel writes, 'the myth was firmly in place and their testimony could only confirm what the press and the public already knew'.[25] In Hayden White's terminology: the 'facts' followed the fiction.

The sense of simultaneity and the uprooting of 'historical reality' through rhetorical devices such as narrativisation and dramatisation—modern media have ever since capitalised on this double matrix across which the truth value of a given historical event is transformed into a commodity value. Daniel Dayan and Elihu Katz give a whole catalogue of criteria defining a media event, each of which, as we shall come to see, seem to apply to Misu's adaptation of the Titanic disaster. Apart from its already mentioned live character ('simultaneity') and transformational quality ('aestheticisation'), a media event transmits an event on a remote location outside the media sphere; it is pre-planned, announced and advertised; it is characterised by a norm of reception which integrates a very large audience; as a 'monopolistic interruption' of everyday routine its cultural performance takes the form of a 'ritual' or a 'ceremony': it is a 'festive viewing' of history in the making and celebrates not conflict, but the reconciliation of a proclaimed 'historic meaning'.[26]

It is against this media scenario that Misu's film becomes readable as a multi-layered palimpsest. The first act of the film largely adopts the documentary aesthetic of newsreel reporting. We are shown the ship in Southampton docks, the taking on of passengers and cargo, the closing of the side hatches and the ship leaving the harbour all in long-shots and pans. The opening sequence also simulates the newsreel aesthetic by picking out of the crowd of embarking passengers later protagonists in the drama, the Strauss couple and the Astors. Their embarkation is pointed up immediately beforehand by two intertitles: 'A millionaire who will go down with the Titanic boards the ship with his young wife. (Front, he wearing a cap, she a scarf)' and 'Another well-known millionaire embarks with his young wife (Front, with a floppy hat.) The young woman was saved while her husband drowned, because he could only think of helping others'. While the two intertitles borrow from newsreel reportage the gesture of 'showing' and the practice of guiding the audience's attention via verbal descriptions, they deviate decisively from this representational formula in their allusion to the audience's pre-knowledge.

These titles presuppose that the audience is in a position to identify the figures portrayed from the information on their later destiny and from the resemblance of the actors, appropriately made up and costumed. Furthermore, the prophetic commentaries establish a temporal structure for the narrative, which marks a change with the present tense of the 'view aesthetic' of non-fictional genres ('this is . . . ') into the paradoxical narrative tense of the future in the past ('it will have been'). Comparable to the nested narrative perspective in *Saved from the Titanic*, Misu's exposition thereby installs a knowing mode of narration and reception, in which the spectator is meant to identify the people portrayed, but not (yet) to identify with them.

Only towards the end of the first act do we find elements of narrative integration and filmic fictionalisation alongside the documentary gestures with which the film refers to the pro-filmic event. With the appearance of Captain Smith as the main character in the film, the function of the camera's look tends to shift in favour of a subjectivisation of the filmic space. His point of view on two other passing ships at first duplicates the previously dominant frontal camera view on events presented in a documentary manner. Unlike the narrative resolution of point-of-view patterns in classical narrative cinema, there remains here a dialectical wavering as to whether the camera assumes the position of the fictional character and thereby anchors the spectator's look within the diegetic world, or whether on the other hand the representation of the character's subjective perception adopts and doubles the previously estab-

lished non-fictional 'view' and thus figures as the fictional agent of the spectator's documentary interest.

The fundamental ambivalence of the camera look, oscillating between narrative absorption and documentary attraction, remains characteristic for the
narrational process of the film, before a distinct difference is marked with the
discovery of the icebergs. At the beginning of the sequence, we see the first
officer on the bridge looking off screen through a pair of binoculars. A masked
shot shows the sea lying calm. After cutting away into a passenger cabin and
into the ship's café, the action jumps back on to the deck. In a diagonal low-
angle shot we see a sailor, looking through a telescope, who suddenly starts
gesticulating. The following shot with icebergs reveals the cause of his excite-
ment. From the masked shot Misu cuts back to the first officer, who is now also
gesticulating and checking with another look through his binoculars. The first
officer then puts the binoculars down and changes the point of view axis
towards Captain Smith who is re-appearing in the frame. The Captain in his
turn looks through the binoculars, discovers the icebergs and initiates the following course of action by signalling to the machine room 'Full-steam to aft'.

It is notable how subtly the film's narrational structure is modified in this
sequence, initially disappointing the spectator's previously aroused expectations of documentary-style shots: the first look through the binoculars goes literally into the void, the field of vision, doubly coded, by the interest of both the
characters and the spectators, being emptied of all narratively irrelevant
objects, so as then to be newly semantically defined and to be able to take over
its function as the trigger for a causal chain of events. While the look at the icebergs is narratively integrated, its extra-diegetic quality as an 'excessive signifier' nevertheless remains preserved in its paradoxical position within the filmic
space. In the fictional sphere of action, otherwise coherently organised by the
first officer's look on the crow's nest and the approaching captain, the perspec-
tively identical, 'impossible' look of all three protagonists towards the icebergs
forms an erratic element. This positioning within the spatial structure can be
understood as a sign retaining the autonomy of a documentary camera-view,
which re-inscribes into the fiction the attraction of the icebergs known to the
audience from the extant newsreel compilations. At this point of the film, the
cinematic process of representation pursues a double agenda, whose central
interest rests not primarily on coherent narrative action but on a *mise-en-abyme*
of the 'act of seeing' itself.

As in all subsequent filmic representations of the Titanic disaster, the discovery of the icebergs marks a decisive point of transition in the narrational
logic. In Misu's film, the sequence serves to mediate between a narratively situated and action-oriented desire for visual information articulated via the look
of the characters and the desire of the audience, reaching beyond the narrative, 'to see how it has happened'. The central aesthetic operation of the film

evolves around the paradoxical identity of two different desires, two different visual and temporal axes: the retrospective look of the spectator and the subjective, action-oriented look of the characters, directed 'forward' in time. In resolving, without neutralising, the split between narrated time and the time of the narration, *Titanic—In Night and Ice* arrives at a radically modern, and genuinely cinematic, narrative temporality which makes the spectator, literally, 'look back into the future'.[27]

In the representation of the collision itself, Misu largely foregoes any claim to authenticity in favour of the spectacle value offered by a head-on collision. The disaster is announced by the distancing intertitle 'Collision with the iceberg and its effect above and below deck', followed by a long shot of the model ship running into a model iceberg. The moment of the collision is repeated another three times, the shock shown in swift succession in the Café Parisien, in the cabin of the millionaire Allinson and his family and in the machine room.

Judged by the standards of classical narrative filmmaking, the serial resolution of the collision scene chosen by Misu might seem surprising. The repeated presentation of something that has happened only once is, however, less to be understood as 'action overlap'—the action overhang so often criticised in early films as inelegant—than as an 'action replay', used here to emphasise and intensify the experience of a singular 'event'. The aesthetic principle of an excessive flood of stimuli, with its cumulative intensification of the experience of shock, consciously disrupts the linear structure of the narrative, but it also shatters any documentary reading of the text: the spatial expansion of the shock effect—which is, according to one intertitle, the central interest of the sequence—spreads from the fictional space of the film action to the perception space of the spectator, whose established patterns of reception, both 'narrative' and 'documentary', are no less severely shaken by the violent event presented as an accumulation of stimuli.[28] In the triple 'Now!' of the simultaneous traumatisation, the differing time planes of the narration are also for the first time integrated into a common logic of experience. The serial lesion of the ambivalent aesthetic fabric stitches narrated time and narration time into a time loop of experience and repetition, whose utopia is represented by that very 'it will have been', with which the virtual spectator's gaze goes back in time only to meet itself in the future of the fiction.[29]

At its climactic point the film veers round to the presence of the observer, from whom any framework for understanding—narrative, documentary—has been pulled away. Their own traumatic experience of the incommensurable aesthetic material must now be processed in the formal organisation of the film: after disrupting all virulent generic fabrics of meaning, the rest of the film sets out to re-fix the unleashed affective energies, recharge the aesthetic material with positive meaning and re-establish the conditions of the pleasure principle.

ALLEGORIES OF NARRATION: SAVING THE AUDIENCE

For this purpose the last act of the film develops far more classical narrative economy concentrated on Captain Smith and the first wireless operator, Jack Phillips, the two characters who had previously been 'spared' the shock of the collision, for there had been no visualisation of the shock on the bridge or in the radio room. Untouched by physical damage, they can act as intact representatives of their respective corporations and technologies—the White Star Shipping Line and the Marconi Telegraph Company.

In alternating shots their efforts to save people are shown as a race against the ship's sinking (intertitle: 'The ship sinks deeper and deeper'). A linear time structure is created, which now vectorises all narrative action in a run-to-the-rescue scenario, which satisfies the melodramatic conventions of tragic self-sacrifice—a rhetorical model familiar to the German public from the press. In the press though there was only unanimity as to the 'devotion to duty'[30] of the Marconi wireless operator—not, however, regarding the role of the Captain. 'Captain Smith?' asked, for example, Maximilian Harden in his journal *Die Zukunft*, with regard to the contradictory reports about Smith in the mass-circulation papers:

Drunkard and good-for-nothing. No: noble hero of duty, as land and sea have never seen one before. At the banquet he got himself into a drunken stupor and missed his duty. In the second of collision, he stood, sober and watchful, on the bridge and afterwards directed the rescue operations with majestic calm. Shot himself on the bridge. Grabbed a helplessly discarded child, carried it on his arm through the waves into a lifeboat and drowned himself with a smile.[31]

That Misu's film should follow the heroic version of the Captain's death—summarised by Harden with deadpan irony—positions *Titanic—In Night and Ice* within a (not last ideologically determined) discourse about the means and possibilities of overcoming social trauma. The poignancy of Misu's filmic intervention in the public debate over the Captain of the Titanic is demonstrated by the fact that the fate of this character is the only one not to be told to the spectator in advance. The prevailing uncertainty over the historical role of the Captain is thereby used to create suspense and involve the spectator into the narrative. The audience's epistemological interest brought to the narrative from outside is in the last part of the film transformed into an identificatory moment, and culminates in the film's final scene which, cross-cutting the Captain's actions and the steady sinking of the ship, takes this character to enforce the notion of emotional catharsis: 'The proud ship sinks into the deep and with it its greatest hero, its Captain! All honour to him!'[32]

It is evident from contemporary sources that the end of the film was conceived as an allegorical duel between the Captain and death. The final shot, in which death appears incarnate behind the iceberg—'And while the waves of the sea strike the iceberg, roaring and surging, we see the ghostly face of death grinning spectrally through the ice colossus, as though pitiless death were satisfied with his horrifying harvest'[33]—has disappeared from the surviving prints of *Titanic—In Night and Ice*. In Continental's description of the film's content, this allegorising reading, meant to work against the traumatic experience of a contingent event, is set up much earlier. Here, already the discovery of the iceberg is accompanied by the words: 'It moves up from behind like a white ghost!'[34]

If the first half of the film aimed to achieve the dialectical synthesis of a camera-eye that was incorporating both the subjective look of the characters and the retrospective view of the spectator, a camera-I whose uncanny identity is established at the moment of the traumatic event, then this synthesis is again discursively dissolved in the last act of the film: the *lecture document-arisante*[35] of a paratactically-structured sequence of views emanates from the sudden shock as an allegorical reading of a melodramatic *mise-en-scène*. In their allegorical stylisation, Smith and Phillips no longer function as autonomous agents of a linear narrative, but coagulate into representatives of a constellation whose true meaning is located outside the horizon of the diegetic world.

In the guise of narrative concretion, this superordinate framework of meaning appears as a dramatisation of that technological transformation responsible for turning the Titanic disaster into a media event: down to individual patterns of mobility, the race against time that the Captain and the radio officer each undertake via their respective systems of apparatus mirrors the innovative logics of locomotion and communication, traffic and information technology, which have become uncoupled in the course of modernisation. What is ultimately articulated via the two characters is, at the moment of its greatest shock, the topos of technological unity—the imaginary reconciliation of what Georg Simmel referred to as 'the wonders and comforts of space-conquering technology'.[36] At the moment of crisis of 'the one misused technology that was on the point of killing everyone', as Gustav Landauer put it, the existential cultural value of the other truly reveals itself: 'The saving of several hundred people by the wireless telegraph was to give the people of our time a signal to reflect on the strength of our spirit. . . . Humanity . . . is made reality by technology'.[37]

Landauer's definition, as radical as it is empathetic, of what can be sublimated as symbolical from the telegraphic 'message of the Titanic', is at the same time an accurate description of the gradual dissolution of individual life experience into the conforming economy of experience of a new community of media consumers, on whom Misu, in his own texts, based cinema's claim to be art and to have cultural significance.[38] Only the reflexive self-integration of the individual into a collective consciousness can achieve the psychic integration of the montage of disparate 'sensations', and media contingency not be felt as terror in the face of a flood of information and sensations, but rather as an instrument of communal self-recognition.

Misu's film aims to convert the individual concern of each spectator into a new community consciousness of collective reception by strongly allegorising the story being told: Intertitles function as a transmission belt between sensory perception and cognitive processing, continually laying down what has happened on the screen against its allegorical readability. The dynamic that unfolds between the shots is coupled with an illustrative representational mode, which charges each narrative development with an anticipated meaning. The culminating point of this tension between diegetic and extra-diegetic meaning is the shot of the last meeting between the Captain and the radio officer. In the intertitle its place within the causal chain of the narrative is removed for the emphatic visualisation of the solidarity between the two technologies that the characters represent: 'Since there is no longer hope of salvation, the Captain releases the first radio officer from his duties. Both are now firmly decided to go down with the ship and are concentrating only on saving the passengers'. Pictorial *mise-en-scène* and melodramatically over-acted gestures coalesce into the arabesque of an allegorical tableau, before they dissolve back as an over-determined plot figuration into the flow of the narrative structure. Once more the characters are unmasked as double agents within and beyond the diegetic horizon, whose movements 'play out' the composition's figurative, or performative, dimension against its narrative significance.

To this double semantic of the visual space the film adds another layer of meaning. Parallel to the visual space it establishes an imaginary sound space, which undergoes its crucial perspectivisation in the final act. Throughout the film, this sound space mirrors individual scenes via linking musical motifs with the ship's orchestra. On deck, when casting off, and in the Café Parisien the ship's orchestra provides a constant motif in the background of the image. The audience's attention is specially directed to this motif at the beginning. The intertitle 'The stewards' orchestra plays "Home Sweet Home"' is to be understood also as a direction to musicians playing in the cinema, to bring the event portrayed into line acoustically with the collective experience of the audience.

Towards the end of the film this imaginary sound space—which, thanks to the way sound and image were synchronised during exhibition, corresponds with the audience's acoustic perception space—is consciously subjectivised within the narrative space.[39] By introducing a shot of survivors of the disaster with the words (in intertitles) 'From the boats in the water, full of saved passengers, one can hear the stewards' band on board playing "Nearer My God to Thee!"' and then firming up the musical concordance by revealing the hymn's musical notation and lyrics, the film aims at the very identificatory moment previously denied by the ambivalent construction of the space of the visual perception of the individualised spectator-subject: not the perspectival identity of a shared individual look of spectator and character enables the collective audience to feel itself part of the community of 'survivors' and join in with the hymn but the 'shared' sound perspective in the acoustic perception space.

Through the creation of a common auditory space, the 'salvation' of the audience is itself inscribed into the central plot motif of the last act, the salvation of individual passengers by the Captain and the radio officer. The duel between death and technology becomes the site of a last allegorical transformation, with which the film symbolically integrates the conditions of its own public reception into the fictional space of the narrative. When at the end the Captain, himself drowning, saves a passenger from going down, the film seems to have come full circle: with the same move, with which Misu—both as Captain Smith and as director of the film—integrates the individual into the collective of survivors, the narrative sinks with its last agent back into the public space of its exhibition.

Notes

1 I am grateful to Clare Kitson for her help with the English translation of this essay. A longer version of this paper has appeared in German under the title 'Schiffbruch mit Zuschauer: Das Ereigniskino des Mime Misu', in Thomas Elsaesser, Michael Wedel (eds.), *Kino der Kaiserzeit. Zwischen Tradition und Moderne* (Munich, 2002) pp. 197–252.

2 *Erste Internationale Film-Zeitung* 17, 27 April 1912, p. 31.

3 'Bekanntmachung', *Erste Internationale Film-Zeitung* 19, 11 May 1912.

4 *Der Kinematograph* 279, 1 May 1912.

5 See Stephen Bottomore, *The Titanic and Silent Cinema* (Hastings, 2000), pp. 69–105. The footage was produced by the American Gaumont-newsreel *Animated Weekly*.

6 Bottomore, *The Titanic and Silent Cinema*, p. 89.

7 'Die Rache einer Tageszeitung: Der "Oberschlesische Kurier" und seine gerechte Abfuhr', *Lichtbild-Bühne* 23, 8 June 1912, pp. 20, 25.

8 'Die Rache einer Tageszeitung', p. 20.

9 Bottomore, *The Titanic and Silent Cinema*, pp. 90–104.

10 See Tom Gunning, 'Before Documentary: Early Nonfiction Films and the "View" Aesthetic', in D. Hertogs and N. de Klerk (eds.), *Uncharted Territory: Essays on Early Nonfiction Film*, (Amsterdam, 1997), p. 15.

11 I am here referring to a German release print of the Gaumont newsreel (length: 119,3 metres) held by the German Federal Archive, Berlin.

12 The film was submitted to the censorship board in Berlin on 6 July.

13 Bottomore, *The Titanic and Silent Cinema*, p. 111.

14 'Die Rache einer Tageszeitung', p. 20.

15 *Berliner Tageblatt und Handelszeitung*, 8 June 1912.

16 Gerhard Lamprecht, 'Interview mit Emil Schünemann, 6 January 1956'. A tape recording of this interview is archived in the collection of the Filmmuseum Berlin—Deutsche Kinemathek.

17 See 'Besuche in Berliner Kino-Ateliers', *Lichtbild-Bühne* 24, 15 June 1912, p. 18; *Berliner Tageblatt und Handelszeitung*, 8 June 1912.

18 Lamprecht, 'Interview mit Emil Schünemann'.

19 'Der Untergang der Titanic', *Lichtbild-Bühne* 28, 13 July 1912, pp. 18, 23.

20 *Lichtbild-Bühne* 41, 12 October 1912, p. 37.

21 *Lichtbild-Bühne* 45, 9 November 1912, p. 50.

22 *Lichtbild-Theater* 40, 3 October 1912, p. 8.

23 Hayden White, 'The Modernist Event', in V. Sobchack (ed), *The Persistence of History: Cinema, Television, and the Modern Event* (New York and London, 1996), pp. 17–38.

24 Stephen Kern, *The Culture of Time and Space, 1880–1918* (Cambridge, Mass., 1983).

25 Steven Biel, *Down with the Old Canoe: A Cultural History of the Titanic* (New York and London, 1996), p. 25.

26 Daniel Dayan and Elihu Katz, *Media Events: The Live Broadcasting of History* (Cambridge, Mass. and London, 1992).

27 On the modern, 'alienated' experience of time, and the role of cinema in this epistemological shift, see Leo Charney, *Empty Moments: Cinema, Modernity, and Drift* (Durham and London, 1998); Mary Ann Doane, *The Emergence of Cinematic Time: Modernity, Contingency, the Archive* (Cambridge, Mass. and London, 2002).

28 See Tom Gunning, 'An Aesthetic of Astonishment: Early Film and the Incredulous Spectator', *Art & Text* 34 (1989), pp. 31–45.

29 On the temporality of traumatic experience, see Cathy Caruth, *Unclaimed Experience: Trauma, Narrative, and History* (Baltimore and London, 1996).

30 'In treuer Pflichterfüllung', *Illustrierte Rundschau* 95, 24 April 1912, p. 29; reprinted in Werner Köster and Thomas Lischeid (eds.), *Titanic: Ein Medienmythos* (Leipzig, 1999), pp. 88–89.

31 Maximilian Harden, 'Titanic: Report', *Die Zukunft*, 15 June 1912, pp. 340–354; quoted from Köster and Lischeid (eds.), *Titanic*, p. 53.

32 *Erste Internationale Film-Zeitung* 25, 22 June 1912, p. 33.

33 *Erste Internationale Film-Zeitung* 25, 22 June 1912, p. 33.

34 *Der Kinematograph* 288, 3 July 1912.

35 See Roger Odin, 'Film documentaire, lecture documentarisante', in J. Ch. Lyant and R. Odin (eds.), *Cinémas et réalités* (St. Etienne, 1984), pp. 263–280.

36 Georg Simmel, 'Die Großstädte und das Geistesleben', in Simmel, *Aufsätze und Abhandlungen 1901–1908*, vol. 1 (Frankfurt, 1995), p. 130.

37 Gustav Landauer, 'Die Botschaft der Titanic', *Frankfurter Zeitung*, 21 April 1912; reprinted in Köster and Lischeid (eds.), *Titanic*, pp. 82, 86–87.

38 See [Mime] Misu, 'Kunst und nochmals Kunst', *Lichtbild-Bühne* 23, 7 June 1913, p. 122.

39 I am here adopting James Lastra's definition of the term 'synchronisation' as 'any fixed or purposeful relationship between sound and image'. Lastra, *Sound Technology and the American Cinema: Perception, Representation, Modernity* (New York, 2000), p. 94.

CHAPTER NINE

Atlantic: The First Titanic Blockbuster

ROBERT PECK

O N 4 MARCH 1929 *The Berg*, a play about a transatlantic liner sinking in the North Atlantic after hitting an iceberg, opened at the 'Q' Theatre in the West London suburb of Chiswick. An immediate success, it moved to the West End eight days later, beginning a four-week run at His Majesty's Theatre, Haymarket. While it was still running on stage the film rights were sold,[1] and the resulting adaptation was to become a landmark of British and world cinema. *The Berg* was the first play by Ernest Raymond, a highly prolific writer (59 novels in 52 years) but one never taken seriously by the literary establishment. Raymond's first effort, *Tell England*, had become a best-seller in 1922, when he was 33 years of age.[2] Eight years earlier he had taken a degree in theology from Durham University, and was then ordained as a priest in the Church of England. As an army chaplain serving throughout the First World War, he saw duty in Gallipoli, Egypt, France, Mesopotamia, Persia and Russia. After the war he became a curate at Brighton Parish Church, but resigned from the priesthood in 1922.

The play is extremely discreet with regard to the identity of the ship. Nowhere in the script is there any mention of the Titanic, nor of any of her actual passengers or officers. Although the author had obviously done considerable background research (most probably on the basis of the Court of Enquiry report), the fact that the ship was not identified by name was consistent with his conception of the narrative—namely a generalised, virtually allegorical situation that transcended any historical event. Nevertheless, the setting is unmistakable: a luxury liner registered in Liverpool and crossing to New York through an ice field south of Cape Race between 11 pm Saturday evening and 2 am Sunday morning. It is not surprising, therefore, that most reviews of the play described it as a dramatisation the Titanic disaster.

Atlantic, the film based on *The Berg* and premiered later the same year, took a very different approach. Here there was no ambiguity; the identity of the ship was not indefinite. Every effort was made to emphasise that the ship in question was not the Titanic, but the eponymous S.S. Atlantic. The only high-profile officer involved was 'Captain F. O. Collins', a new character not present in the play. The ship that rescued the survivors was the 'Oceana'. In short, great care was taken to avoid giving the impression that this ship could possibly be mistaken for the Titanic. This was not by accident. Upon learning that the film was being made, the White Star Line requested the Home Office to intervene with the producers and have the project aborted, on the grounds that it would be extremely damaging to the British shipping industry. This action was not successful, but the producers did undertake not to refer either to the Line or to the Titanic.[3] Concessions to the anxieties of the White Star Line might also explain another small but curious deviation from the play. In the latter, a junior officer upon entering the first-class saloon bar from the freezing deck is offered a drink—which he gladly accepts. In the film he somewhat reluctantly declines, on the grounds that it is 'against orders'. The image of a deck officer imbibing alcohol shortly before the collision with the iceberg would presumably not reflect well on the firm.

Initiative for the production of *Atlantic* was taken by the German director Ewald André Dupont, who had been working as a writer and director in Berlin since 1917. In 1925 he achieved international acclaim with *Varieté*, starring Emil Jannings, which he made for Ufa, whereupon the American journal *Film Daily* had celebrated him as one of the world's 'ten best directors'. The next year, 1926, was spent in Hollywood, at Carl Laemmle's Universal studios, but the situation was mutually unsatisfactory and Dupont returned to Europe. In December of the same year he joined the newly built British National Studios at Elstree as director general. But only four months later the studio was taken over by a new organisation, British International Pictures (BIP). Dupont then signed an agreement with BIP as an independent producer, and began in August 1927 with the shooting of his first British picture, *Moulin Rouge*. This was followed in 1928 by *Piccadilly*, and by 1929 he was ready to make *Atlantic*.[4]

The play had been staged on a single set, the first-class lounge or smoking room. But transferring the action to the screen entailed a major programme of set construction at Elstree, involving the replication of the engine room, the bridge, the chart room, the radio cabin, the grand staircase, a first class suite and the ballroom, as well as the smoking room. In fact, the set design is one of the most impressive features of the film. Exterior scenes were shot on the P & O liner Comorin, berthed at Tilbury Docks, and were completed by the end of June.[5] Production then continued at Elstree during July, and the film received its first certification (in Berlin) on 22 October.

The innovation represented by *Atlantic*, and the reason it has become a landmark in film history, is that it was the first multiple language sound film. The silent cinema had been an international medium—the quintessential 'universal language'. The coming of sound dramatically changed this. Dialogue on the sound track gave the film a specific language, enhancing its appeal at home, but at the same time making it more difficult to market outside its country of origin. One solution was to produce multiple versions for different markets, and it was here that *Atlantic* broke new ground. It was heralded as 'the first *European* sound movie'.

At Elstree two versions were made simultaneously, in English and in German, using separate—and big name—casts from the respective countries. The following year (April 1930) the French director Jean Kemm made a third and somewhat different version, relying heavily on Dupont's material. This version was 67 minutes long—as opposed to the 91 minutes of the British version—and included three English actors and one German actor in the credits. *Atlantic* thus became the first ever trilingual film. It represented, by the standards of the time, exceptionally high production values, and it was also, by the same standards, an extremely expensive project. But, given the economies of scale, it was still far less costly to produce than making three separate films in three different countries.

For the English version, none of the original cast from the play were used, even though the West End run had long since finished by the time shooting began. Instead the roles were reassigned to what the studio publicity heralded as the 'Most Powerful Cast Ever Assembled in any British Picture'. Even making allowances for the customary hyperbole, this was probably a valid claim. Most of the names were indeed well-established figures of the silent cinema or the stage or both. The lead was played by Franklin Dyall in the part of John Rool, a celebrated author on his way to a lecture tour in America. The only names that are likely to be recognised today, however, are those of Madeleine Carroll and John Stuart, who play a young married couple on their honeymoon. Comic relief was provided by Italian-born Monty Banks, perhaps better known as the husband of Gracie Fields and the director of her films, in the part of 'Dandy', a 'lounge lizard'.[6] The only person to play in both versions[7] was Syd Crossley as the wireless operator. This being a non-speaking part, duplication by a non-English actor was unnecessary.

The German cast, led by the veteran stage and screen actor Fritz Kortner, was also quite formidable. Before coming to Elstree to star in *Atlantic*, Kortner had been in no fewer than 68 films, having started his career in 1915. He is probably best known to contemporary audiences for his role as Dr Schön in G.W. Pabst's *Pandora's Box* (1929). In 1933 he was, as a Jew, forced to emigrate, but returned to Germany in 1947 to resume his career. The other cast members were also very well known in Germany, most of them going on to play in dozens of films during the following two decades, and beyond. One of these was Theodor Loos, in the part of the Padre, or, in the German version, Pastor Wagner. Later he was to play the part of Professor Bergmann in the 1943 German version of Titanic.[8] Another was Willi Forst, in the role of 'Dandy's' counterpart 'Poldi', described as 'a young Austrian globetrotter'. A major film personality of the 1930s and 1940s, Forst starred in, and directed, numerous romantic comedies.[9]

The first public screening of *Atlantic*[10] took place in Berlin, at the Gloria-Palast, on 28 October 1929, where it had a highly successful eight-week run.[11] It was billed as 'the first 100 per cent German talking film', a factor which undoubtedly contributed to its success. But it was also an action film, based on a momentous event still within recent memory, and the location shots set it apart from the studio-bound productions that then characterised the German cinema.

Although at the time of its release there were only twenty wired cinemas in Germany, conversion to sound was proceeding rapidly. The sound system adopted was the American RCA-Photophone, and it is interesting to note a further application of the new technology. The soundtrack of the final scene was broadcast live directly from the Gloria-Palast via the local Berlin radio station. It was also relayed to Danzig and Königsberg and broadcast there.[12] *Atlantic* was to have a long run in the provinces over the coming months and years. After all, its potential market was all of central Europe, that is, the whole of the territory previously encompassed by the Hohenzollern and Hapsburg empires and their respective spheres of influence. In a poll of German cinema owners taken in June 1930, *Atlantic* was voted the most commercially successful film of the 1929/30 season.[13] It was, however, an immense success not only in financial terms, but also critically. Press reviews were overwhelmingly positive, observing that the applause at the premiere had 'swelled like an avalanche',[14] and that 'the curtain calls for the cast were too many to count'.[15] Another critic wrote: 'The effect is extraordinary. Seldom have we ever been so gripped by a motion picture, so thrilled to the core, so deeply moved. No film could ever have achieved this exemplary degree of reality if it had passed before us silently, without words'.[16]

In London *Atlantic* premiered on 15 November at the Regal cinema, Marble Arch. This was an exclusive occasion attended by 'diplomatic and parliamentary circles . . . society leaders, notabilities in all professions, and chiefs of the kinema industry'.[17] Press reviews were almost unanimously favourable, and the premiere was considered a great success. The studio also took this opportunity to announce its intention to produce a French version, but the release date was 'not fixed'.[18] The gala premiere could not, however, be immediately followed by public screenings. The Regal was BIP's only West End shop window, and it was already committed to previous bookings. Nor did the studio have access to any other cinema converted to sound, as most of the remaining London venues were booked for (mainly American) films during the approaching holiday season. The studio accordingly decided to lease the Alhambra theatre, a Victorian music hall, as its second first-run cinema and have it wired for sound. Built in 1852 and located on the east side of Leicester Square, the

Alhambra had been a major venue for variety and vaudeville shows for genera-
tions.[19] Variety shows were still being performed there until shortly before 23
December, when *Atlantic* finally opened to the public, eight weeks after its
Berlin premiere.[20]

A week after the opening, the German version was also screened in London
at a special performance at the Alhambra. This offered the possibility of a
comparison, and as *Bioscope* noted, 'perhaps the standard of acting in the
German film [was] raised by the fact that Herr Dupont was directing his own
countrymen in his own language . . . [Comparison] of the two versions certainly proves that the film is one of outstanding merit and will appeal to the
imagination in whatever language it is rendered'.[21] *Atlantic* ran for six weeks in
the West End before going on general release. By October 1930 *Variety* reported that it had 'been a furore in the exhibition houses of Great Britain and the
Continent', and had 'done business all over the European map'.[22]

Ginette Vincendeau's observation that multiple language versions (MLVs)
failed, that aesthetically they were 'terrible', and that 'financially they turned
out to be a disaster'[23] clearly does not apply to *Atlantic*. Indeed, its success
undoubtedly inspired and encouraged the production of the many MLVs that
were made during the following years. The strengths of the film—but also its
weaknesses—are directly related to the way the play was adapted to the screen.
Raymond's original script was constructed around a philosophical dialogue
between the two principal characters, John Rool and the Padre. The glowing
reviews that greeted the play may be largely attributed to this intellectual and
spiritual theme, combined with the skills of the actors playing these two roles.

Rool, middle-aged and confined to a wheelchair because of an unspecified
accident, is an internationally famous spokesman for the modern secular ethic.
His position is rationalist and atheist, and he is scathingly critical of the idealism, romanticism, and what he regards as the general self-delusion of conventional society. Outside the circle of his followers and converts he is regarded as
a dangerous radical. The Padre is an Anglican priest who has lost—not his
faith—but his vocation. He has become increasing unsettled by the fact that
he has ceased to perform any spiritual role in the community. To his dismay
he has become a 'society vicar', who spends his time attending fêtes and functions, presiding at ceremonies, but never ministering to the deeper and more
personal needs of his congregation. A constant round of bridge games and
cocktail parties was not the life he had envisaged. His dilemma is transpar-
ently based on the earlier experiences of the author, and accounts for the conviction and credibility with which it is presented. It is the ship's catastrophe,
the confrontation with imminent death, that brings these two positions into
sharp relief, but not to resolution. When the end comes and the ship is sinking,
the Padre is finally able to carry out his true mission by providing spiritual
comfort and guidance to the doomed company. It is against this background

that the other characters and sub-plots are introduced: the honeymooning couple, the philandering husband and his distressed family, a bluff military man, a vacuous playboy. None of these have any intrinsic dramatic interest; it is only the way in which they relate to Rool and the Padre, and how their destinies are affected by these relationships, that contributes to the plot.

Transferring such a narrative from stage to screen clearly presented some daunting obstacles. First, the play is driven mainly by dialogue rather than by action; although the sinking offstage has cinematic potential, the events on stage do not. Second, the play's philosophical discourse is rather too demanding for a general audience. And third, although this was not the first sound picture made at Elstree,[24] it was still early days and the techniques for successful spoken dialogue had not been perfected. The obvious solution to the first problem was to take as much action as possible out of the lounge and into other parts of the ship, such as the decks, the bridge, the crow's nest, the ballroom and the wireless cabin. This in turn required large numbers of extras to populate these areas. Only one additional speaking part was added, that of the Captain.[25] All these efforts to make the script more 'cinematic' were highly successful, and it is largely due to these additional scenes filmed outside the lounge that the film is gripping and dynamic.

These additions led logically to a solution of the second problem, for in order to create the space for the numerous new scenes, the original dialogue had to be substantially abridged. The sequences most easily deleted were those involving the long exchanges between Rool and the Padre, thereby also removing any danger of losing a less philosophically-minded audience. In consequence, the Padre ceased to have any integral relevance to the plot and was relegated to the position of a minor character. From being the second lead in the play, he fell to near the bottom of the cast lists for the film. Only in the final scene does he become central to the action. Once the intellectual core of the script had been removed, however, only the various sub-plots remained, and these then amounted to little more than bland melodrama. This was frequently commented on by the more perceptive critics,[26] but judging by the film's commercial success, audiences did not seem to mind.

As far as the use of sound was concerned, it was precisely the scenes taken from the play that were least successful. The actors had obviously been instructed to deliver their lines slowly and deliberately for the sake of the sound equipment, and the result was to accentuate any weaknesses in the script and undermine the credibility of the performances. Elsewhere, however, sound was used to brilliant effect. Right from the opening credits, during which the background noises of the ship and the sea provided an evocative introduction, the aural dimension was exploited imaginatively and creatively.

The importance of *Atlantic* does not however lie exclusively in its historical and aesthetic aspects. It also illustrates in an exemplary way the ideological dimension of the cinema and the way in which communal attitudes and values are reflected in narrative. The Titanic is, as Richard Howells has said, 'an event whose mythical significance has eclipsed its historical importance'.[27] Howells examined numerous examples of popular culture produced during the period 1912–14 in order to demonstrate how the incident had been mythologised. He was able to identify a number of distinct facets of the myth, each of which he considered separately, although it should be noted that these categories frequently overlap and are by no means mutually exclusive. These are Heroism, Gender, Class, Religion, Hubris and Nemesis, Nationhood, and Race. To this list might well be added one other, namely Trust. Although this is not dealt with as a separate category, a point that clearly emerges from Howells' study is that in the popular British response to the disaster the question of blame or negligence did not arise. All the participants, in particular the ship's officers, were seen as heroes; no mistakes, no errors of judgment had been made. Hence faith in the competence of the line management and the top management—and, by extension, of the 'system' as a whole—remained unshaken.

One might expect that by 1929, given the experiences of the intervening war, there might have been a more critical or sceptical attitude towards the quality of leadership in the British popular mind. But if human error was in any way involved in the Titanic disaster, there is no trace of it in the film: there is no mention of excessive speed or ignored warnings. When the collision occurs, officers and crew carry out their functions with brisk efficiency. All the lifeboats are successfully launched, completely full, and no men are allowed to leave the ship until all the women have been accounted for. As depicted, it was indeed a system in which one could put one's absolute trust.

The officers and crew were not the only heroes. As Howells has shown, it was sufficient to have gone down with the Titanic to qualify as a hero in the avalanche of tributes that followed the disaster. This perception is carried intact into the film where, in the closing scene, the doomed men face death quietly and with dignity, a memorable image of collective courage. The author of the play, who spent four years ministering to men in peril of their lives, would have known about approaching death and how men deal with it.[28] And it is the heroism of the *men* that is celebrated here, notwithstanding the presence of Mrs Rool, who chooses to die with her husband. These are men who are willing to die, have to die, so that the women can be saved. As Biel has observed, 'As a metaphor for gender relations, the Titanic steamed into the debate over women's rights. Did "the rule of the sea". . . demonstrate that women were better off entrusting themselves to the protection of chivalrous men than trying to claim political power'?[29] This would certainly seem to be the message of the film, as much of the plot is concerned with the rescue of the women.[30]

With regard to the question of class, the Titanic has always been seen as a microcosm of Edwardian society, and 'as a metaphor for class relations the Titanic crashed into the conflict between capital and labour. Did the heroism of the first-class men confirm the generosity and the natural superiority of the rich and powerful? Or...were the real heroes the people down below in the steerage and the boiler room'?[31] As in later filmic versions, the major characters in *Atlantic* belong exclusively to the circle of the wealthy and privileged. The issue of relations between the classes does, however, surface explicitly in the last scene, after the lifeboats have departed and those remaining on board are awaiting the end. Suddenly the bar steward appears, leading dozens of men from the lower decks into the forbidden world of the first class. With the words, 'Come on, my lucky lads. We're all one class now. And the drinks are all one price', he starts taking orders.

This, however, is not a scene that could be interpreted as an egalitarian manifesto or a subversion of the established order. It is understood that only in this situation, *in extremis*, social distinctions cease to be relevant. This no doubt again reflects the author's experiences in World War I, where for all ranks death had been the great leveller. Dramatically this episode prefaces the ending, which—like the (possibly apocryphal) singing of 'Nearer my God to Thee' —'represents a devoutly religious, Christian society celebrating the decorous acceptance of death'.[32] As the Padre leads the assembled company in the Lord's Prayer, the lights go out, the screen fades to black—and we hear the sound of the water rushing in as the ship goes down.

Are any of Howells' mythic categories not to be found in *Atlantic*? For one, the issue of hubris does not arise. There are no examples of pride, greed, or over-confidence, just as there is no hint of negligence, error, or blame. Hence notions of nemesis and retribution—one of the most common morals drawn from the actual disaster—are absent from the film. Nor is there any manifestation in the film of national pride, most often linked with the slogan 'Be British', attributed to Captain Smith. Not only would this have been contrary to the author's intentions, it would also have been most unsuitable for an international production.

One of the most disturbing sequences for contemporary sensibilities, however, takes place on deck as the lifeboats are being loaded. Two men, apparently stokers or steerage passengers, fight their way through the crowd. Kicking and punching, they force their way past the crew and leap into a lifeboat, where other members of the crew try in vain to restrain them. An officer approaches the scrum and draws his revolver. When they ignore his warning, he shoots them both dead; their bodies are tossed overboard. The two men are black. They are virtually the only black faces in a crowd not conspicuous for its ethnic diversity. This scene was even highlighted in the publicity package, which proudly noted that: 'The fight between the niggers was most realistic, the two darkies being erstwhile pearl-fishers. Their fight terminated in their being pistoled by the Captain . . . the bodies thereupon hurtling into the sea'. Biel refers to Titanic as a metaphor for race relations, and asks: 'Was the conduct of the disaster's "Anglo-Saxon" heroes, who supposedly stayed calm and preserved order while swarthier people panicked, evidence of white supremacy'?[33] On the basis of this film, the answer would have to be a regrettable 'yes'.

Atlantic was one of the most successful films of its period—at least in Europe—and it built on and perpetuated the existing myths of the Titanic, reaffirming ideals of courage and self-sacrifice, traditional sex roles, a rigid social hierarchy, the importance of religion and a belief in the innate superiority of the white race. It would appear, then, that the Edwardian values observed before the First World War were still much in evidence two decades into the reign of George V.

Notes

1 Announcement in *Kinematograph Weekly*, 11 April 1929, p. 31.

2 *Tell England: A Study in a Generation* was reprinted five times by April 1922. Set during the Gallipoli campaign, it was made into a film directed by Anthony Asquith in 1931. It had sold 300,000 copies by 1939, and its 40th edition was published in 1965. Ernest Raymond received the OBE in 1972, two years before his death.

3 Letter from Frank Bustard to Sir Haldane Porter, Home Office, dated 9 December 1929. Ministry of Transport 9/2922, Public Record Office, London. A detailed account of this episode may be found in Simon Mills, *The Titanic in Pictures* (Chesham, 1995), pp. 23–31.

4 Further information on Dupont may be found in Jürgen Bretschneider, ed., *Ewald André Dupont: Autor und Regisseur* (Munich, 1992). For an account of Dupont's role in the British film industry, see also Andrew Higson, 'Polyglot Films for an International Market: E. A. Dupont, the British Film Industry, and the Idea of a European Cinema, 1926–1930', in Andrew Higson and Richard Maltby, eds., *Film Europe and Film America. Cinema, Commerce and Cultural Exchange 1920–1939* (Exeter, 1999), pp. 274–301.

5 *Kinematograph Weekly*, 4 July 1929, p. 47.

6 Uncredited parts were played by Norah Baring, Randle Ayrton, and Jack Trevor. The latter played a thuggish character, suggesting an American gangster type, or perhaps merely a typical American as perceived by European filmmakers at the time. As a British actor who appeared in numerous German films during the 1930s and 40s, he was tried after the war for collaborating with the enemy, but acquitted. See entry on Trevor in Hans-Michael Bock (ed.), *CineGraph. Lexikon zum deutschsprachigen Film* (Munich, 1984ff).

7 Perhaps all three; information on the French version is incomplete.

8 See Paul Malone's chapter in this volume.

9 Full cast lists and extensive supplementary material can be found in Gero Gandert, ed., *Der Film der Weimarer Republik* (Berlin and New York, 1993), pp. 34–52.

10 This is the correct spelling of the German film, and not *Atlantik*, as is frequently cited in the literature, e.g. in Alfred Bauer, *Deutscher Spielfilmalmanach 1929–1950* (Munich, 1950), p. 1.

11 Its last performance at the Gloria-Palast was on December 25th. The next film to be screened there was the first American sound film, *The Jazz Singer* (1927).

12 *Licht-Bild-Bühne*, 22/264 (1929), p. 3.

13 Bauer, *Deutscher Spielfilmalmanach 1929–1950*, p. 1.

14 *Berliner Lokal-Anzeiger*, 29 October 1929.

15 *Berliner Volkszeitung*, 30 October 1929.

16 *8-Uhr-Abendblatt*, 29 October 1929.

17 *Kinematograph Weekly*, 21 November 1929, p. 29.

18 *Bioscope*, 8 January 1930, p. 30.

19 It had also intermittently been used as a cinema. Films had been included in variety performances since 1896, and it had been the venue for *Broken Blossoms* in 1920 and *The Cabinet of Dr Caligari* the following year. Cf. Allen Eyles and Keith Skone, *London's West End Cinemas* (Sutton, 1991), p. 118.

20 From this date onwards the Alhambra functioned mainly as a cinema. In 1936 it was demolished to make way for the new Odeon Leicester Square; see Eyles and Skone, *London's West End Cinemas*, p. 118.

21 *Bioscope*, 8 January 1930, p. 30.

22 *Variety*, 8 October 1930.

23 Ginette Vincendeau, 'Hollywood Babel', in *Screen*, vol. 29, no. 2 (1988), p. 25. The article is reprinted in Higson and Maltby, eds., *Film Europe and Film America*, pp. 207–224.

24 BIP had released Alfred Hitchcock's *Blackmail* in June 1929.

25 In order to avoid confusion with the ship's captain, army 'Captain' Boldy in the play had to be promoted to 'Major' for the film.

26 Cf. reviews in *Close Up*, vol.6, no. 2, February 1930; and in *The New York Times*, 6 October 1930.

27 Richard Howells, *The Myth of the Titanic* (New York, 1999), p.1.

28 In the play there is one coward, the 'Excited Passenger' who, contrary to the Padre's counsel, leaves the room with a revolver to take the 'easy way out'.

29 Steven Biel, *Titanica* (New York and London, 1998), p. 12.

30 In the play, however, the iconoclast Rool is ready to challenge this. As his wife declares: '[Jack] says most ideas of chivalry are an insult to women, treating them as weaklings'. Nevertheless, it is Rool who is most instrumental in saving the lives of the womenfolk in his circle.

31 Biel, *Titanica*, p. 13.

32 Howells, *The Myth of the Titanic*, p. 133.

33 Biel, *Titanica*, p. 13.

CHAPTER TEN

Goebbels Runs Aground:
The Nazi Titanic Film

PAUL MALONE

THE 1943 GERMAN film *Titanic* notoriously appropriated the myth of the Titanic disaster in the service of anti-British propaganda. Recent research by Robert E. Peck has exploded many myths surrounding this *Titanic*—particularly the contention that the Nazis banned the film after director Herbert Selpin's death in Gestapo custody.[1] This is in fact untrue, although *Titanic* was indeed shelved for the duration of the war and then banned from German exhibition by the Allies, at British urging, from 1950 until the end of the post-war occupation in 1955.[2] Peck also exposes misconceptions about the film's content, some of which were apparently created by the British press to motivate this later ban.[3] *Titanic* itself, however, remains obscured by such myths; nonetheless, the film is of interest in its own right as a concrete illustration of Nazi propaganda in action, and of its ultimate failure, particularly as regards anti-British material.

In 1937, Propaganda Minister Joseph Goebbels had told his Reich Film Chamber: 'With good reason, no-one would demand that an artist portraying history take the same attitude to history as a historian. . . . Thus it has always been the case that great artists have perceived and portrayed historical events truthfully, in a higher sense than historians'.[4] With this claim to 'truth in a higher sense', Goebbels licensed filmmakers to falsify history to suit National Socialism.[5]

In particular, German history was systematically falsified; but the histories of Germany's neighbours and rivals were also distorted to justify Nazi policy. Thus, for example, new territorial encroachments, from the Sudetenland to the Soviet Union, were prefaced by press reports, stories and films dwelling on the historical ties of the territory to Germany and the present mistreatment in these lands of ethnic Germans yearning to come 'home to the Reich'. Thus, too, at the end of the 1930s, Goebbels's propaganda machine turned to Germany's greatest rival, England.

The demonisation of England was problematic: the racial doctrine in which Nazism was rooted had originally considered the British as 'Aryan' as the Germans. The Anglophile ideas central to Nazi propaganda through the mid-

1930s were never totally eclipsed—indeed, Hitler himself, who admired British empire-building, resisted relinquishing these ideas.[6] By late 1939, however, Goebbels officially set the direction of anti-British propaganda for the entirety of the war, commanding the press to portray England as an 'English-Jewish plutocracy' to be smashed.[7] The film industry had already taken up this campaign: only eight months later *Die Rothschilds (The Rothschilds)*, a film combining Anglophobia and anti-Semitism as desired, was released, though to unreceptive audiences. It was also at about this time, in early 1940, that the *Titanic* film project was initiated.[8]

The vision of history propagated by this 'anti-plutocratic course' depicted the English as belligerent capitalists who had built their empire by cheating rightful conquerors of their colonies. Feigned sympathy was shown with the subjugated Irish, Welsh and Scottish (hence the Nazis often avoided the word 'British' in favour of 'English'), as well as other colonised peoples. Accordingly, Goebbels's ministry oversaw the production of countless articles, lecture tours, and books with titles such as *War Against the Warmongers, The Rule of Force of the British Pound, Under the Knout of Plutocracy, A Hundred Families Rule England*, or *The Social Backwardness of Great Britain*.[9] These materials were disseminated in a number of ways: the book *England: Pirate Nation*, for example, was given out as a cigarette premium.[10]

The cinematic expression of the 'anti-plutocratic course' continued after *The Rothschilds* with several films on Irish Republican themes (*Der Fuchs von Glenarvon* [*The Fox of Glenarvon*, 1940] and *Mein Leben für Irland* [*My Life for Ireland*, 1941]) and films that were critical of British colonialism (*Carl Peters* and *Ohm Krüger* [1941]; *Anschlag auf Baku* [*Attack on Baku*, 1942]; *Germanin* [1943]). This aspect of the campaign came to an end in 1943, however, with the decision to delay the German release of *Titanic*—the delay became permanent, and no further anti-British films were made.

After two years' planning, the direction of *Titanic* was assigned to Herbert Selpin, a director with a respectable box-office record due to his films with matinee idol Hans Albers.[11] Selpin had made *Heiratsschwindler (The Marriage Swindler*, 1938), described by Hull as 'one of the finest German sound films ever made',[12] and the Albers vehicle *Wasser für Canitoga (Water for Canitoga*, 1939), a Canadian-set 'Western' that Courtade and Cadars regard 'a perfect example of the better Nazi commercial cinema', particularly for its inventive cinematography.[13] Selpin dealt ineptly with subjects that did not interest him, however, as with *Carl Peters*.[14] Fellow director Arthur Maria Rabenalt, who clearly disliked Selpin personally, calls him 'an outstanding craftsman who managed to reach the level of a good master, but never of a *maestro*'.[15]

Titanic's screenplay, from a scenario by Harald Bratt, was written by Walter Zerlett-Olfenius, a fanatical Nazi who had scripted five Selpin films—including *Carl Peters*, which had flopped despite starring Albers.[16] Zerlett's politics would play a more obvious role behind the scenes than on the screen: in his hands, *Titanic* merged fact, fiction and folklore into a melodrama—in the sense of a story with 'a thematic concern with personal and emotional life and a stylistic emphasis on spectacle and excess'[17]—focussed on Sigrid Olinsky (Sybille Schmitz), a wealthy Baltic German who loses her fortune while being pursued by both White Star Line president Bruce Ismay (Ernst Fritz Fürbringer) and the ship's German first officer, Petersen (Hans Nielsen).

At the same time, *Titanic* blames the disaster on capitalist rivalry between Ismay and John Jacob Astor (Karl Schönböck). Ismay hopes to cross the Atlantic in record time, salvaging the depressed White Star stocks and making a killing in collusion with the directors. Astor, however, intends to drive the stocks down until he can buy a majority and control the Titanic, 'an effective thing of value that itself creates power . . . the ability to do what you want'.

Subsidiary characters include Astor's wife Madeleine (Charlotte Thiele) and Ismay's fictional fiancée Gloria (Kirsten Heiberg); the Duchess of Canterville (Toni von Bukovics) and her impoverished escort, Lord Archibald Douglas (Fritz Böttger); the brilliant German scientist Dr. Bergmann (Theodor Loos) and his assistant Lorenz (Just Scheu); Captain Smith (Otto Wernicke); and the Cuban jewel thief Señor Cristobal Mendoz (Werner Scharf). Meanwhile, in steerage, working-class Bobby and Henry (Peter Elsholtz and Fritz Genschow) fall victim to the machinations of the Gypsy girl Marcia (Jolly Bohnert, also known as Jolly Maree) and her older partner, 'the Levantine' (Iranian-born character actor Aruth Wartan)—Levantines were considered a mixture of European and 'Oriental' races. Jeffrey Richards rightly refers to *Titanic*, like E. A. Dupont's *Atlantic* (1929), as adopting 'the *Grand Hotel* format'.[18]

Although the cast of characters is ideologically suggestive, the film's explicit propaganda touches are often relatively subtle: Zerlett's dialogue, for example, often revolves around themes of wealth, investment, and competition, even between spouses or lovers, as when Astor explains to Madeleine that controlling the Titanic means 'more power for me, more jewellery for you'. In one notable moment, when Ismay praises the Titanic's record speed, the White Star directors storm the telegraph office to purchase more shares as the orchestra plays 'God Save the King'. Zerlett's most blatant intervention, however, was to make the first officer a German, apparently meant to be in the Albers mould,[19] his presence on board is explained as a last-minute substitution for an incompetent English counterpart.

Hans Albers himself was busy starring in the epic *Münchhausen* (1943), and the part of Petersen went to Hans Nielsen. With only six years' experience in film, and reserved in manner compared to Albers's flamboyant and sometimes bawdy style, Nielsen had most notably appeared in Wolfgang Liebeneiner's pro-euthanasia *Ich klage an* (*I Accuse*, 1941) and Veit Harlan's film about Frederick II of Prussia, *Der große König* (*The Great King*, 1942); Nielsen's acting

career would last, after the two postwar years' hiatus in German film production, until the mid-1960s (in later years he frequently played Englishmen and
Spaniards). Petersen, however, is a role even Hans Albers's charisma could
hardly have salvaged.

Protagonists of Nazi historical films (and sometimes of fiction films as well)
are frequently prototypes of Hitler; such films 'did not concentrate on political
leaders, but included anyone who could be represented as having triumphed
over the prevailing assumptions of his generation',[20] whether in the political
realm (Frederick the Great, Bismarck, Ohm Krüger, Carl Peters) or in the intellectual and artistic fields (Friedrich Schiller, Andreas Schlüter, the physician
Robert Koch). As such, they represent a German 'us', standing alone against
the forces of modernity, internationalism, capitalism, etc.[21] First Officer Petersen clearly fulfils some of this function simply by being a lone German faced
with unheeding Britons; but the frequent confrontations between Petersen and
his superiors become tedious, and offer Nielsen little to play except exaspera-
tion. In the context of the Titanic disaster, he can hardly assume the stature of
a 'Führer figure'—except in Sigrid Olinsky's eyes.

The role of Olinsky, and top billing, were given to Sybille Schmitz, who had
started her career in films such as G. W. Pabst's *Tagebuch einer Verlorenen* (*Diary
of a Lost Girl*, 1929) and in Carl Theodor Dreyer's *Vampyr* (1932). Nicholas
Reeves argues that Nazi-era cinema's use of many of the same stars as Weimar
films gave the German audience a deceptive sense of continuity despite the
propagandistic turn in German film.[22] Like Nielsen, Schmitz had worked with
Selpin in the film *Trenck, der Pandur* (*Trenck, the Pandur*, 1940). With her melancholy beauty augmented by a black wig, and costumed in dark, understated
gowns, she was well suited to play the ambiguous and exotic Sigrid Olinsky.
Erica Carter argues that in Nazi Germany, a Hollywood-style star system
based on individualism gave way to 'the fabrication of ideal types'[23]; and in
fact, a special 1940 issue of the weekly *Filmwelt* (*Film World*) magazine devoted
to six types of women portrayed in the German cinema had classified Schmitz,
along with her *Titanic* co-star, the Norwegian-born Kirsten Heiberg, among
the 'dangerous women'.[24]

Heiberg, however, as Ismay's cynically opportunistic fiancée, is relegated to
a few brief scenes. Schmitz, in contrast, is given ample opportunity to display
Olinsky's conflicted feelings. Olinsky and Petersen have a past, having flirted
once in Egypt; but she jilted him, and he now thinks her superficial. Insulted,
Olinsky forces him, through Ismay, to break ship's regulations by giving her a
tour of the engine rooms. Later, in her cabin, the tables are turned: clad in an
off-the-shoulder peignoir and dwarfed by a bouquet from Ismay, she receives
Petersen, who requests that she use her millions to dissuade the White Star
president from sailing at top speed. Petersen cannot know that she is still holding a telegram informing her that the Russians have expropriated her wealth;

she refuses his plea—without revealing why. He responds before leaving that he had thought her 'a woman with the bad luck to be wealthy, but whom a man could love if things were different'. This scene is constructed entirely around Schmitz's reactions; here, as in the contemporaneous melodramas starring Zarah Leander, 'visual representation of female desire and its constant companion, female suffering, [relies] extensively on extreme close-ups, dramatic lighting, claustrophobic settings, and exaggerated costumes'.[25]

The remaining roles were cast with reliable character actors, many of whose distinguished careers stretched back to silent days (Otto Wernicke and Theodor Loos, for example, had appeared in several Fritz Lang films, and Loos had also acted in E. A. Dupont's *Atlantic*). Others continued to appear in film and television for many decades after the war (Ernst Fritz Fürbringer and Karl Schönböck, for example, worked regularly into the mid-1980s and the early years of the 21st century respectively).

The opulent production design by Fritz Maurischat and Robert Dietrich emphasises excess; while Friedel Behn-Grund's cinematography, concentrating on two- and three-shots against the elegant backgrounds and framing actresses in mirrors, forgoes maritime atmosphere in favour of claustrophobia. This feeling is underscored by the staging, which crowds even the most expansive interior sets; the only long shots that show the enormous ballroom for more than a second precede and conclude the post-collision confrontation between the elegant society in first class and the steerage passengers, who flow down the huge staircase to ask why the engines have stopped.[26] Friedel Buckow's editing builds tension by accelerating the intercutting of multiple scenes just before the collision itself, created through special effects by Ernst Kunstmann, and featuring an impressive model Titanic (though there are problems of scale with the water) and the generally convincing breaching of bulkheads and flooding of gangways.

The message of the film is clear: Astor's and Ismay's venality not only causes the catastrophe, but also alienates their loved ones. Ismay warns Gloria that he may have to seduce the wealthy Olinsky to rescue the White Star Line; Astor, in contrast, finds Madeleine's jewel box missing and falsely accuses her of infidelity with the bankrupt Lord Douglas. Both women ultimately leave angrily for the lifeboats. Alone, Ismay attempts to force Astor to rescue the White Star Line financially in return for a place in the lifeboats, but the deal collapses because only women and children are being rescued. Astor is doomed; Petersen will rescue Ismay in a vain attempt to bring him to justice.

Events proceed similarly in steerage: after Marcia dances provocatively, Bobby and Henry fight over her, and Bobby is sent to the brig for using a knife handed him by the Levantine. Later, as the ship is sinking, the Levantine instigates a riot. In the confusion, Henry leaves Marcia to rescue Bobby; as Marcia and the Levantine attempt to climb a rope ladder into a descending lifeboat, a desperate Mendoz attacks them. The two struggling men fall into the lifeboat, which plunges from its davits into the sea, neatly taking all three racial undesirables with it and demonstrating the fruit of non-Aryan underhandedness.

In contrast, Jan and Anna, simple rural folk (Sepp Rist and Liselotte Klingler), are separated in the final chaos; but the unconscious Anna is placed on a makeshift raft built by Bobby and Henry, while Jan is later revealed to have survived as an amnesiac. Their reunion in the final scene implies that Bobby and Henry, who wisely choose racial solidarity over romance with the 'other', also survive.

Bergmann, meanwhile, resigns himself to death, entrusting his formulae to Lorenz with the Nietzschean words, 'You have the will to make it through this'. The only other real farewell is between the telegraph operators Phillips and Bride (Karl Dannemann and Heinz Welzel). In both cases a quasi-paternal homosocial relationship, rather than a romantic one, makes the separation suitable for sentiment.

The German heterosexual couples, however, fare best: Olinsky's manicurist Hedi (Monika Burg) succumbs to the charm of violinist Franz (Hermann Brix) and breaks her engagement back home by telegramme—the only passenger to use the cable service for anything other than buying stocks. When the ship sinks, Franz remains behind while Hedi boards a lifeboat; fortunately, he too is on hand when Bobby and Henry are constructing their raft.

Finally, after the collision, Olinsky confesses to Petersen: 'I'm as poor as you—perhaps even poorer'. He deputises her with his overcoat, and she helps organise the evacuation; he then declares his love by ordering her into a lifeboat. She adoringly submits, and as her boat is lowered, from her point of view Petersen seems to ascend above her. This farewell, however, is only the 'pleasurable delay of gratification' typical of melodrama:[27] when they at last share a lifeboat, she drapes his overcoat over him, returning it and its authority to their rightful owner.

Thus capitalist competition, unlike the corporatist assimilation and racial solidarity of National Socialism, leads to personal catastrophe; and we are to read the unsavoury effect of 'Jewish-British plutocracy'. There are apparently no Jews aboard this Titanic, though there are Chinese passengers, and of course the Levantine, in steerage. But then, Goebbels himself had once described the English, 'with their blend of ruthlessness, mendacity, pious hypocrisy and sanctimonious holiness', as 'the Jews among the Aryans'.[28]

In the film's closing moments (cut from post-war prints at British demand), a court of inquiry acquits Ismay despite Petersen's impassioned testimony to Ismay's guilt, by placing the blame on the dead Captain Smith; thus leading to the closing title labelling the proceedings 'a searing indictment of English greed'. Notwithstanding the film's message and this final scene, however, *Titanic* ultimately fails in its propaganda aims in several respects.

Most notably, 'in the face of catastrophe, we cannot but feel for the passengers, and the ensemble which was intended as a symbol for perfidious Albion instead becomes synonymous with "us"'.[29] We feel sympathy for the elderly duchess, for example, arriving on deck too late for the last lifeboat; or for Astor, when the ship's detective produces Madeleine's jewel box, taken from Mendoz, and Astor realises that Madeleine is innocent. Also, as Peck points out, the behaviour of the British crew is portrayed as efficient and even heroic.[30] Particularly sympathetic are Captain Smith's final realisation that Ismay and his like are not 'set above me in the order of things', and telegraph operator Phillips's farewell first to his young colleague and then to his pet canary (which he sets free to the strains of 'Nearer My God to Thee').

The 'anti-plutocratic course', however, was aimed mainly at Britain's ruling classes; ordinary Englishmen or women could be portrayed either as oppressed by their own class system, or as rabble displaying English greed and dishonesty *in extremis*. *Titanic* clearly chooses the former: the shots of the engine room, and the confrontation in the ballroom, are reminiscent of Fritz Lang's *Metropolis* (1927). In any case, contrary to some accounts, the discipline of German steerage passengers is not contrasted with the panic of the English in first class[31]: some of the steerage passengers are clearly also English, and none of them, not even Jan and Anna, is explicitly designated as German.

Notwithstanding these apparent weaknesses in the film's propagandistic function, however—and Goebbels's opinion, upon viewing *Titanic* in mid-December 1942, that both directors had failed to inspire decent performances from most of the cast[32]—the completed film was exhibited with great success from 1943 to the war's end in the German-occupied territories, as well as in Spain and Switzerland. Yet despite the film's importance and expense, *Titanic* curiously was not released in Germany until after the war; Peck carefully weighs the merits of the several traditional explanations for the film's alleged 'banning', eliminating some from serious consideration, but leaving the matter open for lack of evidence.[33]

There is, however, one discrepancy in the scholarship on Titanic which has yet to be addressed: this is the fact that the most widely disseminated synopsis of the film, prepared for the programme of the German premiere and printed in the *Illustrierter Film Kurier*, differs in several respects from the actual content of the film. This synopsis describes Olinsky as 'Sigrid Oole', a Dane falsely assumed to be wealthy; it also calls the Astors 'Lord and Lady Astor', conflating the American Astors aboard the Titanic with their English cousins.[34] Karl Schönböck was indeed associated with playing British gentlemen throughout his career; in the three different prints of the film that I have seen, however, the Astors are not titled, as is clear from their introduction in the ballroom scene and the fact that Astor later consistently addresses Douglas as 'Lord Douglas', while Douglas always responds with 'Astor' (Ismay, however, is repeatedly referred to in the dialogue as 'Sir Bruce Ismay', although the actual Ismay was neither knight nor baronet). In all three prints, Sigrid's surname is Olinsky; and her Russian wealth is real, not rumoured.

There is a possible explanation for this discrepancy: in April 1943, when *Titanic* was approved for release, the memory of Stalingrad was still fresh and the Russian front was moving west. Olinsky's telegram from the Baltic ('Lands confiscated . . . return impossible') would certainly have provoked the wrong reaction in a German audience. In the spring of 1943, in fact, Karl Ritter's film *Besatzung Dora* (*The Crew of the Dora*), which featured soldiers fighting at the Russian Front in hopes of being rewarded with eastern farmland after the final victory, was shelved for similar reasons.[35] The decision to delay *Titanic*'s release seems to have been made the same month as it was approved[36]; unlike *Dora*, *Titanic* was salvageable with a minimum of cutting and dubbing, by removing Olinsky's telegram and altering her name and nationality. Yet it remains uninvestigated whether any print corresponding to the altered synopsis, either for domestic release or subtitled for export, was ever prepared. If not, why was the film released at all? And if so, why was no corresponding domestic print made?

Both the Polish and French subtitled prints, for example, apparently survived the war; what version of the film played in Krakow and Paris in the fall of 1943?[37] Courtade and Cadars claim that the French version was dubbed (not subtitled) to accentuate the anti-British aspects[38]—did this include raising the Astors to the peerage; and if so, was Olinsky also transformed into a penniless Dane?

Answers to these questions, of course, would still leave the film's fate unexplained. For whatever reason, only after the war were the West Germans allowed to see a version of *Titanic* cut to British demands; the East Germans supposedly saw a more complete version, since its anti-capitalist and anti-British message suited the Soviet authorities.[39] In the end, despite the propaganda ministry's ambitions to appropriate the mythic stature of the disaster for its own political ends, the failure of the 'anti-plutocratic course' conspired with the monumental nature of the Titanic myth itself to sink Goebbels's *Titanic* as Nazi propaganda. In this, the film may actually be typical: Nicholas Reeves suggests that despite the supposed efficacy of film propaganda in Nazi Germany and elsewhere, close examination of audience reactions does not substantiate the contention that film has ever played a significant role in shaping, as opposed to reinforcing, public opinion: 'For all its considerable skill, Nazi film propaganda was only truly successful when it was giving its audience a message that it wanted to hear'.[40]

Notes

1 The circumstances of Selpin's death are related, with variations, in several sources, including Josef Wulf, *Theater und Film im Dritten Reich: Eine Dokumentation* (Frankfurt, 1983), pp. 329–30. In July 1942, in a heated argument with his screenwriter Walter Zerlett-Olfenius, who had failed to carry out preparations for filming shipboard exteriors in Gotenhafen (now Gdynia), Selpin spoke coarsely and disparagingly of the military, upon which Zerlett gave notice. Selpin was called before Zerlett's friend SS General Hans Hinkel on his return to Berlin. Both Hinkel and the Gestapo were willing to let Selpin off lightly; Zerlett was not. Goebbels then intervened: when the director refused to apologise, Goebbels had him arrested for treason. Two days later Selpin was found, supposedly hanged with his own suspenders, in his cell. His death has commonly been attributed to Goebbels's orders, but Felix Moeller suggests that Goebbels would have preferred a public death sentence to enforce discipline among the film community; Arthur Maria Rabenalt insists that Selpin actually committed suicide. Felix Moeller, *The Film Minister: Goebbels and the Cinema in the Third Reich*, trans. Michael Robinson (Stuttgart/London, 2000), p. 170; Arthur Maria Rabenalt, *Joseph Goebbels und der 'Großdeutsche' Film* (Munich, 1985), p. 174. *Titanic* was completed by Werner Klingler, although it must have been nearly finished; Selpin apparently had time to complete the exterior shooting in Gotenhafen before his arrest, and he had presumably already shot interiors in the studio for six to eight weeks. Wulf: *Theater*, p. 329.

2 Robert E. Peck, 'The Banning of *Titanic*: A Study of British Postwar Film Censorship in Germany' in *Historical Journal of Film, Radio and Television*, vol. 20, no. 3, 2000, pp. 427–53; Robert E. Peck, 'Misinformation, Missing Information, and Conjecture: *Titanic* and the Historiography of Third Reich Cinema' in *Media History* vol. 6, no. 1, 2000, pp. 59–73.

3 Peck, 'Banning', pp. 435–436.

4 Gerd Albrecht (ed.), *Der Film im Dritten Reich: Eine Dokumentation* (Karlsruhe, 1979), pp. 38–39. Unless otherwise indicated, all translations from German and French are my own.

5 Hans-Gerd Happel, *Der historische Spielfilm im Nationalsozialismus* (Frankfurt/Main, 1984), p. 42.

6 Robert Edwin Herzstein, *The War Hitler Won: The Most Infamous Propaganda Campaign in History* (New York, 1978), p. 340.

7 Willi A. Boelcke, *The Secret Conferences of Dr. Goebbels: October 1939–March 1943*, trans. Ewald Osers (London, 1967), pp. 10–11.

8 Peck, 'Misinformation', pp. 59–60.

9 Herzstein: *The War Hitler Won*, pp. 332–35.

10 E. Lewalter, *Raubstaat England* (Hamburg-Bahrenfeld, 1941).

11 Francis Courtade and Pierre Cadars, *Histoire du Cinéma Nazi* (Paris, 1972), p. 287.

12 David Stewart Hull, *Film in the Third Reich* (New York, 1973), p. 122.

13 Courtade and Cadars, *Cinéma Nazi*, p. 162.

14 Courtade and Cadars, *Cinéma Nazi*, p. 90; Hull, *Film*, pp. 222–4.

15 Rabenalt, *Joseph Goebbels*, p. 171.

16 Hull, *Film in the Third Reich*, p. 224.

17 Erica Carter, *How German Is She? Postwar West German Reconstruction and the Consuming Woman* (Ann Arbor, 1997), pp. 177.

18 Jeffrey Richards, *The Definitive Titanic Film: A Night to Remember* (London, 2003), p. 18.

19 Courtade and Cadars, *Cinéma Nazi*, pp. 287–88.

20 Nicholas Reeves, *The Power of Film Propaganda: Myth or Reality?*, London, 1999, p. 106.

21 Leiser, *Nazi Cinema*, pp. 106–120; Happel, *Der historische Spielfilm*, pp. 38–39.

22 Reeves, *Film Propaganda*, p. 128.

23 Erica Carter, 'Marlene Dietrich—The Prodigal Daughter,' in Tim Bergfelder, Erica Carter, Deniz Göktürk (eds.), *The German Cinema Book* (London, 2002), pp. 72–3.

24 The other types were comediennes like Ida Wüst, dancers (Marika Rökk), 'dramatic women' (Paula Wessely), love interests (Irene von Meyendorff) and mothers (Käthe Dorsch). Jo Fox, *Filming Women in the Third Reich* (Oxford, 2000), pp. 12–13.

25 Sabine Hake, *German National Cinema* (London, 2002), p. 75. On the association of Sybille Schmitz with melodrama, see p. 69.

26 Selpin is the first director of a Titanic film to emphasize class difference: Richards, *A Night to Remember*, p. 20.

27 Hake, *German National Cinema*, p. 75.

28 Quoted in Erwin Leiser, *Nazi Cinema*, trans. Gertrud Mander and David Wilson (London, 1974), p. 105.

29 Leif Furhammar and Folke Isaksson, *Politics and Film*, trans. Kersti French (New York, 1971), p. 191.

30 Peck, 'Banning', pp. 440–1.

31 See, for example, Hull, *Film in the Third Reich*, p. 226.

32 Moeller, *Film Minister*, p. 32; Peck, 'Misinformation', p. 67.

33 Peck, 'Banning', p. 65–70.

34 Hull, *Film in the Third Reich*, pp. 230–31; Cinzia Romani, *Tainted Goddesses: Female Film Stars of the Third Reich*, trans. Robert Connolly (New York, 1992), p. 71. The most reliable synopsis to date is in Richards, *A Night to Remember*, pp. 18–21.

35 Moeller, *Film Minister*, pp. 114, 199.

36 Peck, 'Misinformation', p. 61.

37 Peck, 'Misinformation', p. 60; Hull, *Film in the Third Reich*, p. 231. Hull apparently noticed no discrepancy between the French subtitled print he saw and the altered synopsis, which he gives on the same page.

38 Courtade and Cadars, *Cinéma Nazi*, p. 288.

39 Peck, 'Banning', pp. 433–34; Hull, *Film in the Third Reich*, p. 230.

40 Reeves, *Film Propaganda*, p. 129; see also pp. 240–1.

CHAPTER ELEVEN

Reading Titanic Politically: Class, Nation and Gender in Negulesco's *Titanic* (1953)

ALAN FINLAYSON and RICHARD TAYLOR

INTRODUCTION: TITANIC AS POLITICS

WHATEVER else it may be, the Titanic myth is a *political* myth. Even before launching, the White Star Line heralded the building of their new ships as 'a great Anglo-Saxon triumph',[1] while advertising claimed that the Olympic and Titanic 'stand for the pre-eminence of the Anglo-Saxon race on the Ocean'.[2] After the sinking these themes of race and nationality resurfaced. Joseph Conrad bridled at what he regarded as the meddling of American senators,[3] noting the way in which the US inquiry reflected broader geopolitical tensions. G. K. Chesterton and George Bernard Shaw pointedly contrasted the press coverage on both sides of the Atlantic.[4] Ethnicity also made a blunt appearance at the official inquiries. Speaking to the US inquiry, First Officer Harold Lowe said he had been forced to fire his gun because of the unwelcome presence of leering Italian immigrants: he had to withdraw the statement at the insistence of the Italian ambassador,[5] although lingering prejudice against Southern Europeans remained in the roll call of Titanic mythologies. Meanwhile Winston Churchill noted in a letter to his wife:

The whole episode fascinates me. It shows that in spite of all the inequalities and artificialities of our modern life, at the bottom—tested to its foundations, our civilisation is humane, Christian, and absolutely democratic. How differently Imperial Rome or Ancient Greece would have settled the problem.[6]

Not everyone felt so sanguine about these events: racial themes combined with equally charged conceptions of class and the ship became a site for the articulation and contestation of varying politicised interpretations of its fate. Within a few weeks one commentator was declaring: 'The Titanic illustrated in herself and in her destruction within three days after she put to sea, the greed and rapacity and contempt for human life which under capitalism inspired and presided over her creation . . . the White Star Line has millions for the wanton and wicked luxury of the pampered millionaires but not a dollar for a lookout glass'. It was 'a capitalist disaster'.[7]

Nor was the Titanic immune from being drawn into the conflict over the suffrage question and associated gender issues. Churchill noted in another letter to his wife that 'the strict observance of the great traditions of the sea towards women and children reflects nothing but honour upon our civilisation. Even I hope it may mollify some of the young unmarried lady teachers who are so bitter in their sex antagonism, and think men so base and vile'.[8] The feminist and anarchist Emma Goldman, writing from a quite different political perspective, came to a similar conclusion about the damage done to the suffragette cause.[9] To talk of Titanic, then, has long been to engage with issues that are central not only to politics but to human experience. The endless questions about the ship touch on fate, responsibility and the pity of humanity in the face of natural forces, but the answers have turned on assumptions and assertions relating to those central vectors of political dispute: class, nation and gender.

It is thus unsurprising that these themes continue to be articulated in cinematic renditions of the Titanic myth. From Selpin's 1943 conclusion that 1,500 died 'for England's greed' (victims of English and non-Aryan capitalists) to the challenge made by *A Night to Remember* (1958) to the assumption of imperial certainty[10] and Cameron's story of the transition from tight-corseted English prig to born-again American—leaving behind all old Europe's 'square' and adult obsessions with fixed ideas of class and gender—we find the same themes presented from differing angles. For all of them Titanic itself is always the 'index' lying behind the fabrications. They cannot avoid being conditioned by the historical fact of the sinking *and* the subsequent mythologising of which they are a part. Before the screenwriter puts pen to paper Titanic is always *already* a particular sort of story: a cautionary tale, even a fable. There is no choice for the writer but to engage with and extend the myth, even though each film tries, in its own way, to suggest that it is doing something other than engaging with mere myth, that it is getting to the heart, if not of the ocean then of the story and its hidden truth.[11]

Compared to its grander rivals, Jean Negulesco's 1953 *Titanic* is perhaps the least amenable to a political interpretation, appearing as little more than a minor domestic drama somewhat outweighed by the epic background against which it is set. But all films represent realities as well as fictions and so contribute to the use of those realities in a society's conversations with itself. So it is that the writers of the Negulesco version could not help but have real anxieties about class, nationality and gender weave in and out of the fiction: Titanic, like society, comes with baggage in its hold.

The script for *Titanic* was written by Charles Brackett, Richard L. Breen, and Walter Reisch. Brackett in particular had a high profile as a screenwriter—he won the Academy Award for Best Screenplay four times, including the shared one for *Titanic*. His writing credits include Howard Hawks' sparkling *Ball of Fire* (1941, based on a story by Billy Wilder), and Ernst Lubitsch's *Ninotchka* (1939), the latter with Wilder and Reisch. Brackett and Wilder collaborated on several more films in the 1940s, including classics such as *Lost Weekend* (1945) and *Sunset Blvd.* (1950). Walter Reisch, a Viennese émigré, had also contributed to the scripts of Alexander Korda's maritime melodrama *That Hamilton Woman* (1941), and *Gaslight* (1944).[12] Breen, meanwhile, had previously worked with Brackett and Wilder on *A Foreign Affair* (1948), with Brackett and Reisch on *Niagara* (1953), and he wrote Negulesco's segment of *O'Henry's Full House* (1952). In short, *Titanic*'s writing team consisted of successful collaborators with a solid track record in Hollywood who were employed here to undertake quality hack work.

The film's director, Romanian-born Jean Negulesco, was best known as a maker of melodramas and light romantic comedies. Though not the most sparkling of Hollywood directors, he was certainly successful, placed alongside the likes of Hathaway and Hawks in the short-story portmanteau *O'Henry's Full House*. In that decade he was at his commercial peak, contracted to 20th Century Fox and directing Monroe, Bacall and Grable in *How to Marry a Millionaire* (1953); later Fred Astaire in *Daddy Long Legs*, Lana Turner in *The Rains of Ranchipur* (both 1955) and Sophia Loren in *Boy on a Dolphin* (1957).[13]

For the politically minded analyst this is an unpropitious background but it is precisely what makes the film interesting. Because of its 'innocuous' nature, because it is in so many ways a 'routine' Hollywood production, and because, more than the other films, it *appears* to eschew a number of the well-worn themes of Titanic storytelling, Negulesco's film raises questions about the political aspects of everyday and unexceptional film entertainment. Hollywood movies, against varying backdrops and fantastical landscapes, place the dramas of us all—emotional conflicts, conflicting desires and clashing demands of a prosaic sort—at the centre of their world-view. In providing a context for the playing out of these troublesome realities, cinema takes on the old bardic function of story-telling, allowing us to consider at a grander level the banalities that more usually preoccupy us. In so doing cinema becomes not only entertainment but also a vehicle for moral instruction. This is why, when the high drama of the seas met the melodrama of Hollywood—against the backdrop of the last McCarthyite witch-hunts and a studio system that was yet to decline significantly—politics, however hidden, were also along for the ride.

NEGULESCO'S 1953 *TITANIC*

Titanic fits into a pattern of Negulesco movies composed of bankable stars and the promise of spectacle. Negulesco directed his performers to play the types for which they were well known. Clifton Webb depicts the sort of waspish effete snob he had been playing for some time, while Barbara Stanwyck brought with her a screen persona enabling her easily to emphasise the characteristics of the 'desperate' mother and the 'hardened' woman. Audiences knew what to expect from these performers and Negulesco did not disappoint them.

The advertising, from a period when Hollywood was forced to take on television for the first time, declared the film to be 'TITANIC IN EMOTION! TITANIC IN SPECTACLE! TITANIC IN CLIMAX! TITANIC IN CAST! THE MOTION PICTURE AS OVERPOWERING AS ITS NAME!' The trailer went further claiming (incorrectly) that this was the first film to screen the 'strange events' and 'monumental story' while also declaring it 'an immense canvas on which is thrown the gripping story of young love, of cowardice and heroism, of faithfulness and adultery, of sinners and saints', emphasising the epic scale of melodrama. These were important aspects of the commercial appeal of a film that was to win the Oscar for Best Story and Screenplay.

The film begins, before any opening titles, with footage of an iceberg breaking off from an Arctic floe preparing to drift southwards, evoking the spirit of Hardy's poem of natural fate 'The Convergence of the Twain'.[14] But the action of the film is centred on the emotional involvements of the central characters at the core of which—as was typical for melodrama in this period—is a family in crisis. It is they who will play out a story in which a fateful consummation (by two ships passing in the night) will form part of a collision between a seemingly frozen heart and aspirations for familial warmth.[15]

THE LAST SUPPER

Julia Sturges (Stanwyck) is taking her children back home to America, ostensibly on a short family visit. But her husband Richard (Webb) realises that she does not intend to come back to the Europe that he has made their peripatetic home, wishing instead to return to her small-town roots. Bribing a Basque paterfamilias, who was *en route* with his family to a new life in California, Richard secures passage on the ship and surprises his family. It is against this background that the film will portray certain anxieties about family life embedded in wider anxieties of class and gender that will be resolved by the assertion of middle-class American family propriety. That these are the central themes is made plain when Richard surprises Julia at dinner on the first evening. The scene contains a seminal confrontation between Richard and Julia and the worlds and values that they are, initially, to represent. Where Richard is a sophisticated, Europeanised American, Julia is at heart a simple American girl. To Richard's accusation that she is 'kidnapping' their children, she responds that she is 'rescuing' them: 'They're going to stop being rootless, purposeless, superficial hotel children'.

Julia:	Richard, please try to see this sanely. We're Americans, we belong in America. And yet for years we've been galloping all over Europe to be at the proper places at the proper time. Winter in St Moritz, Deauville in season, summer in . . . What's the use? It's the same silly calendar year after year. Look at Annette.
Richard:	I have. With great pride. She's entertaining. She's discriminating. She has grace and style.
Julia:	She's an arrogant little prig.
Richard:	So you've chosen to drag her back to the glories of Mackinac, Michigan?

Mackinac, in the north of Michigan near the Canadian border, is almost as far from the values of Richard's European civilisation as he can imagine. Properly pronounced 'Mackinaw', Richard says it phonetically as 'Mackinack' furthering his intended insult and emphasising his disdain for 'Americanism'.

Julia:	Any town in any state becomes comic on your lips. But, comic or not, that's where she's going. To a big ugly pleasant house with the cheap scent of lilacs in the air . . . Oh, don't worry, she won't turn out dowdy. She'll meet dozens of nice boys.

Here, the world of European high society, with which Richard is at home, is presented by Julia as 'artificial' and contrasted unfavourably with the 'real' world of small-town America, characterised by 'the cheap scent of lilacs' and the 'nice boys'. For Julia, this America (of middle-class, small-town decency and homeliness) is healthy normality: 'And, as for Norman, I can only tell you this. There's not going to be a carriage with two ponies waiting for him at 9 o'clock every morning. From now on he's going to walk to school'.

Identities of class and national identity—or, more properly, their imagined constructions—are thus explicitly raised. But embedded within them are the gender stereotypes that hold the world in place. Annette will be wed to a 'nice boy' and Norman will learn to be a self-reliant man. Yet these gender roles laid out in the dialogue are simultaneously addressed, and perhaps subverted, visually through the appearance of the two main characters. Julia appears to take a dominant role maintaining the upper hand until almost the end of the film. Her 'masculinity' is emphasised in this scene by the suit-like revers on the jacket of her dress, while Richard wears a somewhat 'feminine' flower in the buttonhole of his own suit (placed there by Annette in a routine expression of their European socialite lifestyle). The effeminacy of Richard Sturges is filled out by the screen persona of Clifton Webb continuing a line of sexually ambivalent characters that he had been playing since his role in *Laura* (1944). His magnificently sneering and camp riposte that 'I should have anticipated this. Twenty years ago I made the pardonable mistake of thinking I could civilise a girl who bought her hats out of a Sears Roebuck catalogue. I was wrong', merely leaves him looking more effete, elitist and detached than before, while identifying Julia with the 'average' woman, presumably the film's intended audience. The film invites us to sympathise with the down-to-earth and warm aspirations of a woman who just wants to be a proper mother. Middle-class America becomes identified with the values of 'realistic' community and gentle ambition while Europe is defined as rootless, superficial and, by extension, 'womanly'.

KIPPERS OR GROUNDGRIPPERS?

The morning after the night before, on what she calls 'a brand new day that's never been touched' Julia is drawn into conversation by Giff Rogers (Robert Wagner), a young man who had earlier spied Annette coming aboard only to be rudely rebuffed by her. He quickly explains that the 'P' on his shirt stands for Purdue not Princeton. In other words he is not a rich boy from the European-leaning Ivy League but a student from a solidly Midwestern institution. He has ability, we may assume, yet lacks pretension. As if to make the point even clearer, we are told that he is returning from a college tennis-playing trip to Oxford. He is, we gather, a sportsman not an egghead and just the sort of 'nice boy' Julia wants for Annette.

Then Richard comes to the cabin shared by Julia and Annette, who is just waking for a late breakfast. Richard, whom his daughter worshipfully calls 'angel', examines the dresses Julia has packed for her:

Richard: Your mother seems to have packed everything. Of course, some of them will be a little out of place in 'Mackinack'. *Cut to Julia in the other room: she overhears him.* Still, plenty of practical things. Only high heels? You'll have to have something to walk in. Julia, as soon as we arrive I think you ought to buy her some of those flat shoes. They're called groundgrippers, I believe. She'll need lots of things.

There can hardly be anything more earthbound as a symbol for reality than groundgrippers and they contrast didactically with the Lanvin and Lucille dresses purchased in Paris. Throughout the films clothes of various kinds will be made to bear much symbolic weight.

Richard has skilfully engineered the exposure of Julia's intentions and the imminent confrontation between mother and daughter. As he bones Annette's kipper, he speculates on a social occasion in Warsaw that she was not aware she had missed, deliberately driving a wedge between Europeanised daughter and American mother.

Richard: With the time difference they should just be sitting down to luncheon in that extraordinary room overlooking the fountains. The dear arthritic old princess sitting under the finest crystal chandelier in Europe and Mr

Paderewski complaining about the draught. And at the end of the table one young man next to an empty chair with a tear in his eye. A crystal tear is my guess . . .

Richard's description stands as the formal opposite of Julia's picture of a big family home in Michigan. Where hers suggested that family and community outweigh money and status, Richard seems to revel in the very superficiality of aristocratic life in a declining empire. It is as if he is aware of the emptiness of this existence yet prizes it for the superficiality of which he is master. Forced to admit that she had cancelled the engagement without letting Annette know, Julia resorts to saying 'What's the difference, one party more or less?' only to give Richard the chance to respond cuttingly: 'Now, Julia, a luncheon at the Metternichs is not exactly a wiener roast'. The remark yet again draws attention to cultural differences of nation and class.

Annette: Was there some reason, mother, I wasn't told I was invited to the Metternichs?

Richard: Annette, your mother's a sensible woman. She probably felt something might come of it, some involvement with the young master.

Julia: To be perfectly frank, I was afraid. He's an arrogant little toad.

Richard: He does look a little like a toad, but he's a highly eligible toad. Not many young men are related to both the Metternichs and the Rothschilds.

Again Richard seems aware of the emptiness of this socially formal existence, quite consciously prepared to place an arranged liaison above anything so uncivil as actual romance. Annette though is perhaps too young (and insufficiently absorbed into Europe) to see this. 'I don't think he looks in the least like a toad and I see no reason why we couldn't have left a week later. I'm sorry, mother, but I think it was mean of you', only to give Richard the chance to force all the cats out of their bags: 'Annette, mind your manners. It wasn't a question of a week or two weeks. This was as good a time as any to bow out' and Julia has no alternative but to reveal what is happening:

Annette: Bow out?

Richard: Yes, I'm afraid so. Adieu, great world.

Julia: What your father is saying is that I'm taking you home for good. You may as well know it now. I won't see an arranged marriage, I won't see you jumping from party to party, from title to title all the rest of your life.

Annette: Father, I want to ask you one question. Do you approve of all this?

Richard, putting a carnation in his buttonhole: Annette, I adore you. You know that.

Annette: Are you going to stay in Michigan for good?

Richard: I am a hopeless case . . . far too old to alter my preferences now.

Annette: When are you going back?

Richard: By the next boat.

Annette: Whenever you go, I go with you . . . As for you, mother, I love you very much, but my address is Paris, France!

This fills in the outlines sketched by the dinner scene. The elder of the two children is now directly involved in the tug-of-war between the two parents and their respective worlds. Richard forces Julia to reveal her hand, believing that Annette is not yet ready to be 'turned' into a 'nice' American girl.

REVELATIONS

We have then a family at war: mapped on to that war are the presumed cultural practices and values of aristocratic Europe and middle-class America. Stepping outside the time frame of the film, we can remember that in 1953 this battle was in full swing with audiences perhaps dimly aware that they were to imagine middle-class America to be under threat from a cold Europe not too far away from that luncheon in Warsaw. But still weaving in and out are the proper gender roles that are the ultimate defence against corruption.

As the family prepares for dinner—at the centre of social status, courtesy of Richard, they will dine at the captain's table—Richard is at the tailor's, yet again checking his finery, and young Norman confesses to feeling inadequate as he is still in short trousers. Proudly, Richard instructs the tailor to prepare a suit: 'You're fitting *Mr.* Sturges' he smiles. The spectacle of sartorially based masculinity is thus raised but Richard's pride is about to be dealt a cruel blow. Back in the cabin, after yet more badinage, Annette leaves, so that Richard and Julia are alone. He makes a clumsy attempt at a form of reconciliation:

Richard: Well, Julia, after a few hours, I imagine we've reached the same conclusion . . . We scream, we shout, we hurt each other, but we calm down. Things aren't so bad.

He adds, 'I don't regard this as a victory. It's an adjustment'. But, as he opens the cabin door, Julia turns to confront him:

Julia: Before you go down and eat and drink you'd better know how things are going to be. I've given up on Annette. Her standards will always be the chic club, the best table, the Royal Enclosure—and that's her decision, she's almost of age. But Norman is still a child. I'm not taking any chances with him.

Richard: Now, wait a minute, Julia. What is this all about?

Julia: I should've thought it'd be perfectly clear. I'm not going to see Norman thrown away. He stays with me . . . And, if you try to interfere, I'll be as common as you think I am. I'll fight you tooth and nail. I'll take you to the courts.

'Could you be common in a slightly lower voice?' says Richard, declaring that the boy is 'the most important thing in my life. I have plans for Norman'. His son is to be a 'portion' of himself that will survive. 'Oh yes, I forgot—the best-dressed man of his day. That's what they're going to write on your tombstone,' scoffs Julia in such a way that Richard begins to suspect his wife of 'holding a high trump'. He insists she play it:

Julia: All right, Richard. One question first?

Richard: If it's about Norman, you know the answer. No court in the world, no power under Heaven can force me to give up my son.

Julia: . . . He's not your son.

With this, the story takes an unexpected, perhaps even shocking turn. But the introduction of small elements of sexual impropriety was not uncommon in fifties melodrama. Film was seeking to cover ground that television could not, appealing to audiences able to reflect on occasionally more adult themes. Despite this admission on the part of Julia, we are not encouraged suddenly to despise her. Later we discover that her indiscretion occurred as a moment of madness when she was desperate for meaningful affection. What is more, we find out that she initiated the encounter. For the moment it is enough to halt Richard.

EXODUS AND GENESIS

From this point on the narrative development of character moves more rapidly. Thanks in part to Julia, Giff has softened the icy heart of Annette and even begun to initate her into the delights of American popular culture as exemplified in the Navajo rag, teaching her to dance the steps. But Richard has retreated into all-night card playing, using it to distance himself from Norman's entreaties to join him in a shuffleboard tournament. Julia pleads with him to be nicer to Norman, since none of their troubles are his fault: 'I'm sorry Julia,' he responds, 'You are asking me to do something which involves character. And, as you have pointed out, I'm not a man of character'. When the ship begins to sink, however, things change and true character is revealed. The crisis has been wrought by the effeminate status obsession of Richard Sturges leading to the ultimate expression of marital crisis. But at the point of the sinking roles begin to reverse—or, rather, return to their even keel.

Learning of their impending doom, Richard calmly prepares his family by putting on their lifebelts and reassuring them that 'evidently the steamship company thought we needed something to break the monotony'. He also adapts to his role as substitute patriarch for the Basque family whose ticket he bought, taking charge of them and ordering them up to the lifeboats. As

Richard is placing his family on the lifeboat, Julia repents: 'I beg your pardon, sir. I put you down as a useless man. Somebody to lead a cotillion'. Richard reminisces about their first meeting, showing us that they were once truly in love and they kiss passionately.

Strikingly in the long evacuation scenes that follow there is no background orchestration, only the insistent wail of the evacuation siren, the lap of the water and the occasional horn. The silence adds to an eerie sensibility. Where before we have seen men—Richard and his various vacuous card-playing friends—acting indulgently and weakly, now is the time for displays of true masculinity. When the lifeboat jams as it is winched down, Giff climbs up to free it, doing so only at the cost of a fall that allows him to be retrieved and pulled, injured, aboard the lifeboat. Other men fulfil their duties. Failed priest George Headley descends into the stoke hold to rescue trapped boiler men. Only Earl Meeker (always an aspirant figure) avoids his duty, donning women's clothes to sneak aboard a lifeboat. Richard plays his part and we see him standing firmly on deck pausing at one point to pass his cigarette to an exhausted boilerman. But this is also the moment for Norman in his long trousers as he gives his seat up to a woman and leaves the lifeboat without Julia seeing. He searches for his father who, when they meet, embraces him, acknowledging his bravery. When a sailor tells him a young boy has been looking for him he replies, with marked emphasis, that he has found him and 'He's my son'. Julia meanwhile, aboard the lifeboat, is reduced to the distraught and dishevelled state of helplessness that previously she had seemed incapable of. As the band strikes up 'Nearer My God to Thee' there is no panic. Arm-in-arm Richard and Norman sing before the final engine blows and the ship finally goes down.

CONCLUSION: TITANIC POLITICS

Viewed from the perspective of the present day, a number of things are striking about this film. Perhaps the most obvious are the number of moments that are echoed very clearly by Cameron's film. Like Rose Dawson, Annette is, at first, quite icy and prepared to look down on her lower class suitor. Like Jack, Giff (with similar hairstyle) inducts her into American popular culture. In both the narrative contrasts a corrupt and decadent European culture with a fresh, optimistic and more egalitarian America. But beyond this the differences stand out. Most noticeably the fifties version does not seem overly concerned to apportion blame for the tragedy. In particular there is no strong suggestion that the first-class passengers or the crew prevented the escape of those from steerage. This is easily explicable. It was the period of the Hollywood blacklist after all. But it is perhaps also indicative of the fact that while inequality was a problematic issue in the context of the restructuring of class relations in 1990s

America, in the 1950s a far greater concern was that of gender. Here Negulesco's *Titanic* stood solidly on the ground carved out for mass culture in 1950s America. It was an era trying to imagine that the upheaval of warfare, technological change and the transformations in social roles these had initiated, had never happened. Films tended to eschew the sexiness or the direct confrontation with issues of class and poverty that had given thirties films their depth, or the violence that gave 1940s crime films their illicit appeal. As Jackie Byars puts it, in a study of melodrama from this period:

As women of all ages, races, marital and maternal statuses, and socio-economic classes flooded out of their homes and into the workplaces of America, the family structure began to change, previously sacrosanct gender roles began to alter, and struggles over the meaning of female and male became particularly evident in the cultural atmosphere . . . family values be-came socially and culturally central to Americans, and Hollywood films interpreted and helped to make sense of this basic social institution symbolically deploying it across a panoply of permutations.[16]

Titanic's permutation begins with a world askew, in which gender relations are already unbalanced. The father of the family acts too much like a woman, the daughter has surrendered her nurturing characteristics to the vapidity of social grace, and the young man is kept in a state of emasculated pre-adulthood. As a result the woman has been forced to take charge. Where, in some renditions, the fateful collision stands for the underlying tensions of society or civilisation, literally turning upside down a world that was already metaphorically so, here the sinking constitutes the confrontation that puts things the right way up. By the end Julia has prostrated herself before her husband and he has recalled the days when his sexuality was lacking in apparent ambivalence. When death confronts, things are made plain and it is time for women to cry and men to die.

And yet it is not so simple. For, in portraying gender roles in need of being 'restored', the film has already exposed their fictitious nature, showing that they are matters of social convention and not nature, deriving from the dress worn rather than the one wearing it. Richard is able to adopt the fatherly role for his adopted migrant family and to accept that he is the father of Norman, even if not biologically so. Julia has taken charge of her life and it will be her vision for Annette that comes true in the end. She is not directly punished for her adultery, it is Richard who pays the price for his previous lack of manhood. But these openings to a different way of understanding gender are, in the end, only openings. For 'correctness' in gender roles is tightly articulated with (American) nationality and (middle) class. Effete old Europe has sunk and folksy traditionalism survived to sail another day. Ninety years after the sinking of Titanic, fifty years after the making of this film and six after Cameron's blockbuster, Hollywood—and America—is still telling us the same old story.

Notes

1 Cited in John Wilson Foster (ed.), *Titanic* (Harmondsworth, 1999), p.255.

2 Foster, *Titanic*, p. 256.

3 Foster, *Titanic*, pp. 194–5.

4 Foster, *Titanic*, pp. 196–8; 214–16.

5 Foster, *Titanic*, pp. 258–9.

6 Dated 20 April 1912, cited in: Randolph S. Churchill, *Winston S. Churchill. Vol II: Companion, Part 3: 1911–1914* (London, 1969), p. 1543.

7 Foster, *Titanic*, pp. 165–7.

8 Dated 18 April 1912, Churchill, *Winston S. Churchill*, p. 1542.

9 Foster, *Titanic*, pp. 238–9.

10 Jeffrey Richards, *A Night to Remember: The Definitive Titanic Film* (London, 2002), p. 69.

11 *A Night to Remember* adopts a pseudo-documentary and 'realist' style, starting with the launch and ending with a title telling us of the progress in safety measures made since. Cameron's film makes a virtual fetish of fidelity to historical detail recreating parts of the ship, claiming faithfully to copy the interior design from the curtains to the crockery. This urge to convince that one is 'telling it like it really was' is only evidence of the impossibility of so doing.

12 It is suggestive, though beyond the scope of this chapter, to speculate about an émigré European perspective contributed by Reisch and Negulesco in particular, which might illuminate the ways in which the latent and manifest content of the movie contradict themselves. For more on Reisch, see Thomas Elsaesser, '*It's The End Of the Song*: Walter Reisch, Operetta and the Double Negative', in *Weimar Cinema and After. Germany's Historical Imaginary* (London and New York, 2000), pp. 330–358.

13 Arguably, Negulesco's best artistic work was already behind him—the classy noir *Road House* and the unusual *Johnny Belinda* (both 1948), the latter taking an Oscar for Jane Wyman as best actress.

14 Foster, *Titanic*, pp. 269–70

15 Unfortunately there is no space here to consider fully the subsidiary characters in this domestic drama. Principal among them are the defrocked alcoholic priest Rev. George Headley (Richard Basehart), returning home to disappoint his doting and doubtless devout family; the Molly Brown substitute, Maude Young (Thelma Ritter) and the stoical British captain (Brian Aherne). There are also a family of Basque migrants and walk-on parts for a cowardly salesman and the celebrated self-sacrificing Ida Strauss. A longer analysis could fruitfully show how these figures provide both harmony and counterpoint to the main dramatic orchestration.

16 Jackie Byars, *All That Hollywood Allows: Re-Reading Gender in 1950s Melodrama* (London, 1991), p. 8.

CHAPTER TWELVE

Questions of Authenticity and Realism in *A Night to Remember* (1958)

SARAH STREET

A S THE FIRST British feature film to depict the Titanic disaster, *A Night to Remember*, based on Walter Lord's book first published in 1956, was widely perceived to be semi-documentary. Producer William MacQuitty referred to it as a 'gigantic, documentary film' in which 'all of the cast seemed to become part of reality'.[1] The drama of this spectacle was emphasised in the film's publicity of 'the greatest sea drama in living memory'. The budget was rumoured to be over £600,000, a very high sum for a British film of that period, as part of the Rank Organization's push to revive ambitious, prestige filmmaking. Discourses around the film's realism were at the heart of its marketing campaign and persist in the release of the DVD, complete with a feature on the making of the film. When James Cameron's *Titanic* was released in 1997 many reviewers compared it unfavourably to *A Night to Remember* on the grounds that the earlier film took few liberties with 'the truth'. Despite Cameron's access to technology capable of representing the sinking of the ship with a degree of realism that was previously impossible, for many viewers *A Night to Remember* remains 'more authentic'.

The film's codes of cinematic realism reinforce this impression in a style of filmmaking that was praised by critics as representative of 'quality' British cinema. As Nina Hibbin commented: 'It has that rare quality of integrity which is the hallmark of the best of British films'.[2] The reviewer for the *Hollywood Reporter* described it as 'one of the best documentary-style movies ever made'.[3] Geoffrey Unsworth, the cinematographer, chose black and white to emphasise authenticity, explaining that his general strategy aimed to 'avoid artiness' and 'reflect the realism of the situation'.[4] In the absence of much actual surviving footage of the Titanic, *A Night to Remember* has therefore come to stand in for the 'missing' actuality footage, particularly the 'found' shots at the opening which while from the period are not of the Titanic. Shots of the ship, which was recreated with a model and from location footage of a ship about to be scrapped on the Clyde, are almost fetishised, creating a close relationship between 'spectacle' and 'realism'. As well as exploring the textual dynamics of suspense, spectacle and realism, this chapter will examine the extent to which

A Night to Remember can be termed a 'classic realist text'. In particular, it will focus on the conventional and unconventional strategies it employs to convince us of its verisimilitude. In terms of its broader, intertextual address, the film's status as a 'truthful' document will also be analysed with reference to contemporary reviews, commentary and to Walter Lord's novel. The key argument is that despite its quest to be authentic and realistic, *A Night to Remember* remains closely aligned with the late 1950s context of its release. In its concern to represent the past with accuracy it nevertheless relates to trends within contemporary British filmmaking as well as to debates about social class. While the release of James Cameron's *Titanic* has suggested scope for comparative analyses with previous films based on the disaster, a study of *A Night to Remember* with reference to its own textual strategies and contemporary concerns is long overdue.[5]

For many contemporary reviewers, the emphasis on realism in *A Night to Remember* was seen to conflict with the film's ability to deliver entertainment. While she admired the film's 'integrity', Nina Hibbin wrote in the *Daily Worker* that it was 'lacking the imaginative personal touch', and Jympson Harman ended his review of the film in the *Evening News* by stating that 'it is a moot point with me whether this kind of detailed, honest reconstruction of the facts…does not suffer from lack of intimate human drama'.[6] The impact of the film's realist style was at the heart of every review of the film, whether from a critical standpoint as above, or in praise of the film's approach to the subject which was considered by the *Variety* reviewer, for example, to be appropriately respectful: '*A Night to Remember* is a sincere and conscientious reconstruction of a tragic event, which will satisfy all but those who like their entertainment glossed over with contrived fiction'.[7] On balance, a greater number of reviews were critical of the film's 'documentary', realist style than in praise of it, and I will use these criticisms as a basis for analysing the codes which seek to convey verisimilitude in *A Night to Remember*.

The film's claim to be authentic arises in great part from its debt to Walter Lord's best-selling book, *A Night to Remember*. The emphasis on authenticity is stressed throughout the film which declares proudly at the opening that Joseph Boxhall, fourth officer on the Titanic, acted as technical adviser, along with Captain Grattidge, ex-commodore of the Cunard Line. The trailer announces that the 'true story' of the Titanic is 'greater than any fictional imagination'. The film's producer, William MacQuitty, had seen the Titanic being built and launched in his native Belfast and was keen to make a film about the sinking when Lord's book was published in the UK.[8] Lord was consulted during the scripting process, and by and large, the film adheres closely to the events detailed in his book which was based on many years of research and on the testimony of survivors. The book makes no claim to provide definitive answers to the many riddles surrounding the disaster, Lord demonstrating the aspirations of objectivity held by many traditional historians 'to weigh the evidence carefully and give an honest opinion'.[9] Yet his evidence highlighted some theses which MacQuitty retained, and even elaborated in the film adaptation: the failure of all the ice warnings reported to the Titanic to reach Captain Smith; the nearby Californian's misinterpretation of the Titanic's distress rockets; the heroism of second officer Charles Lightoller and contrasting cowardice of J. Bruce Ismay, Managing Director of the White Star Line.[10] Indeed, the film gives no sense that any of these 'facts' are in dispute, departing from the book in the sense that the 'riddles' are not presented as being in any way contested. With its reliance on the testimony of survivors, Lord's book acknowledges the role of embellishment in recollections and the varying accounts of particular incidents that have produced a number of myths about the disaster, including how many men got into lifeboats disguised as women and whether Captain Smith died while trying to save a baby. So although the film is described as a 'documentary' in several reviews, it is unable to provide an impression of the contested nature of the material on which Lord based his book.

The reviews pick out many attributes of the realist film. Several mention the accumulation of period detail that was one of the film's codes of realist verisimilitude.

Philip Oakes wrote in the *Sunday Dispatch*:

Eric Ambler [screenwriter] has gone all out for documentary detail and this is impressive enough if you care to know how many pots of marmalade and how many crates of caviar the ill-fated vessel carried. But men and women are submerged beneath a welter of facts. Reconstruction is fine; detail is certainly important. But a perfectly proportioned model of the drowned stateroom is no substitute for one flash of real characterisation which would turn the doomed puppets of the screenplay into living and suffering people.[11]

Yet the attention to detail is arguably an integral aspect of the film's visual strategy, exemplifying the workings of what Colin MacCabe termed 'the classic realist text', in which visual detail is connected with a film's meta-language, often taking precedence over dialogue in communicating a dominant discourse.[12] In *A Night to Remember* there is the same attention to 'authentic' period detail that so obsessed James Cameron for *Titanic* (1997). But the detail does more than provide surface authenticity, as is implied in Oakes' review. It is the major technique used to convey the detail necessary to highlight the film's theme of rigid class inequality. In this sense it qualifies as a 'classic realist text' in its consistent stress on visual detail which, as I shall go on to argue, combined with 'spectacular realism' makes a convincing case about the hierarchical nature of the class-ridden world of 1912.

This is signalled at an early stage in the film when Lightoller (Kenneth More) travels with his wife by train, on his way to join the ship in

Southampton. To the dismay of another couple in the carriage, Lightoller makes a joke about an advertisement (reproduced in Lord's book, and so 'authentic') for 'Vinolia Otto Toilet Soap', designated for first-class passengers. Lightoller comments with irony that 'the rest don't wash'. On hearing this quip the other couple conclude that Lightoller must either be 'foreign' or a 'radical', a position they are forced to revise when they find out that he is about to join the Titanic as an officer. This humorous incident prepares us for many subsequent observations about class which are conveyed by the *mise-en-scène*. With the assistance of deep-focus photography, the detail of the first-class restaurant, and of the accommodation occupied by the first-class passengers, is meticulously reproduced in a way that replicated the ship's own pre-maiden voyage history, when its fine and expensive features were conspicuously advertised. Attention to such detail was integral to *A Night to Remember*'s claim to authenticity since it conveyed a general attitude towards 'the truth' that encompassed fidelity to Lord's book, with all its implications of respect for those who perished. An awareness of the subtle material differences between second- and first-class, for example, reinforced the film's depiction of a watertight class-system, understood by all but questioned by few. In this sense the film's *mise-en-scène* is used to deploy critique of a system that was implicitly depicted as anachronistic.

As well as through *mise-en-scène*, the class theme is represented via a number of key techniques. Montage and thematic counterpoint are used, for example, when the steerage passengers are shown dancing in a state of ebullient camaraderie in contrast to the following scene of the first-class passengers in their restaurant, genteel music being played in the background, restrained and stuffy in comparison with the lively rowdiness of the previous scene. The upper-class are identified by their codes of manners and decorum. They are seen to be aware of subtle social distinctions, most notably between a *nouveau riche* passenger (not named but obviously Molly Brown), and titled aristocrats who look down on her for having money rather than breeding. When the ship has hit the iceberg, an upper-class couple watch some steerage passengers improvise a football match, kicking the ice that fell on the deck as the iceberg scraped the ship. The couple look down from a higher deck and when the man comments to his female companion that the game looks fun and maybe they might go down and join in, he is rebutted by a firm repost: 'But they're steerage passengers!' While I would agree to some extent with Richard Howells that on the whole *A Night to Remember* tends to limit its critique of the upper classes, it nevertheless displays an acute awareness of the class inequalities Walter Lord so highlighted in his book.[13] The film made no attempt to conceal the fateful delays in assisting steerage passengers to the upper decks; their ghettoised existence out of the sight of second- and upper-class passengers, and their slim chances of gaining a place in a lifeboat. These details unquestionably do much work to highlight the class theme. As I have discussed elsewhere, costume is also used to delineate class and class distinctions in *A Night to Remember* in a very particular way.[14]

The film adaptation of *A Night to Remember* shares with Lord's book a desire to depict the world of the Titanic as a lost one. He wrote of the impact of the disaster: 'The Titanic somehow lowered the curtain on this way of living. It never was the same again. First the war, then the income tax, made sure of that'.[15] The end of the film includes a reassurance that after the sinking of the Titanic no ship set sail with insufficient lifeboats for all passengers. 1912 was another era, a tragedy which had been vividly re-created but designated as firmly in the past. Lightoller's status as middle-class, sensible and the only character with insight into the restrictions of the class system, stands in for the man of the 1950s, for the post-war world where class distinctions were rendered anachronistic. This was consistent with Kenneth More's star persona as an uncomplicated and reliable professional, which pervaded his other roles, most notably in *Chance of a Lifetime* (1950). Yet as Derek Hill, reviewer for *Tribune*, pointed out, there was perhaps not such a gulf between 1912 and 1958:

Underneath this daring social comment, a mere half-century late, is the implication that the days when wealth bought privilege at the expense of others ended the night the Titanic went down. But that's a night we can't remember—it hasn't yet come![16]

It is significant that *A Night to Remember* was produced in 1958, at the end of a decade of conservatism in British cinema, but on the eve of the 'new wave' when class became even more of a key theme. Examined in the context of this trend, the film looks more like a precursor of changes in British cinema than as merely representative of anachronistic ways of living. As the 'new wave' was preoccupied with showing the consequences of class rigidity, *A Night to Remember* questions, albeit gently, the assumptions on which that system was based. As Lightoller reflects on the disaster from the safety of the Carpathia: 'I don't know that I'll feel sure about anything again'. Just because the film is set in the past does not mean that it has no relevance for the present.

To reinforce this argument, an analysis of the film's approach towards characterisation reveals that it is indicative of a style of filmmaking which seeks to provide social comment. In their concern to measure claims of authenticity against norms associated with popular cinema such as melodrama, love-interest or 'the imaginative personal touch', critics perhaps missed the point that *A Night to Remember* was working within well-established codes of political realism.[17] Many of them commented on the film's refusal (with the exception of Lightoller), to deliver sustained character portraits, but failed to connect this to an overall system, or meta-language, of political commentary. The approach to character bears resemblance to Eisenstein's *typage*, in which characters are largely representative of a group, or class of people. The advantage this has for political filmmaking is that these 'types' eschew individuality, thus encouraging the audience to identify them as members of one social group in contrast to others. Political issues are therefore foregrounded rather than subsumed by individuation. Thus the opening of *A Night to Remember* introduces us to three major social groupings which on the ship are clearly equated with first-class, second-class and steerage. First, we see an upper-class man and his wife leave their country house to board the ship. They are waved off by workhouse children who, according to servants who comment cynically on their fond farewell, are interested in 'making sure of their Christmas turkey from the home farm'. We then see a middle-class couple leaving after their wedding, followed by a scene of an Irish family leaving in a pony and cart, being seen off by a priest and a large group of well-wishers. These three groupings are followed throughout the film, but we do not even know their names. Presumably the upper-class couple are meant to represent Sir Cosmo and Lady Duff Gordon (although the man is referred to as 'Sir Richard'), but such familiarity is frustrated. Their wider lives are hinted at, but never explored; they serve the purpose of illustration. The young married couple in second-class pledge to stay together as the ship sinks; the upper-class couple are saved, but disagree with their companions who want their lifeboat to go back and rescue the host of people who are drowning; some of the steerage passengers manage to get in the boats, and one or two are picked-out as characters, but by and large they are an undifferentiated mass.[18] The overall effect of this strategy is to develop a clear register of social stratification which is reinforced by the ship's spatial organization of cabins and decks designated for particular classes, with barriers between staircases to prevent accidental social mixing. As such the ship acts as a microcosm of Edwardian society.

With its emphasis on individuation and characterisation, it becomes clear that Cameron's *Titanic* takes many cues from *A Night to Remember* by embellishing the stories of several characters, or character-types. In *A Night to Remember*, for example, a young couple in steerage are shown to be attracted to one another and it is not difficult to see where the idea of a romance came from, although Cameron's crucial change in this respect was to conceive a cross-class romance. The likelihood however of Cameron's Rose and Jack actually being able to meet on a ship whose very design reinforced class distinctions, is questionable. By refusing to go down this route, *A Night to Remember* arguably maintains its focus on class distinction that might have been lost if fictional embellishments had distracted from the impact of the representative 'types' so clearly presented from the beginning. *A Night to Remember* makes the ship's stratified spatial organisation a major feature which reinforces the notion that the ship was symbolic of Edwardian class society with its instantly recognisable 'types'. Thus the first-class 'types', who are representative of a class and of a lifestyle, can be aligned with the technology of the ship at crucial junctures.

The ship's celebrated possession of Marconi wireless equipment, for example, is shown to be at the service of the first-class passengers who keep the operators busy by sending frivolous messages. These messages distract the operator from keeping track of all the ice warnings and, most seriously, lead him to urge the Californian to 'keep out' when it attempts to send a vital message that warns of the treacherous icepacks ahead. While there is no explicit link (as there is in Cameron's film) between the ship's speed and its upper-class passengers' desire to have been on a record-breaking voyage, there is nevertheless an insinuation that speed was an issue which might have influenced Captain Smith's decision not to stop the ship when the ice warnings became more frequent. In this sense the ship is geared to privilege first-class desires above the safety of all passengers.

Several reviewers pointed to the fact that although the film was episodic in structure and did not present 'intimate human drama', there was a major character, namely the ship.[19] Indeed, in its realisation of the Titanic the film deploys the spectacle normally reserved for film stars. In this respect its emphasis on authenticity and realism is accompanied by instances of 'spectacular realism' which reinforce codes of verisimilitude. As Hallam and Marshment have argued: 'For realism to become foregrounded as visual spectacle, there have to be iconographic elements which centre attention on the performance of realism as a signifying value within the film's narrative structure'.[20] The film opens with a montage of shots revealing the ship 'in bits', just as stars are often introduced partially in order to create suspense and eager anticipation of their first, 'whole' appearance. This emphasis on the performative value of the ship continues when we see the Titanic being launched with the customary champagne bottle crashing on the bow. This departs from reality in the sense that the Titanic did not have such a 'christening' ceremony, but the incident is necessary at a narrative level to enhance the ship's monumental status, as well as perhaps adding a symbolic portent of disaster, as the crash prefigures the ship's later collision with the iceberg. Since audiences would have been familiar with the major events of the ship's sinking, it was all the more important to register those 'iconographic elements' of a lost object in a spectacular way. The fetishisation of the ship therefore acquires extra poignancy since what we are offered is the horrific contrast between its perfect incarnation and its spectacular demise.

In keeping with a *mise-en-scène* which is associated with realism, there are many observational shots of the ship from afar, conveying its profile at a distance which emphasises both its isolation and its spectacle. Indeed, the triumph of engineering represented by the Titanic is referred to several times in subsequent scenes, and there are many shots of the ship, the decks, funnels and boilers that are reminiscent of classic documentary's tendency to fetishise technology. One of the film's strategies is to use such indicators of science and progress in a relationship of symbolic counterpoint, as noted above with the champagne bottle breaking on the ship's bow. Similarly, the hooting funnels we see early on in the film can be likened to monumental towers, signalling the ship's stature and efficiency. This is subverted however in a tragic way when we later see the funnel breaking off and crashing down on terrified passengers as the ship sinks.[21] This contrasting technique adds dramatic resonance to a *mise-en-scène* which in this instance combines realism and spectacle. Many of the ship's other celebrated features which we have seen early on in the film are returned to as the ship sinks.

The emphasis in *A Night to Remember* is not on technology as a problem but as a wonder. Rather, the story is of human failing, mismanagement and fallibility. While the Marconi wireless system saved some lives, it could have saved more if the Californian's operators had picked-up the SOS message in time. Similarly, if human assumptions about the ship being 'unsinkable' had not been taken for granted, the Board of Trade's regulations about the number of lifeboats on ocean liners would have been revised as ships became bigger. It is this story—of how the ship was let down by human error—that provides *A Night to Remember* with drama and suspense. Although Walter Lord's book had been a major success, the film relied on the assumption that people still had an insatiable curiosity about how the disaster occurred. As the reviewer in the American magazine *Saturday Review* commented: 'A large part of the audience has a passionate interest in just *how* something happened'.[22] The film is careful to provide audiences with key details, such as the number of passengers to lifeboats, and the details about why the ship could not float with all five 'watertight' compartments flooded. Designer Thomas Andrews' comment about the ship's sinking being a 'mathematical certainty' indeed gains tragic momentum when combined with these facts. Added to this is the deployment of classic narrative suspense, when the audience has 'privileged' knowledge over the characters. The scene is agonising, for example, when the wire giving a serious ice warning gets buried beneath a pile of passengers' personal messages, as is the sight of the sleeping wireless operator on the Californian, as his friend puzzles over a strange signal which we know is the Titanic's desperate call for help but which he cannot decipher. All this is the stuff of melodrama, when the audience experiences the frustration of seeing and hearing what the characters do not, but is powerless to intervene. As the star of the film, the Titanic suffers from these tragic strokes of fate, as do the steerage passengers who through human design have been consigned to a place on the ship which ensures their death. It is no wonder that MacQuitty made the drama of the ship's sinking the major feature of the film's suspense, rather than a 'human interest' angle which might have detracted from the greater tragedy.

Why a film about this subject should appear in 1958 is an interesting question. The publication of Lord's book was of key significance, but it has been argued by Howells that it is also crucial to place the film in a context of the rise of the middle class in the 1950s, and associated optimism that class barriers were being erased.[23] Some reviewers, like Derek Hill mentioned above, concentrated on the film's depiction of class, showing that it did provoke debate about class even if for him it did not go far enough. As mentioned earlier, as an example of British filmmaking of the late 1950s, it relates both to conventions of 'quality realism' which had dominated British cinema, but in its class thematic to the 'new wave'. Like the 'new wave' films that followed, *A Night to Remember* connects with British cinema's examination of class at a time when there was tension between claims that class barriers were being eroded and evidence that they were still very much in operation.[24]

While the class theme is not underlined at the end, as I have shown, *A Night to Remember* nevertheless contains strategies associated with political realism.[25] These reinforce the film's serious engagement with Lord's exposure of a patrician social system which was so replicated by the ship's spatial organization and management, that by far the greatest proportional loss of life was accounted for by steerage passengers.[26] Indeed, to relate this drama convincingly, the film combines many elements of realism, particularly its emphasis on an 'authentic' mise-en-scène which is used to spectacular effect in the filming of the ship. This combination of realism and spectacle enhance the film's general critique of the Edwardian class system, reinforced by the use of techniques such as 'typage' and symbolic counterpoint. These elements make *A Night to Remember* an important film of the disaster, a film which set a standard for subsequent adaptations, particularly James Cameron's *Titanic*. With continued fascination with all the 'what if' questions about the disaster that preoccupied Walter Lord, nearly fifty years after its release, *A Night to Remember* has proved to be as durable as the book on which it was based.

Notes

1 William MacQuitty, in documentary on the making of *A Night to Remember* on the DVD of the film (Carlton).

2 *Daily Worker*, 5 June 1958.

3 *Hollywood Reporter*, 18 Dec 1958.

4 Geoffrey Unsworth, interviewed by Derek Hill in *American Cinematographer*, Oct 1958, p. 642.

5 There are few studies of *A Night to Remember*, but of note is Jeffrey Richards' 'British Film Guide', *A Night to Remember* (London, 2002).

6 *Daily Worker*, 5 June 1958; *Evening News*, 3 July 1958.

7 *Variety*, 9 July 1958, p. 16.

8 Although Roy Baker, the film's director, claimed to have read Lord's book and went to John Davis at Rank with the idea for the film. See interview with Baker in *Film Review*, April 2000, p. 74.

9 Walter Lord, *A Night to Remember* (London, 1976), p. 202.

10 All of these propositions are controversial, as revealed in the US Senate's investigation. In the transcripts Lightoller, for example, said that Ismay was told by Officer Wilde that all the women had left on lifeboats and that he could therefore board. In Lord's book Ismay climbs into a boat at the last minute. In the film First Officer William Murdoch witnesses this, but does nothing to prevent Ismay from leaving. The Captain of the Californian was severely criticised in the investigations, and in the preface of the 1976 edition (pp. 10–11) of his book Lord concludes that after re-examining the evidence, he reaches the same conclusion about the Californian's culpability as he had done in the first edition.

11 *Sunday Dispatch*, 6 July 1958.

12 Colin MacCabe, 'Realism and Cinema: Notes on some Brechtian Theses', *Screen*, vol. 15, no. 2, 1974.

13 Richard Howells, 'Atlantic Crossings: Nation, Class and Identity in Titanic (1953) and *A Night to Remember* (1958)', *Historical Journal of Film, Radio and Television*, vol. 19, no. 4, 1999, p. 430.

14 Sarah Street, *Costume and Cinema: Dress Codes in Popular Film* (London, 2001), pp. 18–19.

15 Lord, *A Night to Remember*, p. 136.

16 *Tribune*, 11 July 1958.

17 Nina Hibbin, *Daily Worker*, 5 June 1958 described the film in this way.

18 The Duff Gordons' escaped in boat no. 1 which did not row back to pick up passengers who had jumped off the ship when it sank. See Lord, *A Night to Remember*, p. 148.

19 Frank Majdalany of the *Daily Mail*, 4 July 1958, complained that the film lacked 'intimate human drama'. He named the film's major star the Titanic.

20 Julia Hallam with Margaret Marshment, *Realism and Popular Cinema* (Manchester, 2000), p. 117.

21 Although it is ironic that, as Lord demonstrates in *A Night to Remember*, p. 120, the breaking off of the funnel saved the lives of Lightoller, Bride and others as its fall just missed the overturned collapsible B to which they were clinging. The thrust of the falling funnel washed the boat clear of the sinking hull, saving it from being sucked under the water when the ship sank.

22 *Saturday Review*, 13 Dec 1958.

23 Howells, 'Atlantic Crossings', pp. 432–3. Richards, *A Night to Remember* (2002) pp. 99–102, prefers to relate the film to British films of the Second World War which depicted classes as 'pulling together'.

24 For a study of British cinema and social class see John Hill, *Sex, Class and Realism: British Cinema and Society, 1956–63*, (London, 1986).

25 This was in keeping with director Roy Baker's insistence that although the clearly depicted 'a hierarchical structure', this theme was not over-emphasised. See *Film Review*, April 2000, p. 77. William MacQuitty wanted the class theme to prevail, and saw the disaster as representing 'an end of an era of arrogance', DVD commentary.

26 As Richards in *A Night to Remember*, pp. 7–8, has shown, loss of life amongst steerage passengers was often absent from contemporary commentary about the disaster.

PART III

James Cameron's Titanic

CHAPTER THIRTEEN

Titanic/*Titanic*: Thoughts on Cinematic Presence and Monumental History

GAYLYN STUDLAR

Two FICTIONAL SWEETHEARTS romp on the deck of a ship, bound for New York. Their antics distract the ship's lookout from observing an iceberg looming nearby in the darkness. Thus, too late, he sounds the alarm, 'Iceberg right ahead'. The ocean liner, Titanic, heads, inexorably, towards ice and disaster.

This scene from James Cameron's *Titanic* (1997) may call to mind philosopher Gilles Deleuze's remarks in *Cinema 1: The Movement-Image* where he says: 'It is easy to make fun of Hollywood's historical conceptions'.[1] It may appear to confirm just how easy it is to make fun of a film in which the distracting presence of an unlikely cross-class romance 'causes' what is perhaps the 20th century's most famous—and controversial—maritime accident. It is less easy to make fun of *Titanic* (or of any film) that grosses more money at the box-office than any previous production—for making lots of money is a serious matter in contemporary culture, especially so in Hollywood. Through its unprecedented moneymaking prowess, *Titanic* acquired the status of a film phenomenon—of a contemporary media event. In a postmodern context it also became an important cultural event, for *Titanic*'s box-office gross of 1.8 billion dollars signifies an enormous number of viewers, a global audience, as well as unprecedented economic success within the film industry.

Why did *Titanic* succeed, or, as one scholar has quipped, 'float triumphantly' with audiences?[2] There are many possible explanations, but I am interested in how the film's success with audiences relates to its status as a distinctly Hollywood articulation of history. In pursuing this primary question, I wish to couch the film's success in terms of its *cinematic presence*. I am defining cinematic presence as a textually based phenomenon experienced by the viewer, who registers the impact—psychological, physiological, perceptual, and emotional—of the film as it is viewed, as it unfolds. In some ways, the notion of cinematic presence attempts to articulate what is often referred to under the rubrics of 'spectacle' and 'excess' in film criticism and theory. But I would like to depart from those terms because I believe they are not always helpful in coming to an understanding of cinema as a phenomenon of movement, movement that takes place across time and requiring organisation, most obviously and often, narrative organization, to make its images meaningful to viewers. In the case of *Titanic*, this meaningfulness must succeed for three hours and seventeen minutes as the film unfolds as the only 'thing' in 'the room'.

We would probably all agree that James Cameron's *Titanic*—the film event —uses the White Star's Titanic, both pre- and post-sinking, as a milieu, a space, an 'architectural presence' upon which it projects contemporary anxieties and fantasies that appeal to a broad, indeed, multi-million member audience. This projection could be denigrated as a process that almost inevitably involves a perversion of history, for viewers' historical recognition becomes conflated with or replaced by emotional allegiance or psychological identification with fictional characters. However, some United States critics, including Michael Wilmington of the *Chicago Tribune*, point to *Titanic*'s fusion of history and fiction to suggest something of the presence and power of the film. He says: 'Cameron is not really making a realistic film . . . . He gives us instead a wild romance and supreme cliffhanging melodrama, laced with thrills, shocks, and ecstasy . . . It's easy to scoff at this movie, but how can you look at it for long unmoved?'[3]

What does this merging of putative historical reality and Hollywood romantic fiction suggest? In particular, what does it suggest about the structure required to forge *Titanic* into an effective cinematic presence—one in which an historical era and its cultural moment are re-imagined through/for a contemporary consciousness—and unconsciousness? In fact, what I wish to argue is that, in order to give greater meaning to the original event, in order to make White Star Titanic's maiden voyage and sinking of 1912 matter to audiences of 1997 and beyond, Cameron's *Titanic* depends upon a formula of realism, history, and genre filmmaking that combine to make the film-as-text less postmodern and more classical Hollywood. In this respect, there is some irony in the fact that the film's success in turning a real life disaster of the past into what Deleuze would call 'real-make believe' succeeds also in making it into an effective cinematic presence of the 'now'.[4] For, if *Titanic*'s content depends crucially upon its reconfiguration of the past, so too it depends upon narrative strategies and aesthetic structures that re-articulate a traditional mode of Hollywood's fictional reproduction of 'the real'.

First, we must acknowledge that the fictional and the cinematic are almost analogous in classical Hollywood 'realist' filmmaking. While 'redeeming' the real through fiction—and spectacle—may seem to be a particularly postmodern occurrence, as Thomas Elsaesser has suggested, it is worth considering how the merging of *Titanic*, the film, and Titanic, the doomed liner, suggests another model of cinema's actualisation of history.[5] After suggesting that

Hollywood conceptions of history are easy to make fun of, Deleuze goes on in *Cinema 1: The Movement-Image* to remind us that while we may consider classical Hollywood films laughably simplistic in their depiction of history, such a response is unjustified because: 'on the contrary . . . they bring together the most serious aspects of history as seen by the 19th century'.[6] Borrowing from Nietzsche, Deleuze distinguishes three of the dominant modes or aspects of history favoured by classical cinema: (1) monumental history (2) antiquarian history, and (3) ethical history.

Here, in Deleuze's remarks, I believe we have the beginnings of a useful avenue for exploring how exactly Cameron's *Titanic* created such a wildly successful cinematic experience for viewers from the historical event of the sinking of White Star's Titanic. Cameron's film, we may quickly conclude, belongs in the category of the 'monumental history film'. According to Deleuze, the monumental history film operates, first and foremost, in the domain of 'the action image' where affects and impulses are embodied in behaviour (emotions, passions made visible). These behaviours inhabit a world made visible that is placed in a determinate, geographical, historical, and social space-time. For Deleuze, this is the basis of 'realism' as a filmic style, manifested in realist illusion made from a milieu and the modes of behaviour necessitated by it.[7] This model of historical representation is found in D. W. Griffith's depiction and destruction of Babylon in *Intolerance* (1916), in C. B. DeMille's *The Ten Commandments* (1923 and remade in 1956) with the successful escape of the Hebrews from Egypt through the memorable parting of the Red Sea, and in James Cameron's depiction of the voyage and sinking of Titanic.

The primary milieu in *Titanic*, most expensive film made in the 20th century, is the liner Titanic, in 1912, the most advanced and expensive sea-going vessel ever built. Within the film, the liner is the sublime monument; it embodies powers and qualities that are actualised in its cinematic presence as a milieu. Following Deleuze, this milieu is not a benign or passive backdrop to action, but a set of forces that must act and be acted upon if the film is to exist in the domain of the action image and realism.[8] This actualised milieu in Cameron's film thus situates characters that exhibit a mode of behaviour merging the melodramatic and the psychological. This merging is typical of realism.

In Cameron's *Titanic*, it is neither the cold Atlantic, nor the forces of capricious nature, nor of careless capitalism that constitute the strongest force acting upon characters. Instead, it is the *ambience* represented by the ship that takes this role of a force that elicits characters' reactions. As a result, it is not the ocean coming up, but the ship going down that threatens characters and creates the narrative. It is in this milieu that Rose DeWitt Bukater (Kate Winslet), the youthful female protagonist, acquires a new mode of being and emerges into her new self. This adheres to Deleuze's formula of the classical narrative structure of *SAS₁: Situation/Action/Situation Altered*. Rose's transformation also provides the symbolic centre of the film's re-articulation of the birth of a modern nation-civilisation, of the American democracy as a milieu that releases individuals from class and gender oppression associated with European tradition.

Rather than being the source of historical instruction, the presence of White Star's Titanic in Cameron's film functions in this American *ur*-myth as the monumental milieu. It represents the tempting but decadent state of things that must be altered, destroyed, overcome through *action* in order for a healthy individual and the new nation-civilisation to emerge.[9] Thus, the 'silly' scene in which Rose and Jack Dawson (Leonardo DiCaprio) distract the lookout and cause the collision with the iceberg may seem ridiculous by our standards of historical reality, but those standards are usually detached from notions of film as a fictional construct that organizes history for its own purposes. On the contrary, in the context of the film and of 20th century Hollywood realism, this scene is absolutely necessary in providing the 'binomial action' that Deleuze associates with monumental history. More simply stated, in the duel between milieu and characters, this scene proves that White Star's Titanic, the monumental milieu, may be the film's primary antagonistic force, but it is not one imper-vious to love. In fact, in this scene, love in a nascent form (flirtation) literally starts the action that will ultimately sink the ship.

Monumental history, says Deleuze, considers effects in and of themselves; the only causes such a model of history understands are simple duels of opposing individuals or forces.[10] Such duels are commonly organised according to the ethical image of Good vs. Evil. Not only did this ethical duel influence Hollywood through its status as the *sine qua non* of 19th century melodrama, but it is also the structure insinuated in Hollywood's conventional response to the Production Code guidelines that determined on-screen morality from the early 1930s through the early 1950s.

The impact of this ethical image on James Cameron's *Titanic* is clear: the past must submit to the truth in order to disclose, not what happened in the real, historical sinking of the Titanic, but what it is that produces Evil and what it is that produces, by way of contrast, new life. By way of explanation, this might usefully be illustrated by a DeMille orgy scene, such as the worship of the fatted calf in *The Ten Commandments* (either version of DeMille's film) vs. the presentation of the sign of the cross. In Cameron's *Titanic*, such an organisation of forces explains the otherwise inexplicable presence of Cal Hockley (Billy Zane), Rose's hysterically violent fiancé. Cal's attempt to shoot the lovers might seem redundant as it occurs in the midst of a mid-Atlantic sinking with no hope of timely rescue. However, Cal's presence is demanded by the action image; his 'power-qualities' (in Deleuzean terms) expand outward from the milieu and situate him as an antagonistic force, an excessive but logical extension of the already excessive milieu. The logic of monumental history and the action-image that embodies it also combine to explain why most of the film's action takes place within the first-class accommodations of the liner. While the spectator is encouraged to enjoy the sight of *Titanic*'s lavish sets and the vicarious experience of being situated within the liner, we also know that this ship must sink, not because of 'history' as we know it, but according to the logic of Hollywood monumental history. Not only must the ship sink into order to free Rose, but it also must sink because it is pathological. Its pathology, social and spiritual, is represented architecturally by the ship's absolute separation of the classes. The cinematic presence of this separation constitutes the primary force that the lovers must overcome spatially as well as emotionally.

Typical of monumental history and the Hollywood classical style that serves it, this division of a single civilisation into classes has no real causation assigned to it. Cal Hockley may be a vile, sneering villain, but he no more causes the existence of steerage than the mild-mannered shipbuilder, Mr. Andrews (Victor Garber), who designed the hierarchical accommodations that literally keep third-class passengers trapped behind bars as the water rises and the last lifeboats leave. Even as the film condemns those, like Cal, who desire to possess as opposed to those who seek to love, *Titanic*'s governing moral order, its ethical judgment, condemns the injustice of things—the division of class that means that the crew and the majority of third-class passengers, including the free spirited artist, Jack Dawson, will go to watery graves.

The intermediary duels, feints, and parries of the action operate on multiple levels and work to move the film between *Situation* and *Situation Altered*. The oft praised last half of the film that marks Rose as a heroic survivor modifies the narrative into the *S1* transformational situation. This helps to explain the emotional force of the sequence in which Rose, adrift on a piece of wreckage, realises that her lover is dead of hypothermia. She says goodbye, unfastens his body from the wreckage, and she (and we) watch as he sinks away into the frigid depths of the ocean. Acting upon Jack's admonition for her to live, no matter what, Rose then responds to the sound of rescuers. When they cannot hear her voice, she vigorously swims over to the body of a dead crewmember, commandeers his signal whistle, and uses it to summon help.

Under a rough peasant shawl, Rose sits among the third class passengers as the rescue ship, Carpathia, pulls into New York harbour under the shadow of the Statue of Liberty. Rose's emergence in *S1* (*Situation Altered*) as a surviving third-class passenger is not based on an *accident*, but it is a result of her *acting upon* her promise to Jack. She now calls herself 'Rose Dawson', and her new name reflects her emotional debt to and bonding with Jack. It also provides the actualisation of the 'melting pot' and fusion of nationalities that typifies, not only third-class, but also the ideal of the American nation-state.[11]

The Statue of Liberty provides the objective correlative for Rose's redemption from the soul-destroying, pseudo-European milieu into which she is originally bound in first-class. Instead of DeMille's sign of the cross, we have the sign of an open democracy in this cinematic version of history's New American civilisation on the march toward the pursuit of happiness. Thus, Rose's story emerges as an American dream/myth/rebirth in which the ship's sinking had to occur. Without it, the required transformational situation could not have taken place. Rose could not become a new person, a transformed American citizen freed of the class divisions and prejudices embodied in the architecture of the liner that now rests in ruins at the bottom of the ocean.

Just as Rose is re-configured to move beyond class divisions, so too Titanic the ship is reconfigured from the degraded wreck depicted at the beginning of the film into something else by the end. In the flashback that forms the bulk of the film, the ship becomes an enjoyable spectacle of class privilege and yet, at the same time, an obstacle to love. Rose's recounting of her story of love, loss, and renewal teaches the true meaning of Titanic to the film audience as well as to greedy treasure seekers who admit they 'didn't get it'.

Before she dies, Rose dreams. In the *mise-en-scène* of her dream, civilisation is reconstituted and redeemed through Rose's re-imagining of the milieu of the White Star's Titanic. Made visually manifest in Rose's dying dream, the ship becomes a classless milieu by virtue of the heroine's inner life. Thus, the ship is reclaimed, not by the treasure-seekers who find the wreck through advanced technology, but through the force of love. We see Rose, Jack, and the lost Titanic passengers, regardless of station, gathering on the first-class Grand staircase to celebrate love, Rose's and Jack's. Just as the lovers caused the ship's wreck, in the end, Rose's love for Jack is the decisive action that causes the extraordinary reconstitution of the wreck. As is typical of the 'action-image' as a form, what happened 'inside' to the main characters (Rose's taking on a new identity as Rose Dawson) happens also on the 'outside'—visually— to the architectural monument; in the elderly Rose's imagination, the ship takes on a new identity as a monument to classless society.[12]

So also, I would argue that Cameron's *Titanic* re-imagines White Star's Titanic in an unexpected way. It does not do this through an ultra-contemporary, cultural-cinematic form dominated by aggression, irony, parody, and the 'making false' that 'becomes the sign of "new realism"'.[13] Instead, *Titanic* returns to the old Hollywood's mode of realism, where visual and aural impact can be harnessed, and, indeed, *must* be, to effectively create a powerful cinematic presence bound to the action-image at its source. Thus, for all the discussions of Cameron's film as a postmodern spectacle, *Titanic* operates beyond the level of 'sheer astonishment'. Instead, we can understand it as an incarnation of a very classical Hollywood approach to the intersection of narrative and the cinematic possibilities of a visualisation of history. Although I would not offer it as the only cause, *Titanic* may be proven so popular among and so powerful an experience to so very many because, like its ostensible historical subject, it is a *relic*. As such, it returns filmmaking to familiar tensions and 'primitive' pleasures attached to the narrative logic of a 19th century concept of history sustained in the classical Hollywood action-image. In this light, we cannot fail to see that Cameron's *Titanic* is not indicative of a postmodern disregard of history but instead demonstrates the cinematic strategies of a monumental history essential to the classical Hollywood paradigm in its parallelist conception of events and nations.[14]

Whether illustrated by D. W. Griffith, C. B. DeMille, or James Cameron, American monumental history, played out through fictitious situations and sham actions, can form the basis of a cinematic presence that is invested with and elicits real emotions. How else do we explain the tears shed over the death of the fictitious character, Jack Dawson, or pilgrimages, even, to 'his' grave in Halifax, Nova Scotia?[15] Considered through the framework of Deleuzean notions of the large-form action-image and the monumental history film, *Titanic* puts forward a coherent conceptualisation of 'universal' history, but Deleuze also calls the historical film 'a great genre of American cinema . . . formed out of conditions peculiar to America'.[16]

One can argue that the worldwide appeal of *Titanic*, as a quintessential 'American' story, is as complex a phenomenon as the film's evocation of monumental history. In this respect, the success of *Titanic* suggests that this model genre of American cinema has the potential to play 'big' and assert the appeal of the large form action-image outside of its original cultural moment and into the 21st century. Although the conceptualisation of history that *Titanic* shares with so much of classical Hollywood may not fit our contemporary tastes as we would like to conceive of them, it is one that made the film a cultural phenomenon and appealed to millions of viewers who are likely to know little about the fundamentals of classical Hollywood realism but, nevertheless, know what they like when they see it—and there is no arguing with the fact that they liked *Titanic*'s version of history very much, indeed.

Notes

1   Gilles Deleuze, *Cinema 1: The Movement-Image* (Minneapolis, [1986] 1997), p. 149.

2   Matthew Bernstein, 'Floating Triumphantly: The American Critics on *Titanic*,' in Kevin S. Sandler and Gaylyn Studlar, eds., *Titanic: Anatomy of a Blockbuster* (New Brunswick, New Jersey and London, 1999), p. 14.

3   Michael Wilmington, 'See-Worthy: Romance and Catastrophe Make for a Highly Entertaining Mix in the Three-Hour-Plus Epic Thriller *Titanic*', *Chicago Tribune* (North Sports Final, CN Edition), December 19, 1997, page 2A. See also *Chicago Tribune* website: www.chicagotribune.com.

4   Deleuze, *Cinema 1*, pp. 140–148.

5   Thomas Elsaesser quoted in Michael Hammond, '"But it was True! How Can You

Laugh?" The Reception of *Titanic* in Britain and Southampton', in Sandler and Studlar, *Titanic*, p. 255.

6 Deleuze, *Cinema 1*, p. 149.

7 Deleuze, *Cinema 1*, p. 140.

8 Deleuze, *Cinema 1*, p. 141.

9 Deleuze, *Cinema 1*, p. 148.

10 Deleuze, *Cinema 1*, p. 142.

11 Deleuze, *Cinema 1*, p. 144.

12 Deleuze, *Cinema 1*, p. 158.

13 Deleuze, *Cinema 1*, p. 213.

14 Deleuze, *Cinema 1*, p. 149.

15 A headstone marked 'Jack Dawson' resides among the graves of Titanic victims whose bodies were recovered and brought back to Halifax. Unclaimed by relatives or unidentified, these remains were interred in the cemetery there.

16 Deleuze, *Cinema 1*, p. 149.

CHAPTER FOURTEEN

'Far Across the Distance': Historical Films, Film History and *Titanic* (1997)

PETER KRÄMER

THE ELDERLY WOMAN is asleep. In her dream, she is floating along a huge shipwreck at the bottom of the ocean. When she enters one of its corridors, the wreck gradually transforms itself into the brand new ship it once had been. Doors are held open for her, and she moves inside a room crowded with people expecting her, and up a grand staircase towards her young lover. She herself is young again now. The two lovers embrace and kiss to the applause of the crowd. Then, after briefly looking up at the bright ceiling, the dream scene dissolves into whiteness—and then fades to black. The words 'written and directed by James Cameron' appear, and the music that has been accompanying the dream begins to take the shape of a song. A female voice can be heard:

> Every night in my dreams,
> I see you, I feel you.
> That is how I know you go on.
> Far across the distance
> And spaces between us
> You have come to show you go on.

This is the ending of James Cameron's 1997 blockbuster *Titanic*. Whether one loves or hates the film (and Celine Dion's hit single), its ending is, I think, remarkable for a number of reasons. First of all, the film's final scene places us in a character's dream, and within that dream it transports us back to the past that the 101 year old Rose has been telling us about in the preceding three hours. The story she has told us ended with the death of her lover and countless others, and with her own liberation from social restrictions. In her dream this ending is revised, and history is rewritten: The lovers are united, surrounded by many of the disaster's victims, and the ship, presumably, will never sink. The final scene, then, reminds us that most of the film did in fact take place in Rose's mind, that it was all her memory. The scene also exposes the tensions between the objective facts of history and the subjective longings of fantasy, and, dreamlike as it is, it can erase the distance between the present and the past.

The second remarkable aspect of this ending is its ambiguity. The camera's final movement upwards and into the light and the subsequent fade to black suggest that what we witness is Rose's death (experienced from her vantage point, no less), yet this is never stated explicitly. Furthermore, the bright light that Rose's mind is engulfed by becomes the whiteness of the very screen on which the film we have seen has been projected and the whiteness of the light which is the source of that projection. The end of Rose's dream (which may or may not be her death), therefore is also the end of our participation in the fantastic adventure of the film, and a return to the banal realities of everyday life (the blank screen, the light of the projector, the people in the seats next to us).

Thirdly, the end of the film provides us with a remarkable commentary on the relationship between cinema and life. After James Cameron's signature credit, which seems to assert male authorship and authority, Celine Dion's song again places us within the subjective experience of a woman. Echoing Rose's narration and final dream, the singer evokes an absent lover who returns 'every night in my dreams' and is 'here in my heart', reviving past experiences which will 'last for a lifetime'. Thus, the singer, like the elderly Rose, can feel the presence of the past. However, the song also serves as a bridge between the fantasy of the film and the reality of the audience, sitting in the dark and getting ready to leave the cinema. The song suggests that, like the singer's absent lover, the *film* may come to haunt them in their dreams, becoming a constant presence in their heart and lasting them for a lifetime. 'Far across the distance' between past and present, cinema and reality, then, the film's sounds, images and emotions will go on, and on, in the audience's memory.

In this essay, I relate the ending of *Titanic* to a number of contexts. I begin with James Cameron's statements on his approach to the task of making an historical film. Taking a cue from his references to *Gone With the Wind* (1939) and *Doctor Zhivago* (1965), I then outline the tradition of historical epics, of which *Titanic* is a rare recent example. Finally, I discuss how the film engages with this tradition.

HISTORICAL FILMS

In the two major book tie-ins with his blockbuster film (a making-of volume and an illustrated screenplay), James Cameron outlines his approach to the difficult task of making a film about the Titanic disaster.[1] He highlights his extensive historical research and 'the challenge of sorting out fact from misinformation, misperception and downright lying'.[2] A lot of effort was put into giving the audience a sense of the physical reality of the ship, its majestic size, its luxurious decor and elaborate fittings. Indeed, by incorporating footage of the actual wreck into the film, Cameron wanted to push documentary realism to the limit: 'When old Rose stares at the video screen and imagines herself stepping through the entry doors into Titanic, the ghostly doors are real, just as they sit now down in eternal blackness'.[3]

While aiming to reconstruct the materiality of the ship and the precise series of events leading to its demise, Cameron also admits that he had to go beyond the historical record. Speaking about the ship's musicians, for example, he says that their legendary sense of duty in the face of certain death 'is not based so much on what the band actually did, but what we hope they would have done'.[4] More importantly, Cameron felt that he had to complement actual historical events with a purely fictional love story, so as to offer audiences something new, and to provide them with an emotional entry point into the disaster scenario: 'The fact that you are perceiving the tragedy through the subjective vantage point of these two young people who you care about makes it a completely different type of experience than all of the other docu-drama-like films that have been made about Titanic'.[5] And to further his aim 'to make history alive and palpable', he decided on a framing story: 'I thought this would connect the event to our time, and through the doorway of her (Rose's) memory invest it with an added layer of poignancy'.[6]

Perhaps quite surprisingly, Cameron also points out the continuities between *Titanic* and his earlier work, stating that 'all my films are love stories'; *True Lies* (1994), for example, is about 'a marriage in jeopardy', and *Aliens* (1986) about 'unconditional parental love'. What's more, he states: 'I've based my cinematic career on creating a sense of unity between the audience and the characters on the screen, through whatever means necessary. I wanted to try the same stylistic approach with an historical event and see if I could create that unity through recognizable emotions and situations'.[7] The necessary cinematic means include, very prominently, special effects. Cameron emphasises that the deployment of up-to-date digital technology to create images (notably of the ship itself) and to enhance the film's slow dissolves, is not to be noticed in its own right. Instead, he says, computer generated visual effects are meant to be 'advancing the story . . ., creating and sustaining an emotional state'.[8]

The dissolves between the events of 1912 and the framing story are of particular importance. There is, for example, '(t)he morphing of Rose from a young girl to an old woman at the end of the scene where Jack is sketching her. There's an amazing sense of a connection of that character across time. Her emotional state at that moment—a trembling, anticipatory longing for Jack—carries over across the gulf of time to a moment when she's an old woman, and you can see her still experiencing that'. The earlier scene of their first kiss on the bow of the ship is similarly connected to the present: 'the moment when Jack and Rose fade as the ship transforms into the wreck turned out to be a kind of effects epiphany, because it shows the power visual effects can have to merge concepts in poetic ways'. They enable him to show the central characters as 'youthful spirits, somehow still alive and attached to the ship in the depths'.[9] These transitions between the past and the present, then, together with Rose's present-day voiceover commentary, establish a particularly intimate link between the events of history and the audiences of today.

The spiritual, ghostly presence of the characters and events of 1912 in the lives of the film's present-day characters, mirrors the imaginary presence of the film's actors and actions in the cinema auditorium.[10] And in the same way that, within the film, the elderly Rose and the people listening to her story are overwhelmed and indeed transformed by the events and emotions of the past, Cameron wants the cinema audience to be overwhelmed and transformed by their experience of the film. As we have seen, this intention to equate the audience with Rose and her listeners, and the film with Rose's absent lover and past love, is made explicit by Celine Dion's song:

> Love can touch just one time,
> and last for a lifetime,
> and never let go 'til we're gone.

Indeed, audiences were unwilling to let go of the film, many returning to see it again and again, and many more trying to relive the experience of the film outside the cinema. As Jeff Smith points out, the most effective memento of *Titanic* was Celine Dion's 'My Heart Will Go On'. Smith notes that all across the US, 'radio stations were flooded with requests for the song just after screenings of *Titanic* were let out'.[11] The single 'broke broadcasting records by racking up the largest number of radio performances measured in one week' and by reaching the largest radio audience ever recorded.[12] The two albums on which the song was featured, namely Celine Dion's *Let's Talk About Love* and James Horner's *Titanic* soundtrack, also broke records. They were the two top selling albums of 1998 in the US; *Let's Talk About Love* sold 10 million units and Horner's album 11 million units, making it by far the biggest selling classical album ever.[13] The music allowed *Titanic*'s viewers to re-visit the emotional experience of the film, thus fulfilling the wish expressed in the song's lyrics: 'Once more, you open the door, and you're here in my heart.'

FILM HISTORY

The use of music as a promotional tool for, and memento of, major Hollywood films is nothing new. The 'Gone With the Wind' theme or 'Lara's Theme' from *Doctor Zhivago*, for example, had an impact on audiences which is comparable to that of 'My Heart Will Go On'. Indeed, when Cameron talked about the filmic models for *Titanic*, he referred specifically to 'epic romance in the traditional vein of *Gone With the Wind* and *Doctor Zhivago* where you're telling an intimate story on a very big canvas'.[14] As Matthew Bernstein's study of the critical reception of *Titanic* in the US has shown, such Hollywood epics of the past provided writers, and also, presumably, audiences, with an important reference point for their understanding of, and response to, the film.[15]

While the film's detractors found *Titanic* to be lacking in aesthetic coherence, convincing characterisation and engaging storytelling when compared to past masterpieces, the film's supporters saw it as a welcome departure from the action-oriented blockbusters that have become so closely associated with contemporary Hollywood, and indeed with Cameron's previous work. Positive critical responses to *Titanic* described it as a return to a long neglected tradition in Hollywood filmmaking which combined hugely expensive and awe-inspiring cinematic spectacle with character-centred storytelling, grand emotions, human values and mythic resonances, and aimed at an all-encompassing mass audience rather than the more restricted young target audience of most of today's blockbusters. Critics noted that the film transported audiences back in time, not only to the events of 1912 but also to a by-gone era in Hollywood's own history, which spanned from the last successful burst of epic filmmaking in the mid-1960s, exemplified by David Lean's *Doctor Zhivago*, via the biblical epics of the 1950s such as *Ben-Hur* (1959) and via David O. Selznick's *Gone With the Wind* all the way back to D. W. Griffith's *The Birth of a Nation* (1915).

A closer look at this tradition of epic films about crucial events or periods in Western history shows that they were absolutely central to Hollywood's operations until the mid-1960s, both commercially and culturally (in terms of the public's perception of Hollywood). According to Joel Finler, by far the top-grossing film of the 1910s was the Civil War epic *The Birth of a Nation*.[16] The top hits of the 1920s (before the coming of sound in 1927) were the World War I dramas *The Four Horsemen of the Apocalypse* (1921) and *The Big Parade* (1925), the biblical epic *Ben-Hur* (1925) and the epic Western *The Covered Wagon* (1923). By far the biggest hit of the 1930s, and indeed of all time (if revenues are adjusted for inflation), was another Civil War epic, *Gone With the Wind*. Unusually, the 1940s list is headed by a contemporary drama about soldiers returning from the war, *The Best Years of Our Lives* (1946). Yet this is followed by Selznick's large-scale romantic Western *Duel in the Sun* (1946) and the first of Cecil B. DeMille's post-war biblical epics, *Samson and Delilah* (1949). The top hits of the 1950s, again by a wide margin, are two more biblical epics, the 1959 remake of *Ben-Hur* and DeMille's *The Ten Commandments* (1956). The first half of the 1960s represents the final years of the historical epic's dominance at the box office. The list of top-grossers is headed by an extravagant musical about family life and romance set against the backdrop of the rise of fascism—*The Sound of Music* (1965). This is followed by *Doctor Zhivago*, an epic love story set amongst the turmoil of World War I and the Russian Revolution, and *Cleopatra* (1963), another epic romance.[17]

Until the mid-1960s, historical epics did not only account for the majority of Hollywood's top grossing films, they also were its most prestigious productions, the films that the industry itself, and also probably the public at large, saw as Hollywood's most important and culturally resonant achievements. For example, in 1940 the Academy of Motion Picture Arts and Sciences awarded *Gone With the Wind* ten trophies (eight regular Oscars plus two special awards). This was topped by *Ben-Hur*, which won eleven Oscars, a record only matched decades later by *Titanic*; between them *The Sound of Music* and *Doctor Zhivago* won ten Academy Awards in 1965.[18] Furthermore, almost all of the top historical epics also gained prestige through their road-show release, an exhibition strategy, which equated the cinema with the legitimate theatre.[19] Unlike regular releases, road-shows played only in very few cinemas across the country, had long runs, reservable seats and high admission prices (several times the cost of a regular ticket). In addition to their long runs (which often went on for years), several of these films, most notably *Gone With the Wind* and *The Sound of Music*, also confirmed their importance and continued cultural resonance through their successful theatrical re-releases and through the tremendous ratings their television broadcasts achieved.[20] With almost half of all sets tuned in, the two-part 1976 broadcast of *Gone With the Wind* is still the highest rated film ever shown on American TV.[21]

Last but not least, from *The Birth of a Nation*'s unprecedented million-dollar budget to the notorious excesses of *Cleopatra* (probably still the most expensive film of all time, if inflation is taken into account), historical epics have consistently been the most expensive Hollywood productions of their time. Cameron's *Titanic* connected with this venerable tradition, in which cost was meant to signal quality and import, by being far more expensive than any of the action-adventure films whose huge budgets have received so much (and often negative) attention in recent decades.[22] As Vivian Sobchak has pointed out, the publicity for historical epics has always foregrounded and praised their 'extravagant generality and excess—of sets, costumes, stars, and spectacle, of the money and labour that went into the making of such entertainment'.[23] This excess (which, amongst other things, results in the excessive length of historical epics) can be understood as a *positive* quality because a 'correlation is clearly established here between the present events of the film's production and the past events it is intended to represent'. The size of the production is seen as a prerequisite for representing, and indeed repeating, 'the transcendent magnitude of past events'.[24] Momentous historical events require a momentous production, so that the impact of the filmic spectacle on cinema audiences can hope to echo the impact of the represented events on subsequent history.

Sobchak also notes that of all Hollywood genres the historical epic 'calls the most explicit, reflexive, and self-authorizing attention to its own existence as a *representation* . . . (T)he most obvious example is the frequent written or spoken narration with which the majority of historical epics begin and which later punctuate their dramatic action'.[25] The narration, in conjunction with extensive trailers and spoken pre-credit prologues, serves to reiterate the historical importance of the events about to be depicted, to emphasise the historical distance that separates filmmakers and audiences from these events, and to assure audiences that a huge effort has been made to reconstruct the past, and that this past is still relevant in the present. Indeed, trailers, prologues, titles and voiceover narration may spell out what this relevance is. In many cases, it is said to lie in an ongoing conflict between the desire for freedom and the forces of oppression, between a lawful, moral democratic order and lawless, amoral dictatorship. Or as DeMille put it in his prologue to *The Ten Commandments*: 'The theme of this picture is whether men are to be ruled by God's law, or whether they are to be ruled by the whims of a dictator like Rameses. Are men the property of the State, or are they free souls under God? This same battle continues throughout the world today'.

In this way, several of the most successful historical epics present the liberation of the Israelites from Egyptian slavery and the challenge that Christ's teachings posed to the Roman Empire as important models for contemporary political struggles (especially, but not exclusively, during the Cold War).[26] While this also applies to epics dealing with both world wars (which the Allies fought against undemocratic European regimes), the contemporary significance of Westerns and Civil War films has to be understood in quite different terms. These films focus on the formation of the American nation state, yet they also nostalgically evoke the archaic forms of social organisation (the Wild West as well as Southern plantation life and slavery), which had to be overcome for the modern United States to emerge. It would appear that these more specifically American epics were particularly important before World War II, whereas the dramatically increased internationalisation of Hollywood's operations in the post-war period moved biblical and European epics to the centre.[27]

TITANIC

So how does *Titanic* fit into this tradition of epic filmmaking? In terms of its budget, prestige and box office returns the film is a worthy successor to the epics of the past. Costing $200 million, it is the most expensive film ever made (if inflation is not taken into account). Winning 11 Academy Awards, it matches the record of *Ben-Hur*. And with North-American theatrical revenues of $601 million, it is by far the highest grossing film of all time (again without considering inflation). Perhaps even more remarkably, *Titanic*'s foreign gross of $1.235 billion is more than twice the amount the previous record holder had generated abroad.[28]

To what extent does the film engage with the traditional thematic concerns of historical epics? To begin with, *Titanic* literally deals with a transatlantic topic, thus bridging the gap between the tradition of American national epics and that of European/biblical epics. Like the American epics, the film displays, and evokes in its audiences, a nostalgic emotional investment in an archaic social order, which is destined for oblivion. The film foregrounds, and invites us to admire, the grandeur of the ship, the splendour of the first-class, the nobility of many of its passengers, while also emphasising the injustice, oppressiveness and self-destructiveness of the class-based, capitalistic society which the ship is a microcosm of. In his writings, Cameron expresses the film's ambiguous attitude towards Edwardian society by referring to 'the juxtaposition of rich and poor, the gender roles played out unto death (women first), the stoicism and nobility of a bygone era, the magnificence of the great ship matched in scale only by the folly of the man who drove her hell-bent through the darkness'.²⁹ Like the Southern plantation and the unruly West, then, the class-based European social order which Anglo-Saxon pioneers and immigrants transported across the ocean, needs to be removed for modern America to come into existence. Yet while the necessity of this removal is acknowledged, the disappearance of the old order is also mourned. In this way, *Titanic* connects to the tradition of Civil War and Western epics.

At the same time, like the European and biblical epics, the film's central focus is on the conflict between the desire for freedom and the forces of oppression, and the main narrative revolves precisely around the protagonist's initial lack of freedom and final liberation. However, unlike most of its predecessors (with notable exceptions such as *Gone With the Wind*), *Titanic* tells this traditional epic narrative from a woman's perspective.³⁰ Indeed, with only a few minor gender-related changes, DeMille's prologue to *The Ten Commandments* describes *Titanic* rather well: 'The theme of this picture is whether women are to be ruled by their hearts, or whether they are to be ruled by the whims of a dictatorial husband like Cal Hockley. Are women the property of men, or are they free souls? This same battle continues throughout the world today'. Thus, Cameron's revival of the grand tradition of the Hollywood historical epic has a distinctly feminist flavour, suggesting that women's liberation is at the heart of 20th century history, that this history can best be accessed and understood through women's memory, and that the actions of men have been most important where they served this liberation—by facilitating it like Jack Dawson, or commemorating it like Cameron himself.

Notes

1 For a sympathetic assessment of Cameron's objectives and the resulting film, which notes the film's connection to Hollywood's tradition of historical epics, see Robert Trent Toplin, '*Titanic*: Did the Maker of *True Lies* Tell the Truth About History?',

Perspectives: American Historical Association Newsletter, vol. 36, no. 3 (March 1998), pp. 1, 29–31. Cf. David M. Lubin, *Titanic* (London, 1999), pp. 15–27. For information on Cameron, see, for example, Christopher Heard, *Dreaming Aloud: The Life and Films of James Cameron* (Toronto, 1997); Paula Parisi, *Titanic and the Making of James Cameron* (London, 1998); Marc Shapiro, *James Cameron: An Unauthorized Biography* (Los Angeles, 2000).

2 Ed W. Marsh, *James Cameron's Titanic* (New York, 1997), p. p.xiii.

3 Marsh, *James Cameron's Titanic*, p. xii.

4 Randall Frakes and James Cameron, *Titanic: James Cameron's Illustrated Screenplay* (New York, 1998), p. xviii.

5 Frakes and Cameron, *Titanic*, pp. xii–xiii.

6 Marsh, *James Cameron's Titanic*, p. viii.

7 Frakes and Cameron, *Titanic*, p. ix.

8 Frakes and Cameron, *Titanic*, p. x.

9 Frakes and Cameron, *Titanic*, p. x.

10 Interestingly, Cameron also stated that his filmmaking was guided by a kind of ghostly presence from the future: 'I answer to a kind of phantom audience I carry around with me all the time. They ultimately are the arbiter of what should and should not be in my films'; Frakes and Cameron, *Titanic*, p. xxi.

11 Jeff Smith, 'Selling My Heart: Music and Cross-Promotion in *Titanic*', in Kevin S. Sandler and Gaylyn Studlar (eds.), *Titanic: Anatomy of a Blockbuster* (New Brunswick, New Jersey, and London, 1999), p. 60.

12 Smith, 'Selling My Heart', pp. 53–4.

13 *2001 People Entertainment Almanac* (New York, 2000), pp. 226–9.

14 'Captain of the Ship', *Preview*, November-December 1997, p. 18.

15 Matthew Bernstein, '"Floating Triumphantly": The American Critics on *Titanic*', in Sandler and Studlar, *Titanic*, pp. 23–5.

16 Joel Finler, *The Hollywood Story* (London, 1998), pp. 276–8.

17 The fact that the Disney musical fantasy *Mary Poppins* (1964) and the Bond spectacular *Thunderball* (1965) were placed on this list between *Cleopatra* and *Doctor Zhivago* points to future developments, namely the rise to dominance of male-oriented action-adventure films and of what I have elsewhere called 'family-adventure movies' in the 1970s. Cf. Peter Krämer, 'A Powerful Cinema-going Force? Hollywood and Female Audiences since the 1960s', in Melvyn Stokes and Richard Maltby (eds.), *Identifying Hollywood's Audiences: Cultural Identity and the Movies* (London, 1999), pp. 93–108; and Peter Krämer, 'Would You Take Your Child To See This Film? The Cultural and Social Work of the Family-Adventure Movie', in Steve Neale and Murray Smith (eds.), *Contemporary Hollywood Cinema* (London, 1998), pp. 294–311.

18 John Harkness, *The Academy Awards Handbook* (New York, 1994).

19 Sheldon Hall, 'Tall Revenue Features: The Genealogy of the Modern Blockbuster', in Steve Neale (ed.), *Genre and Contemporary Hollywood* (London, 2002), pp. 12–5.

20 For successful re-releases and TV ratings see Cobbett Steinberg, *Film Facts* (New York, 1980), pp. 25–7, 32–6. Re-releases have helped several historical epics to achieve high

rankings in *Variety*'s inflation-adjusted all-time chart for the US. The Editors of *Variety*, *The Variety Insider* (New York, 1999), p. 66.

21 Steinberg, *Film Facts*, p.32; *2001 People Entertainment Almanac*, p. 162.

22 For a discussion of the reception of big budget films from the 1920s to *Titanic*, see Justin Wyatt and Katherine Vlesmas, 'The Drama of Recoupment: On the Mass Media Negotiation of *Titanic*', in Sandler and Studlar, *Titanic*, pp. 29–45.

23 Vivian Sobchak, '"Surge and Splendor": A Phenomenology of the Hollywood Historical Epic', *Representations* 29 (Winter 1990), p. 28. Cf. Wyatt and Vlesmas, 'The Drama of Recoupment', pp. 30–31.

24 Sobchak, 'Surge and Splendor', p. 30.

25 Sobchak, 'Surge and Splendor', p. 34.

26 For an excellent discussion of the contemporary meanings of biblical epics, see Bruce Babington and Peter William Evans, *Biblical Epics: Sacred Narrative in the Hollywood Cinema* (Manchester, 1993).

27 On Hollywood's increased dependence on, and targeting of, foreign markets after World War II see, for example, Peter Krämer, '"Faith in Relations Between People": Audrey Hepburn, *Roman Holiday* and European Integration', in Diana Holmes and Alison Smith (eds.), *100 Years of European Cinema: Entertainment or Ideology?* (Manchester, 2000), pp. 195–206.

28 *Variety Insider*, p. 64; http://us.imdb.com/Charts/intltopmovies.

29 Marsh, *Titanic*, p. v. Cf. Frakes and Cameron, *Titanic*, p. xiv.

30 For a more extensive discussion of this, see Peter Krämer, 'Women First: *Titanic*, Action-Adventure Films, and Hollywood's Female Audience', Sandler and Studlar, *Titanic*, pp. 108–131.

CHAPTER FIFTEEN

Unsinkable Masculinity: The Artist and the Work of Art in James Cameron's *Titanic*[1]

DAVID GERSTNER

NOT MANY YEARS before Titanic sank in 1912, Thorstein Veblen wrote in *The Theory of the Leisure Class* that the 'modern feminine [code] . . . leaves no alternative direction in which the impulse to purposeful action may find expression'.[2] This, in particular, Americanist economy of functionalism and efficiency threatened by the excesses of the 'feminisation of American culture' (to borrow Ann Douglas's phrase) shared a similar relationship with the economy of the American arts. Walt Whitman, for example, urgently called attention to what he perceived as the European decadent 'feminised' art forms endangering America's emerging national aesthetic. Woman's presentation of self, in Whitman's mind, is to suggest both 'a strong and sweet Female Race' that must be 'raised to become the robust equals' of man.[3] To secure America's claim to a financially sound and aesthetically viable culture, a masculinist rhetoric intervenes where cultural feminisation purportedly occurs. Titanic, the ship, and *Titanic* (James Cameron's 1997 film) re-inscribe this tradition in contemporary cultural mythology as moral reminders of the necessity to contain the economies of this feminine excess. In addition, Cameron's *Titanic* rehearses this cultural ideology through the filter of the American artist and his work of art. At stake here, as we might suspect, is the body of the woman.

To identify the aesthetic of the work of art that serves to contain the cultural excess of the 'feminine' and reappears in *Titanic* I turn to what Michael Davitt Bell has described as the 'problem' in the American literary tradition: Realism. Undoubtedly burdened by contradiction and unending variation, the term (particularly under the aegis of *American* Realism) is often associated with a complexity of cultural ideals. In fact, as art historian Barbara Novak has suggested, the problem with 'American Realism' rests in the 'dilemma' artists confront precisely between notions of the 'Real' and the 'Ideal'[4] because American realists sought an aesthetic that conceptually delivered the ideal *thing*.[5]

Realism's uneven relationship to idealism is traceable through Whitman's elegiac yet 'virile' poetry, Thomas Eakins' scientific-painterly aesthetic that embraced the photograph and Darwinism, Frank Lloyd Wright's architectural Machine as 'Forerunner of Democracy,' and Robert Henri's non-'sissified' painterly temperament. What underscores idealist realism is the masculinist ideology that defines those problematic terms of the aesthetic we call American Realism. Common sense. Democratic. Virile. Balanced. Scientific. Ordinary. Natural. In other words: an *ideal Sameness*. More to the point: ideal sameness *as masculine* where, in the American arts, the perceived 'feminine' hand of the artist is put under erasure. As Bell argues, the formulation of the *non*-artist-position at the end of the 19th century was essential for the male artist's sense of gendered self. 'It is surely no coincidence', writes Bell of William Dean Howell's enthusiasm for Realism, 'that Howell came to associate realism with "masculine" normalcy, and to distinguish it from concern for "art", at a time when modern stereotypes of male sexual identity—rigidly differentiating "effeminate" homosexuality from "virile" heterosexuality—were being solidified into what sociologists call master status traits'.[6]

This is not to say that the artist entirely disappears. Rather, through the rhetoric of realism the artist and His work of art are made to appear *natural*. To say that the American artist puts *the* Artist under erasure is to say that the American male artist (in order not to be associated with 'effeminacy' or indeed homosexuality) re-negotiates the terms for both masculinity and creativity. American Realism and masculinity emerges only through a series of fits and starts and, often, ironic inconsistencies. Cameron, I will argue, fits into this anxiety-ridden tradition of the masculine aesthetic of American Realism that dreams of the perfect melding of the Ideal and the Real. A man's work is never done and is always on display for us to see.[7]

Situating the historical relationship between the work of art/machine and gender is central to identifying the aesthetic that reduces gender difference to the masculine ideal. Cameron's *Titanic* presents the American male artist and his work as something ideologically derived through 'masculine' common sense. Following the American tradition of 'problematic' realism, Cameron frames his film through an aesthetic paradigm that champions this common sense over 'effeminised' excess.

What I sketch below is the ideological relationship between gender and the American work of art. As we will see through a study of *Titanic*, the woman's body, following the modern masculine anxiety over American aesthetics, is reconfigured by the filmmaker's doubling of himself with the fictionalised artist so as to achieve an ideal masculinist work of art that stitches together a female body from a painterly and industrial arts' palette of culturally defined 'feminine' traits.

At the centre of my discussion is the role of the male American artist in the film who stretches over and through the detail of cinematic and painterly imagery. The Hollywood filmmaker is indeed the decisive American Realist artist since the historical contradictions that burden American Realism are successfully (or so it is thought) managed in the Hollywood film. The merging of 19th century pictorialism and mechanical invention has, in the *ideal* sense, satisfied the 'problem of American Realism'. In the film *Titanic*, I would argue, the filmmaker announces realism's successful resolution through an idealist construction of what constitutes the traditional and industrial arts.

The film itself plays with the doubling effect of the filmmaker-as-artist both on and off the screen. The presence of the author's hand is no secret in this film. Indeed, Cameron's placement of his hand is actually part of the film's publicity strategy. In an interview Cameron discusses how his own hand stands in for Leonardo DiCaprio's in the scene in which Kate Winslet is sketched.[8] The finished drawing of Rose is actually that of the filmmaker. I do not need engage an *auteur* argument here because Cameron has inserted his authorial presence thus underscoring the privileged creative enterprise of the (American) male artist. Cameron, a true manly democratic American artist (albeit an émigré), manages the great American myth: He vigorously promotes himself and is popularly perceived as Artist, Technologist, Entertainer, and Cultural Wizard. With *Titanic*, Cameron is at once Robert Henri, Thomas Alva Edison, and P. T. Barnum.

What is it that the American Realist creates with his 'vision of democratic action'?[9] What significance does the female body offer the American male artist? American Realism, as Bell reiterates, is the hope to contain the perceived threat of 'effeminacy'. To be precise: American Realism seeks an ideal aesthetic that masculinises the feminine. The creative application of such an aesthetic is fruitfully manufactured in the classical Hollywood cinema; the historical concept of realism in the Hollywood film is, to say the least, over-determined in its success.[10] The formal mode of cinema production indeed follows the realist tradition of narrative (something identified early on by the likes of Eisenstein). More importantly, classical cinema seemingly resolves the creative tension of which Novak has suggested: cinema's technology weds the Ideal and the Real.[11]

And, of course, cinematic hysterical women, *femmes fatales*, and aristocratic *dilettantes* share the honour of deliberately leading morally efficient capitalist production. The trope of feminised mechanical chaos—a cultural mayhem often unleashed by the uncontrollable and gender-'neutral' forces of Nature—is ubiquitous in the Hollywood tradition of storytelling. From Cecil B. De-Mille's Progressivist uplift film, *Male and Female* (1919), to Howard Hawks' shrill homosocial repartée in *Only Angels Have Wings* (1939) man (using truculent skills and modern machines) has had to defend himself against the dangerous temptation embodied in over-feminised culture. With this in mind we can (and as the film asks us to do) 'return' to *Titanic* where classical Hollywood storytelling and the creative arts' tradition of masculinising femininity repeats and reminds us of our moral obligation to withstand the lure of cultural excess. There is, however, one last feminised obstacle in the mechanical age that calls our attention: the great ship *herself*, Titanic.[12]

It is not only the creative arts where the woman-as-masculine ideal is upheld. The builders of machines have for centuries engaged a similar rhetoric around their industrial designs. Sometime around 1796, for example, shipbuilders in Europe scaled down ornamentation on the body of the ship leaving a simplified decorative focal point on the ship's bow known as the figurehead. Often modelled after the young daughters of sea captains and the 'sweethearts of many sailor's dreams', the figurehead was 'believed capable of calming angry seas'. Since no actual women were permitted on board the 19th century vessel (they were considered 'unlucky'), the representational figurehead of a woman stood in and served to 'protect and defend [the sailors] from the evils of a mythological sea'.[13]

During the same period a creative compromise was made over the design of the female figurehead. In order to alleviate perceived over-aestheticisation of a ship's external design, shipbuilders agreed to limit the use of figureheads to one per vessel. The reduction of excessive exterior detail proved a more efficient and faster vessel. The figurehead itself saw a reduction in the amount of aestheticised detail that went into its final shape. In the end, the work was sculpted so as to conjure an image of both mother and sexual object. Usually bare breasted, the figurehead eased the anguish of 'lovesick sailors [who] often confided in the motherly figurehead'; the young lad's desire for both mother and sexual-object choice was met.[14]

On board Cameron's *Titanic* we literally confront the historical figurehead as it comes to life in the body of Rose (Kate Winslet). The positioning of the female as ship's figurehead in the film's text demonstrates the popular and moral rhetoric issued during the Gilded Age regarding women's perfidious and 'unlucky' effect on the machine; it is an idea contemporaneously tied to the notion that Titanic's sinking marks the end of the age of excess.[15] As one of the ship's British passengers, Colonel Archibald Gracie (Bernard Fox), not unceremoniously reminds us following Rose's attempted suicide: 'women and machinery do not mix'. But, in fact, at the heart of the film's narrative is the assertion that indeed Woman and Machine can and *do* mix.

I would suggest that the role of the filmmaker (Cameron) and fictionalised artist (Jack Dawson played by Leonardo DiCaprio) is to create the appropriately designed figurehead—the ideal 'mix' of Woman and Machine—both on the ship itself and on the body of the film's female protagonist. The construction of these ideal feminised bodies effectively demarcates a 'balanced' and functional female form, or a body that solidifies the gap between Nature and Machine. Moreover, the creative commingling of filmmaker with the film's protagonist illustrates the harmonic juxtaposition of the traditional with the industrial arts. Jack is the painter while James is the filmmaker. The creative conjoining of these two figures celebrates the masculinist dream of 20th century American Realism.

The feminine body, the film's work of art, is released of its aristocratic excess through the guiding hand of the male artist(s) in order to emerge as an ideal American middle-class Woman.[16] It is here that Cameron's authorial hand inserts itself at two important junctures in the film. The intersection of these points serves as the anchor for the construction of Rose. The first reconstructed representation of Rose passes through the filter of the non-industrial arts (sort of a blueprint for the industrial model). Rose is sketched by the artist's hand; her womanly essence is captured through the romanticised vision of the traditional Artist. But the industrial arts (film) elicit the same gendered essence. Cameron's 'camera-stylo' (following Alexandre Astruc's term) demonstrably sets itself the task of fusing Machine and Nature in the name of creating the work of art. *Titanic*, through the work of art (the female body), signals the successful and historical alliance between the *idea* of art as unique (Walter Benjamin's 'aura') and art as mechanically reproduced. Woman and Machine successfully mix through the art of the cinematic enterprise.

THE BRIDE STRIPPED BARE BY HER BACHELORS, EVEN

Before Rose is constructed as the ideal feminine centrepiece of the Machine age, the terms for American art are first established in the film.[17] The work of art (the female figurehead) in *Titanic* emerges only through the film's contradictory relationship to modernist art. Cameron, on the one hand, wants to side with early modernists (Picasso and Monet) because they are perceived as reactionary to aristocratic-bourgeois lack of taste (characterized by Cal, Billy Zane). Picasso and Monet, on the other hand, are also presented as nemeses to the American-style realist drawings of Jack: ultra-modernist Paris (1912 Cubists) stands in direct opposition to the Robert Henri-like paintings and Whitmanesque prescriptions of down-to-earth 'Americana' art.

The relationship to art in the film is strikingly reminiscent of America's response to the 1913 Armory Show in New York where Americans for the first time witnessed the paintings of the major European artists. A scandal soon followed the exhibit's negative reviews in the popular press. Most reviewers posited Cubism as cartoon-like and the works of Matisse as insane and blasphemous. One of the major criticisms of the works (particularly those by Duchamp and Matisse) was the artists' rendering of women -Duchamp's *Nude Descending a Staircase* the most infamous of them all. The perceived deformation of the modernist female nude was anathema to the 19th century dictum of the sacred female body in artistic representation. For Americans in 1913, European modernism was a grotesque bastardisation of bourgeois artistic sentiment.

It is noteworthy that several of the key American artists who exhibited at the Armory Show, especially members of the Ashcan Group (led by Robert Henri), were spatially and critically sidelined in the face of the attention garnered by the Europeans. What is striking about this sidelining in relationship to our discussion of *Titanic* is that Jack Dawson's first set of sketches recall the American Realist perspective espoused by the Ashcan members. It is, in fact, this American Realist sensibility that is finally championed in Cameron's film.[18] Like the Ashcan's paintings of prostitutes and urban street life, Dawson's sketches, as Rose remarks, are 'drawn from real life'. [19]

When Rose sees Jack's sketches she is mesmerised by art that is so like 'real life'. After encountering Jack, her Picassos and Monets apparently have nothing to do with her 'life'. Thankfully, such European dross sinks right along with the other European pretensions of the day. Jack's sketchbook that illustrates real life for Rose indeed serves as a catalogue where Rose's ideal womanhood is inserted. Somewhere between the prostitutes, the disenfranchised bourgeoise, and the dancers of his artwork, Jack will artistically situate Rose. Lest we underestimate the value of this sketch, we should bear in mind that it is precisely the re-discovered drawing that is the catalyst for the film's narrative.

The emphasis on 'real life' in Dawson's sketches highlights the notion of a consecrated rendering of the woman's body. Unlike the so-called artificial life with which Rose is associated, Jack unveils his 'pure' vision of womanly form. Legless prostitutes, a forgotten bejeweled bourgeois woman, and struggling ballerinas are dignified by the hand of the sympathetic young male artist.[20] Jack, however, is in search of the female form that falls somewhere between Mother and Whore.[21] In Rose he finds her. What is vital to the masculinist creation of Rose is the 'seeing', or the artist's look, his point of view, toward the bodies of the women in the film. Rose, indeed, tells Jack that he 'has the gift to see'. The gift of vision for the artist, here, is the ability to find, re-draw, and re-train Rose into an exemplar of the American middle-class Woman. Through a series of extreme close-ups during the sketching of the nude Rose, the young artist's intense glance on the woman's body suggests the artistic integrity with which Jack takes his work and his ability to penetrate into Rose's womanly essence. Rose, as the artist's model, is no mere sex object who is lasciviously displayed for perverse observation—she is pure work of art. This tightly edited sequence also draws together, if you will, the important commingling—through Cameron's hand—of auteur, actor, director, and work of art (painterly and cinematically).

Moreover, it is the bodies of the other women in the film's narrative to

whom Jack directs our vision and who are ultimately fragmented to complete
the portrait of the ideal Rose. The images of the other women are images of
negation and difference that enable Rose to come into being. Rose is thus the
amalgamation of the film's representation of the extremes of economic class.
On the one hand, the artist directs our attention to the primitive women in
steerage while, with the other hand, he observes the artificial dilettantes in first
class. In steerage Jack finds the truculent pleasures that provide the essential
earthiness of a mythic past that necessarily balances modern-world knowledge.
On the upper decks, we see Rose's mother (Frances Fisher) and her first class
cultural milieu occupying their positions of an embalmed aristocracy. The
'vulgar Brown woman' (Kathy Bates), however, promises an American-upper
class who never forgot their 'down-to-earth-work ethic that got-them-where-
they-are-in-the-first-place' beginnings.

The selected bodies of women in *Titanic* are presented along several different levels of feminine strata. They are articulated as object-studies for the film's
resident artists (Jack and James). It is precisely Jack's and James' point of view
that finally constitutes the site of the ideal woman through his process of artistic
selection. Rose appears as the sanctified image that has been pieced together
by these fragmented traces of women displayed in the film. Rose is the body
where the American-masculinist dream of the feminine is re-written through
the creative practices of painting and, subsequently, filmmaking.

Jack's final sketch of Rose goes one step further under the terms of hetero-
normative democracy marshalled through American Realism: Jack, in the
classical Hollywood tradition, falls in love with his subject. The realist sketch of
Rose (on canvas and on the cinematic screen), the film's figurehead, no longer
represents the Ashcan's (or Jack's) gritty rendering of prostitutes and the forgotten, nor does it reach the modernist pretences of Picasso. Cameron's/
Dawson's design of the ideal Woman suggests a moral balance—an American
common sense in the arts—that satisfies a female figurehead in the service of
the perfect Machine. Located between the figure of the prostitute and the misguided airs inculcated by her European-minded mother, the stripped-bare
portrait of Rose appears.

Like the changing history of the decorative ship figurehead that coincides
with a history of efficient capitalism, Rose's body will be re-dressed, re-shaped,
and re-created until it finally disappears—stripped bare—into middle-class,
democratic sameness. It is through Jack's look and deft craftsmanship that the
training ground for Rose's disciplining into a manly woman will occur. To do
this Jack (and James) re-draw the parameters of Woman and Machine by containing the excesses of the bourgeois feminine body.

For Rose to achieve the status of efficient and masculinist figurehead, her
body is cinematically melded with the design of the ship. The Titanic is a
training ground for Rose where the weight of her domestic past puts at risk her

own ability to see, as Jack promises, a 'way out'. It is on the ship where she is modelled into the dream of man. The ship is also where the violent ripping apart of her past takes place—a past significantly embodied in the great ship. Her break from the mother-ship occurs in four distinct phases in the narrative: her attempted suicide at the stern of the boat, Jack's Shavian (albeit Americanised) re-education of Rose, her filmic transcendence from the confines of her dilettantish past, and, finally, the sinking of the ship. The process of masculinising Rose, like that in the design of 18th century figurehead, alleviates the repressive obstructions that hinder a free-flowing, efficient, and functional model of production.

The freedom to move freely, to function smoothly is the *sine qua non* of masculinist cultural production. An over-feminised aristocratic culture forbids a male character like Jack Dawson to move (as he tells Rose) through the world like 'a tumble-weed blowing in the wind'.[22] Rose, once she meets the liberated artist, admits that she too longs for freedom from the 'inertia' in which she feels bound. The masculinist dream of unrestricted movement in a crowded industrial age must necessarily reject the excesses of bourgeois production. In *Titanic*, unchecked femininity delivers the unlucky blow to the 'unsinkable' and over-feminised machine.

Rose's first attempt at assuming the figurehead position is a mistake. Prompted by an act of feminine hysteria, Rose, emotionally responsive to her rebellious spirit (read here a misguided but essentially healthy American girl), feels smothered by her bourgeois (read here European aristocratic pretence) upbringing. Conflicted by the nightmare of the family romance that awaits her at the end of her voyage, Rose tearfully runs to the ship's stern assuming a misplaced figurehead position. Rose's hysteria seemingly skews her (historical) judgment. The traditional, unadorned ship's figurehead is historically positioned on the ship's bow; Rose runs to the stern. Her error in judgment (to commit suicide or choose the wrong end of the boat?) elicits Colonel Gracie's earlier comments on the impossibility of mixing woman and machine. Rose's poor directional skills will be corrected by Jack.

Rose, fascinated by her saviour's artistry, can hardly resist Jack's mobility and common-sense approach to life: 'Why can't I be like you, Jack', Rose exclaims. Jack is more than happy to oblige her wish. He is direct in his questioning, simple in his dress, he rejects creative excess but not creativity; he is, in short, the romanticised vision of the ideal American Man. Through and with the body of Rose, Jack carries Whitman's exegesis soundly into the 20th century. The progress and capitalist success of America insists on the *de*-effeminisation of culture. Furthermore, the strength of American culture depends upon woman (in relationship to man) to define herself as Whitman has, as *masculinely* feminine ('a strong and sweet Female Race, a race of perfect Mothers', *Titanic* follows Whitman's feminine body to the extent that the film's narrative and cinematic presentation of the feminine is not about getting rid of Woman as much as it is about neutralising (balancing nature), therefore masculinising, her cultural effects. If Rose is to be freed of her inertia she must become like Jack. Through the hands of the film's two American male artists who have achieved the privilege to move freely through the modern world, the perfect Woman—a figurehead embodying both Mother and Lover—is constructed as the false promise of liberation.

Hence, Jack/James build the American woman. Rose's query, 'why can't I be like you', is answered by Jack putting Rose through the rehearsal of becoming a man. Jack promises to teach Rose how to drink beer, ride horses like cowboys (none of that sidesaddle stuff she learned in finishing school), and (the rehearsal we see) spit like a man. When Rose feels uncertain about leaving her past, Jack lures her into the ship's gymnasium to convince her that, while she is a 'spoiled little brat, but under that . . .the most amazingly, wonderful girl . . . woman that I've ever known', they are now the *same* ('you jump, I jump'). The consummation of the heterosexual coupling that follows in *Titanic* is precisely a coupling of masculinist sameness (note Rose's simplified clothing she now wears as she and Jack ride the bow of the ship). Rose's excessive femininity is eschewed in the service of a representation of corporeal difference (male and female) conditioned by a masculinist ideology. The figurehead, a 'liberated' Rose, trained by the creative American man, is now correctly positioned with Jack's guidance and James's direction at the ship's bow.

PROTO-FEMINISM AND MASCULINIST EQUALITY

Titanic presents a cinematic fusion with, and separation from, the film's two feminised bodies: Rose and Titanic (Nature and Machine, respectively). Rose's body—the new figurehead of middle-class Progressivism—stabilises the ostentation of old world bourgeois-ness by streamlining the figurehead position that allows for efficient transactions in a functional society. She is a work of art made possible through an admixture of the traditional and industrial arts. The bringing together and subsequent tearing apart of the over-feminised bodies forges a model of (American) feminine balance. Once Titanic sinks Rose emerges as the ideal Woman as masculinised Machine. Woman and Machinery successfully mix. In *Titanic*, the work of art, the female body, and the machine are combined. They are stripped from cultural excess and presented as models of American creativity and masculinity.

As the ship's proxy figurehead, Rose registers the new (American) woman/ mother/sweetheart. She emerges from the wreckage of the Gilded Age as the new liberal middle class unfettered by the decadence of the aristocratic bourgeoisie. Rose's survival is the essential split between and balancing of the ages of excess and streamlined efficiency. Importantly, her survival serves to protect the future of the American middle-classes from another European creation similar to that other excessively bourgeois body: Titanic.

Rose's decision to break from her past and run away with Jack is cinematically rendered by Cameron through their conjoined (masculinised, Americanised) bodies at the site of the boat's bow. Ironically, with all the spectacle, excess, and computer-generated imagery that Hollywood can muster, the stripped-down and simplified work of realist art appears to emerge victorious.[23] The new American figurehead—the ideal American woman secure in the arms of her creators—is ready to break free from the excesses of capitalist production in order to remind those who nostalgically yearn for the dream of Titanic that we have fulfilled the dream of the future: American progress, creativity, equality.

When the elderly Rose (Gloria Stuart, barefoot, simply dressed) decides to toss her diamond necklace, named the 'Heart of the Ocean', into the sea, she throws away the vestiges of excessive femininity. The film concludes with the soundly sleeping Rose (some suggest she has died) who survived her second visit to Titanic. She sleeps secure surrounded by photos that display her 'new woman' consciousness following her trauma in 1912. The photographs present to us an American proto-feminist (aviator, horse-'man') who has been apparently equalised under the terms of American masculinity.

If the 'problem' of the American Realist aesthetic has been the tension between the Real and the Ideal that ideologically sets itself the task of masculinising the threat of effeminacy through an erasure of the male artist *as* feminine/homosexual, *Titanic* presents itself as the successful resolution to this tension. The body of the woman and the body of the machine are useful in this logic of masculinist culture because they at once defend against the male artist's fear of homosexuality and (once properly masculinised) contain the purported excess of cultural production.

The Hollywood artist (here Cameron, but certainly Hawks, Ford, De-Mille)[24] is the ideal American Realist (the *non*-artist) because the creative enterprise of the Hollywood film industry seamlessly (or so it appears) merges Machine and Nature through an aesthetic practice crafted on the terms of realism. The Hollywood director's hand fulfils the dream of the American *non*-artist by embodying the creative principles of the American arts: invention, craftsmanship, techno-wizardry and, above all, masculinity.

Notes

1 This is an abridged version of an essay that appeared under the same title in *Cultural Critique*, no. 50, winter 2002, pp. 1–22.

2 Thorstein Veblen, *The Theory of the Leisure Class* (New York, 1931), p. 358.

3 Walt Whitman, 'Democratic Vistas' in Mark Van Doren (ed.), *The Portable Walt Whitman* (New York, 1974), pp. 328, 343.

4 Barbara Novak, *American Painting of the Nineteenth Century* (New York, 1969), p. 61.

5 For a list of works discussing American Realism see Gerstner in *Cultural Critique*, 2002, p. 16.

6 Michael Davitt Bell, *The Problem of American Realism: Studies in the Cultural History of a Literary Idea* (Chicago, 1993), p. 37.

7 See David Gerstner, 'Dancer from the Dance: Gene Kelly, Television, and the Beauty of Movement', *Velvet Light Trap*, 'Beauty Marks' issue, winter 2002, pp. 48–66.

8 *MSN Online Tonight* with James Cameron, 21 January 1998; http://onlinetonight.msn.co.uk/titanic/transcript.htm

9 Alfred Habbegger, *Gender, Fantasy, and Realism in American Literature* (New York, 1982), p. 110.

10 'Realism, said J. A. Berst, vice-president and general manager of Pathé's next Gold Rooster release, 'is the essential quality in a picture—that goes without saying' (quoted in 'Does Color Enhance Dramatic Realism', *The Moving Picture World*, 1 July 1916, p. 84.

11 Novak, *American Painting of the Nineteenth Century*, p. 198

12 'For seamen . . . ships have a high emotional value. One of the main reasons for this is probably the fact that the ship is a living thing, which explains why, in the English language, it is a feminine gender'. See Hans Jürgen Hansen (ed.), *Art and the Seafarer: A Historical Survey of the Arts and Crafts of Sailors and Shipwrights*, (London, 1968), p.130.

13 Hansen, *Art and the Seafarer*, pp. 106–07

14 James Clary, *Superstitions of the Sea* (St. Clair, MI, 1994), p. 107.

15 Titanic's sinking is often recognised as a moment of moral comeuppance. See, for example, Cameron's journal on *Titanic*, (Writers' Guild of America website: http://wga/journal/1997/12/97/titanic.html).

16 For discussions of class in *Titanic*, see Laurie Ouellete, 'Ship of Dreams: Cross-Class Romance and the Cultural Fantasy of *Titanic*' in Kevin S. Sandler and Gaylyn Studlar (eds.), *Titanic: Anatomy of a Blockbuster* (New Brunswick, New Jersey, London, 1999), pp.169–188, 185 and David Anshen, 'Out of the Depths and Through the Post-Modern Surface: History and Class Figuration in *Titanic*' in *CineAction*, no. 51, February 2000, pp. 23–29.

17 Duchampian irony is evoked because Duchamp's transgendered 'alter-ego,' named Rrose Sélavy (eros, c'est la vie), suggested gender and sexuality play. Rose in *Titanic* (*sans* the all important doubled 'r') stands in for the model bride stripped bare in more ways than one—even.

18 Peter Lehman and Susan Hunt discuss Jack's 'highly conventional, realist style' in 'Something and Someone Else: The Mind, The Body, and Sexuality in *Titanic*' in Sandler and Studlar, *Titanic*, pp. 89–107, 97.

19 Additionally, see David M. Lubin's recounting of the Cameron film in *Titanic*, (London, 1999), p. 57.

20 It is instructive to consider DiCaprio's 'feminine' demeanour in relation to the sham of 'kinder, gentler' heterosexual masculinity about which Eve Kosofsky Sedgwick speaks in *Epistemology of the Closet* (Berkeley, 1990), p. 145.

21 Jack tells Rose (after her suicide attempt) that he lost his mother as a young boy and has since had to wander the world in search of, if we follow a psychoanalytical reading, his mother.

22 When Rose finds it difficult to articulate Jack's financial condition, she states that he is a person of 'limited means'. Jack smirks and insists she speak plainly: 'go on and say it . . . a poor guy'.

23 Cameron's over-aestheticised realism in *Titanic* ironically highlights the inability of masculine discourse to claim itself as 'simple and natural'.

24 But not, for example, Vincente Minnelli. See David Gerstner, 'Queer Modernism: The Cinematic Aesthetics of Vincente Minnelli' in *Modernity*, no. 2, 2000, http://www.eiu.edu/~modernity/modernity.html.

CHAPTER SIXTEEN

Romancing Disaster: *Titanic* and the Rites of Passage Film

SUSAN SYDNEY-SMITH

THE HOLLYWOOD BLOCKBUSTER *Titanic* (James Cameron, 1997) produced a wealth of critical material aimed at illuminating how and why it
so successfully seduced a worldwide audience. Affinities have been drawn between the film and frames of reference including a new, female-centred action-
adventure cinema; democratic escapism signified by the 'Ship of Dreams'
motif; material profit versus love; the emblematic significance of 'The Heart of
the Ocean' and the cross-class desires of contemporary America.[1] In terms of
romance, or indeed romancing disaster, much has been made of the film's
framing story and its foregrounding of the fictional star-crossed love story
between the characters Rose Bukater (Kate Winslett) and Jack Dawson (Leonardo DiCaprio), narrated in the present tense by the surviving female protagonist.[2] Whilst some critics have located *Titanic*'s past-present narrative structure
within a post-modern aesthetic discourse, there are others who see it as connected to the British 'heritage' genre.[3] Critics have also located the film's narrative structure within a contemporary mode of analysis, and related it to
millennial *Angst*. However, there has until now been little attempt at relating
these concerns to what I want to identify here as rites of passage films, narratives which enable us to cross over from one millennium to the next. Homi
Bhahba offers us new ways of understanding such shifts with his concept of
'the beyond'. This, he argues is neither a new horizon, nor a leaving behind of
the past:

Beginnings and endings may be the sustaining myths of the middle years, but in the *fin-
de-siècle* we find ourselves in the moment of transit where space and time cross to produce complex figures of difference and identity.[4]

What rites of passage films offer are transitional, borderline moments were
questions of cultural difference and self-hood intersect with new ways of representing history. The 'moment of transit', where past and present collide, arguably also facilitates a return to older mythologies, in particular to the chivalric
romance. This evokes the so-called dialogical imagination that Mikhail

Bakhtin has written about, citing the importance of the medieval form of the *Roman* as central to pre-modern cultural discourse.[5] I want to argue in this chapter that these ancient generic negotiations are very similar to those today, not least in their articulation of *fin de siècle Angst*.

As a millennial narrative, *Titanic* shares characteristics with a cluster of historical films of the late 1990s dealing with sea-journeys and voyages, including *Amistad (1997)*, *The Piano* (1997) and *Oscar and Lucinda* (1998). These films represent a conscious cinematographic re-writing of a previously elided, or 'whited-out', diaspora. In this context, Paul Gilroy has pointed out how a magnificent 19th Century William Turner painting of a galleon in full sail turns out on closer examination to be a portrait of a slave ship.[6] As Gilroy further discusses, such ships plied their trade across the notorious 'middle passage', that of the slave trade route across the Atlantic. Steven Spielberg's *Amistad*—eponymously named after a Spanish slave ship—offers an inversion of this story, when its own cargo overthrows the galleon. In *Oscar and Lucinda*, the ship which carries Oscar on his fearful journey to Sydney and provides the meeting ground for his romantic encounter with the heiress Lucinda, bears the name Leviathan, suggestive of a metonymic structure which parodies the ambivalent nature of the newly formed Australian society and the colonial discourse which served it.[7] *Titanic* articulates a similar sense of guilt when Rose declares that although for some *Titanic* was 'the Ship of Dreams', for her it was 'a slave ship taking me back to America in chains'. Unlike the Irish emigrant Jack, for whom America is 'the promised land', the 'dream ticket'—with democracy written into its very constitution—for others it was a ticket to bondage unless, as Peter Krämer puts it, 'something should happen along the way'.[8] Both *Amistad* and *Titanic*, negotiating events of piracy on the one-hand and shipwreck on the other, offer consecutive moments of liberation and catharsis. Each—but *Amistad* in particular—negotiates hitherto 'forgotten' colonially induced horrors. In so doing, they disrupt both the mythology of Empire as 'natural' and the discourse of another heritage sub-genre, the Raj cycle of the 1980s, including *A Passage to India* (1984) and *Heat and Dust* (1982).[9] Gilroy also notes in respect of the ship as metaphor, 'As it were, getting on board promises . . . to reconceptualise the orthodox relationship between modernity and what passes for prehistory'.[10] It is arguably this aspect above all that *Titanic* is seen to negotiate and which is especially appropriate in terms of the *Roman*.

Another cluster of 1990s films figure a more symbolic journey, through their developmental *Bildungsroman* narratives, centred upon canonical figures or texts, including *Orlando* (1992), *Elizabeth* (1998), and *Shakespeare in Love* (1999). *Titanic* too, sits comfortably within a configuration of the rites of passage film as a developmental or psychical journey. Symbolising the precarious move from Rose's girlhood to womanhood, the maiden voyage offers an undreamed of opportunity, where future expectations can be overturned, patriarchal structures questioned, sexual knowledge realised and female identity arrived at. The fact that the older Rose is a Centenarian is crucial to the story. Her whole life is presented as a celebration of 20th century female emancipation; it is a *Bildungsroman* we too can applaud. Rose's modernity is conveyed amongst other attributes, by her knowledge of French art, Freud, and her lack of modesty, in posing nude for Jack. She is negotiating her own feminism, eschewing what is essentially an arranged marriage. We are soon made aware that the fabulous Heart of the Ocean diamond with its royal pedigree is not so much a love gift, but more a token of exchange, for pre-nuptial sexual favours. Rose's anger at the situation is self-directed and she tries to end her life by jumping over the side of the ship. A significant step to her recovery arrives when Jack saves her, and, at the bow of the ship, physically transforms her into its figurehead, arms akimbo. From that heady place grows the awareness that Rose, too, can be self-determining.

Despite the rigidity of its hierarchical structure, the geography of the ship also presents a transformative space. Jack's invitation to the steerage party allows us to witness Rose's embrace of a wild, defiant freedom, unavailable within the artificial constraints of her first-class life-style. When Hockley becomes aware of her growing attachment to Jack, he calls her 'whore to a gutter-rat'. Rose's riposte, that 'I would rather be 'Jack's whore than your wife' is an expression of her newfound ability in the art of self-defence. As we learn after the disaster and her lover's demise, Rose carries a torch for Jack Dawson, adopting both a bohemian life-style and his name. All these aspects, as well as her escape from marriage (the *white* slave trade), are signifiers of Rose's successful reconfiguration as a 20th century, thoroughly modern, woman. Rose's rejection of Old World values—Europe, class, and materialism on Titanic's maiden voyage—can be seen as a *Girl's Own* adventure story, offering undreamt of freedom from gender and class constraints, as well as the embrace of artistic values *vis-à-vis* the non-productive figure of the artist.

What both groups of films I have identified hold in common, apart from their physical and psychical journeys, is a new take on the historical film. In narrative terms they do away with clearly demarcated beginnings and endings. Rites of passage films frequently query what happens *before* the 'official' story commences. For example, in *Elizabeth*, we see the sequence of circumstances preceding the young princess's histrionic accession to Virgin Queen-dom, 'the moment at which Elizabeth became historical'.[11] Similarly, the BBC television adaptation of Dickens' *Oliver Twist*, *Oliver* (2001), dramatises events leading up to the eponymous protagonist's arrival in the orphanage. In each case, what we are offered is a prequel to the main event, and a far more playful, alternative version, to the 'authentic' heritage: one that subordinates the 'As if' narrative, to the more open-ended 'What if?'

The British historical films of the 1980s and 1990s has been defined by

Andrew Higson and others within a heritage discourse, interpreted as articulating predominantly inherited middle-class values in 'quality', 'authentic' products, exemplified by Merchant Ivory's *A Room with a View* (1985), *Howard's End* (1992) and *The Remains of the Day* (1992).[12] Higson argues that heritage discourse operates in a similar way to early 19th century landscape photography in which 'the pictorialist landscape photograph . . . organises and displays the landscape as precisely something to be looked at, primarily from the point of view of the outsider, a spectator as opposed to a participant'.[13] *Titanic* can be connected to heritage films because of its features including the British ship; a depiction of the past in lavish settings and costumes; and Cameron's quest for 'authenticity'. Julian Stringer, for example, has interpreted *Titanic*'s connection to the British heritage film through its intertextual references, 'via the casting of DiCaprio, Winslet, Billy Zane—in the roles of Jack Dawson, the young Rose Bukater, and Cal Hockley respectively—and others to such revisionist titles as *Orlando* (1992) and *William Shakespeare's Romeo + Juliet* (1996)'.[14]

In a discussion of recent 'British' historical films, including *Elizabeth*, Claire Monk queries the suitability of both 'British' and 'heritage' in films whose dependence upon American co-funding, distributor backing and international casting is paramount.[15] She further argues that the socio-political ground upon which the extended heritage debate is premised has radically altered. [16] She asserts that it is because of, rather than despite, their revisionism that films like *Orlando*, *Shakespeare in Love* and *Elizabeth* more fully subscribe to a category she has designated as 'post-heritage', a term that may usefully be extended to the rites of passage film, including *Titanic*.

In order to further justify the uses of terms such as post-heritage and the rites of passage film—it will be helpful at this juncture to look at the way in which 'revisionist' films such as *Orlando*, *Shakespeare in Love* and *Elizabeth* direct our attention away from the 'authentic' seductive aesthetics of heritage discourse. What they promote instead is a *mise-en-scène* that is depictive rather than pictorial. In order to comprehend this crucial difference it is worth noting that *Titanic* not only moves away from the hierarchical relations of early pictorial photography, it also dismantles the implied separation between audience and spectator that exists both in classical Hollywood and British heritage cinema. In each case, events are enacted, and the 'invisible' spectator watches them unfold from the dark of the auditorium. However, *Titanic* mixes modes of both enacted and spoken narrative. Rose's address to camera in the framing story shatters the 'transparency' conceptually engendered by that invisible fourth wall, which separates the audience from the spectacle.[17] The elderly Rose's (Gloria Stuart) strong presence, and her insistence on telling the story 'like it was', interpellates and thereby draws us into a new version of a female-centred history. As she tells us near the beginning of the film, hers 'was a somewhat different experience', one that relies not so much on the 'forensic' data upon which salvage-expert Lovett and his crew are so reliant, as that of memory, nostalgia and reverie.

Another sense in which this group of films is highly depictive is in terms of their 'prosthetic' realism. For example, *Elizabeth*'s 'authenticity', as Moya Luckett has noted, is predominantly achieved by its allusions to the famous portraits of Queen Elizabeth I; in most other respects, the film shows 'scant respect for actuality'.[18] Similarly, although *Titanic* glories in the perfect 'patina' of its objects, and its 'museum imagination', from the minutiae of the china to the liner itself—such that it has been said to resemble a 1930s Cunard poster— its realism is surface deep.[19] Indeed, critics have compared the blockbuster's minute attention to superficial detail, plus the stupefaction-inducing *scale* of the film, to a formula directly dating back to the large-scale nineteenth century history academic painting.[20]

The post-heritage film is not only 'spectacular'; it is also 'artful' in a highly self-regarding manner. *Titanic* contains manifold allusions to 'making pictures', both in fine art and cinematic terms. These are implicit in Jack's occupation as an artist and his sepia drawings of Rose wearing the Heart of the Ocean neck-lace. Hockley's collection of paintings, including those by Picasso, strikes an anachronistic chord within the Edwardian encoded *mise-en-scène*. The collective sense they engender, of experiencing the shock of the new from the wrong end of history, alerts us to the film's own status as a time-specific, cultural arte-fact. *Titanic*'s sheer scale in terms of the construction of the ship and budget has also been seen as part of its blockbuster appeal, used as a marketing tool in ancillary media which promoted claims for the film as the most expensive ever made, whilst hinting that, like its real-life referent, it too might sink before it had begun.[21] There is no doubt that the hype surrounding the film was highly successful. *Titanic*'s enormous appeal however goes beyond its box office block-buster allure, to a more *symbolic* reality. As American critics have noted about the framing story centred on the diamond, rather than being a waste of time, it is a metaphor for the film itself:

At first a symbol of commercial profit, the diamond becomes an image of the place the past occupies in the present, as memory and as inspiration. That's the same ennobling route that *Titanic* takes as it leaves the port of enterprise and arrives on the far shore of art.[22]

It is the framing story that ensures the audience experience is different in *Titanic* to that of a conventional Hollywood or heritage film because of the way in which its double diegesis creates not only two, but arguably three time-scapes: the present where we, the viewers, are both witness to the events and fellow travellers on a voyage of self-discovery; the period in which the *Titanic* story takes place and finally, a trans-historical, symbolic time, that relates to the earliest form of the romance, from the *Roman de la Rose*, through the

Arthurian legends and the nineteenth-century Waverley Novels by Sir Walter Scott. It is in this sense, of *Titanic* in its incarnation of an older form of the romance, whose relevance has to do with the narrative's symbolic axis, that this chapter further proceeds. Bakhtin's work on the presence of certain chronotopes in chivalric romance includes the important analysis of new hybridised versions of Greek epics alongside a newly introduced 'adventure' or journey 'chronotope'.[23]

In order to contextualise *Titanic*'s relationship to the romance in more recent generic terms, it is worth recalling the 'archetypal' categories John Cawelti constructs: 'Adventure, Romance, Mystery, Melodrama, Alien Beings/ States'. *Titanic* certainly embodies 'Adventure' and 'Romance', both these being further regarded by Cawelti as the most influential ur-genres; that is, the basic paradigms that inform all generic creation.[24] As he notes further, in the adventure story the central fantasy is that of the individual hero or group overcoming obstacles and dangers and accomplishing some important and moral mission. For example, in nineteenth-century literature the adventure archetype was popularly fulfilled by the 'knightly adventure', which consisted of the quest for the Holy Grail. But it is with the even earlier *Roman* that *Titanic* displays close affinities.

The *Roman* narrative centred upon a form of knightly love whose trajectory was part of young man's rite of passage into the world, as expressed in Guillaume de Lorris's translation of the *Roman de la Rose*, and its continuation by Jean de Meung. In medieval literature, the quest of the male knight for the rose—the allegorical emblem of devotional and sexual love—forms the basis of his courtly rite of passage.[25] It is important to point out that it was not the rose itself but its chimerical image reflected in crystal, at the bottom of a well, that represented the ultimate prize.

In these terms at least, Rose's name is significant, as is the Heart of the Ocean diamond. The two become inextricably intertwined within the symbolic diegesis of the film, as is the quest, Rose's personal quest to be free, Lovett's treasure hunt, and the over-arching narrative of the maiden voyage. There are also similarities between the novelistic discourse of *Titanic* and that of the *Roman*. In explaining the magically comfortable existence of the itinerant chivalric knight as arising out of the symbolic time of chivalric romance—which operates in contradistinction to the 'real time' of the Greek romance—Bakhtin explains that:

In this world the hero is 'at home' (although he is not in his homeland); he is every bit as miraculous as his world. His lineage is miraculous, as are the conditions of his birth, his childhood and youth, his physique and so forth. He is flesh of the flesh and bone of the bone of this miraculous world, its best representative.[26]

Jack indeed seems to spring from nowhere within the enacted *Titanic* narrative as Rose's youthful saviour. As the elderly Rose explains to Lovett and his team in her rhetorical address to camera, 'he saved me in every conceivable way that a person can be saved'. When the two lovers face death together in the water, Jack predicts to Rose that, 'you're gonna go on . . . and you're gonna die an old, old lady warm in her bed . . .'.

Travelling light in every sense, as Jack himself states within the main story, he has 'everything I need right with me . . . I figure you'll never know what hand you'll get dealt next.' Associated with the positive side of the egalitarian American Dream, Jack is a gambler, having embarked on the voyage (of life) with a lottery ticket.[27] In his privileged role as bohemian artist, in social terms, Jack is all licensed: he can 'pass' for class. As Cal further determines, during his reward dinner in the first-class restaurant, Jack is 'almost a gentleman'. But Jack also knows his place. Whereas Hockley seeks to bribe his way to safety when class barriers break down, as the water sluices into the ship—acquiring a child in order to gain a place on a life-boat—Jack honours the unwritten gentlemanly edict that allows women and children to go first. Such heroic qualities accord with the codes both of the 'parfit gentil knight' whose latter-day status as heartthrob teen idol runs congruent to his earlier incarnation.[28]

Bakhtin claims that the temporality of the miraculous world of the *Roman* is achieved by a 'subjective playing with time'. This in turn 'has a corresponding playing with space, in which elementary spatial relationships and perspectives are violated'.[29] Although this essay has addressed the implications of the framing narrative in temporal terms, it has not yet noted the way in which *Titanic*'s emotional and ideological registers are articulated through a continuous visual dynamic of macro/micro relationships, and of ascent and descent. In terms of the former, Vivian Sobchak sets the diminutive Heart of the Ocean necklace against the immensity of the ship as part of a system of reversibility and reconciliation, whereby the large image of the ship is juxtaposed with the miniature jewel, small enough to be slipped into a pocket.[30] Just as the *Roman* 'provides a model for the primarily non-allegorical use of myth in a new, allegorical framework, that of the dream vision of love', so too *Titanic* may arguably be seen to produce in the daydreaming viewer a 'consciousness of enlargement'.[31]

The dialectics of space and material objects form an integral part of the medieval and poetic imagination, epitomised by courtly practices such as the painting of miniatures, the keeping of lockets, and the creation of garden mazes. All imply a 'secret', and in the latter, a journey and quest, motifs which, as we have seen, are similarly reworked in *Titanic*. The dynamic of ascent and descent is noticeable from the beginning of the film, when the camera depicts the ship-space in tune with an imperial hierarchy: migrant lower classes at the bottom, American first-class cabins at the top and amongst them the distinction between new money versus old. Extra signification is communicated by the light at the top of the ship, cascading through the upper decks and reflected in the fabulous chandeliers, glass and cutlery of the first-class dining hall. Metaphors of class are spatially mapped onto the eating order of the first-class restaurant. On being flummoxed by the order of the cutlery, the good-hearted Molly Brown tells Jack 'start out and work in'. By contrast, steerage is dark, the place of more bodily functions, signified by wild dancing and sexual energy, symbolised by Rose and Jack's making out in the back-seat of Cal's motorcar.

After surviving the disaster, Rose is shown arriving at the docks of America looking up at the Statue of Liberty, whose symbolic value as a gift from France, the birthplace of republicanism, can hardly be lost upon the film. Rose's triumphant personal *Bildungsroman* is that she eschews the notion of inherited wealth for an independent life and by the end of the film, we know that she has come through, without recourse to inherited money or gifts (the precious Heart of the Ocean jewel) having worked her way up from the bottom. In narrative terms, those at the top of the hierarchy are not spared. Hockley lacks both intellectual substance (despite the art collection) and emotional intelligence (real 'heart', not diamonds). We later hear of his subsequent descent into despair and suicide.

Titanic's combination of realism with symbolism and allegory, is finally exemplified by the ascent up the staircase in Rose's 'vision', just before she dies, where protagonists and antagonists unite in a tableau. This same functions as a standing ovation: *we* are the ones responsible for her (our) survival, and her (our) on-going refusal to capitulate to any form of subordination. From this perspective, the scene can no longer be pronounced, as some critics have done, as 'dangerous' because of its 'levelling' fantasy; it is rather part of the film's utopian 'vision', rendering an ideological analysis, inappropriate.[32] In a superb moment of disavowal shared only with the audience, we watch aghast as the elderly Rose throws the precious Heart of the Ocean diamond back into the ocean. Now she is free to die, as Jack has promised her, in a warm bed, at peace with herself and the world, thereby bringing the narrative to an end. As the screen fades to white, Peter Krämer argues that, 'by sharing in Rose's transition from dream to death, the film audience dissolves its connection with her and begins to awaken from the dream of the to the reality of the film theatre and the blank screen in front of it'.[33]

In conclusion, what Bakhtin finds exceptional about the *Roman* seems to fit perfectly with what the audience takes away from the experience of watching *Titanic*:

What is most remarkable in these works is the fact that . . . there lies at their heart an acute feeling for the epoch's contradictions, long overdue; this is in essence, a feeling for the end of an epoch. From this springs that striving toward as full as possible an exposition of all the contradictory multiplicity of the epoch. [34]

The statement's congruence with Bhabha's pronouncement about the state of culture in general today, helps to prove that powerful iconographies do not disappear but remain submerged, to reappear any time. In their collective imagining of an interstitial, or threshold space, rites of passage films such as *Titanic* grant us permission to grieve or mourn the 'passing away of a former world', alongside our more apocalyptic fears that we too may not survive the voyage. Nonetheless, we know that, like Rose, we too must go on.[35]

In summary, it is evident that *Titanic*'s success has to do with the way in which Cameron has utilised an innovative format and modes of narrative address for the feature film whilst at the same time drawing, either consciously or unconsciously, upon timeless, epic traditions, including the *Roman*. From this perspective, Cameron's revisionist take on history may be seen as a rein-terpretation of the traditional adventure-romance, aided and abetted by a rad-ical new mode of digital transmission. This liberates the director, just as the camera freed the artist during the nineteenth century, from the necessity of reproducing 'documentary authenticity'. The post-heritage rites of passage film allows its audience to dream of possible worlds, divesting them of anxieties produced by 'facts', such as the knowledge that over a thousand people were drowned. Instead, we take comfort from the fact that one good soul was saved, and in far more ways than one. In this sense at least, *Titanic*, the blockbuster film, has to be the ultimate Romance.

My thanks to Mary Ellen, with whom I originally collaborated on this project and which we hope one day to extend.

Notes

1 All these views are to be found in Kevin S. Sandler and Gaylyn Studlar (eds.), *Titanic: Anatomy of a Blockbuster* (New Brunswick, New Jersey, London, 1999).

2 See Peter Krämer's 'Women First: *Titanic*, Action-Adventure films, and Hollywood's Female Audience', in which he analyses the way in which the framing story takes up the first twenty minutes and the last seven minutes of the film and is also present in the main body of the film (its love and action parts) through the voice-over and several inserts. See Krämer in Sandler and Studlar, *Titanic*.

3 See Julian Stringer, '"The China Had Never Been Used!"': On the Patina of Perfect Images in *Titanic*' in Sandler and Studlar, *Titanic*, pp. 205–219 and *Titanic* is mentioned in connection with heritage films by Andrew Higson in *English Heritage, English Cinema: Costume Drama Since 1980* (Oxford 2003), pp. 11, 260.

4 Homi Bhabha, *The Location of Culture* (London and New York, 1994), p. 1.

5 Mikhail Bakhtin, *The Dialogic Imagination: Four Essays*, ed. Michael Holquist (Austin, 1981).

6 See Paul Gilroy, *The Black Atlantic: Modernity and Double Consciousness*, (London, 1993), pp. 17–18.

7 Graham Huggan 'Is the (Gunter) Grass Greener On the Other Side?: Oscar and Lucinda in the New World', in *World Literatures in English*, vol. 30, no. 1, 1990, p. 5.

8 Peter Krämer, 'Women First', p. 119.

9 For an excellent new discussion on these see T. Muraleedharan's 'Imperial migrations: Reading the Raj cinema of the 1980s' in Claire Monk and Amy Sargeant (eds.), *British Historical Cinema*, (London, 2002), pp. 144–62.

10 Gilroy, *The Black Atlantic*, p. 18.

11 M. Hirst, *The Script of Elizabeth*, (London, 1998), p. 7 cited in Kara McKechnie, 'Taking liberties with the monarch', in Monk and Sargeant, *British Historical Cinema*, p. 232.

12 Charles Barr coined the term 'heritage' with reference to British films of the 1940s which drew upon aspects of the 'national heritage', including *This England* (1941) and *A Canterbury Tale* (1944). See 'Introduction: Amnesia and Schizophrenia' in Charles Barr (ed.), *All Our Yesterdays: 90 Years of British Cinema*, (London, 1986), pp. 1–30.

13 Andrew Higson, *Waving the Flag: Constructing a National Cinema in Britain* (Oxford, 1995), p. 53.

14 Stringer, '"The China Had Never Been Used!"', p. 206.

15 Claire Monk, 'The British heritage debate revisited', in Monk and Sargeant, *British Historical Cinema*, pp. 176–198.

16 Monk relates the turn away from 1990s Higsonian heritage discourse to the demise of Thatcherism and the altered ideological conditions promoted by New Labour. See Monk in *British Historical Cinema*.

17 John Corner describes the crucial difference between spoken and enacted forms of address in *Critical Ideas in Television Studies*, (Oxford, 1999), p. 48.

18 Moya Luckett, 'Image and nation in 1990s British cinema', in Robert Murphy (ed.), *British Cinema in the 90s*, (London, 2000), p. 90, cited in Kara McKechnie, 'Taking Liberties with the monarch', in Monk and Sargeant, *British Historical Cinema*, p. 230.

19 For a discussion on *Titanic*'s prosthetic realism see Stringer's '"The China Had Never Been Used!"', pp. 205–199.

20 This similarly featured a prosthetic rather than referential realism. For a discussion about *Titanic*'s blockbuster status, see Alexandra Keller, 'Size Does Matter: Notes on *Titanic* and James Cameron as Blockbuster Auteur', in Sandler and Studlar, *Titanic*, p. 147.

21 Justin Wyatt and Katherine Vlesmas, 'The Drama of Recoupment: On the Mass Media Negotiation of *Titanic*', in Sandler and Studlar, *Titanic*, p. 34.

22 *The New York Times* cited by Matthew Bernstein in '"Floating Triumphantly": American Critics on *Titanic*' in Sandler and Studlar, *Titanic*, p. 17.

23 Bakhtin's notion of the chronotope, translates literally as 'time-space', a term borrowed from Einstein's theory of relativity.

24 John Cawelti, *Adventure, Mystery and Romance*, (Chicago and London, 1976), p. 39.

25 Bakhtin, *The Dialogic Imagination*, p. 156.

26 Bakhtin, *The Dialogic Imagination*, p. 154.

27 The OED significantly describes a Jack as 'a man of the common people, a lad, fellow or chap, especially a low-bred or ill-mannered fellow . . . a knave'.

28 See Melanie Nash and Martti Lahti, '"Almost Ashamed to Say I Am One of Those Girls": *Titanic*, Leonardo DiCaprio, and the Paradoxes of Girls' Fandom', in Sandler and Studlar, *Titanic*, pp. 64–88.

29 Bakhtin, 'Forms of time and chronotope in the novel', *The Dialogic Imagination*, p. 155.

30 Vivian Sobchack, 'Bathos and Bathysphere: On Submersion, Longing, and History in *Titanic*' in Sandler and Studlar, *Titanic*, p. 196.

31 Renate Blumenfeld-Kosinski, *Reading Myth: Classical Mythology and its Interpretations in Medieval French Literature*, (Stanford, 1997), pp. 51, 197.

32 As argued by Laurie Ouellette in 'Ship of Dreams: Cross-Class Romance and the Cutural Fantasy of *Titanic*' in Sandler and Studlar, *Titanic*, p. 185.

33 See Peter Krämer 'Women First', p. 122.

34 Bakhtin, *The Dialogic Imagination*, p. 156.

35 Diane Negra discusses the concept of survival and *Titanic* in her chapter 'Survivalism and the Millennial Myth' in Sandler and Studlar, *Titanic*, p. 227.

CHAPTER SEVENTEEN

Titanic: Whiteness on the High Seas of Meaning

SEAN REDMOND

JAMES CAMERON's *Titanic* (1997) is a cultural text that succinctly and power-fully captures the often unstable and contradictory nature of 'whiteness'.[1] My argument in this chapter is that in *Titanic* whiteness is made 'invisible', and displaced by issues of social class, national identity and gender. This displace-ment is in part given embodiment in the character of Rose (Kate Winslet) whose whiteness is hidden behind a melodramatic plot line and tokenistic lib-eral and quasi-feminist attributes and motivations. At the same time, whiteness in *Titanic* serves the narrative, and thus is also explicitly visible, in fuelling con-tradictory and competing forms of whiteness and non-whiteness.

Titanic conjures up a negative and self-destructive version of whiteness through the character of Cal (Billy Zane). According to the ideology of the film, this is made manifest through his exaggerated and mistaken higher ideals, superciliousness, 'imperialist' manner, and cold and calculating reasoning in his pursuit of Rose. In this instance then, Cal's whiteness is marked out as ide-ologically excessive. Cal's negative, English-inflected and bourgeois, version of whiteness is set-up in binary opposition to Rose's 'invisible' but nonetheless modern, American-inflected liberal whiteness, and to bohemian Jack's all-inclusive form of 'Otherness'. Cal's destructive tendency is explicitly placed in a framework of more desirable 'ethnic' oppositions, and oppositions that also directly reference his whiteness as the source of all narrative and ideological problems. In this dynamic, Cal's whiteness is shown to be a destructive, death-like force. Rose, by contrast, embodies an invisible form of whiteness that is hidden behind democratic values of independence and inclusiveness. Rose is presented as a bourgeois liberal who while recognising and articulating the failings of an English imperialist past in the film does so from the vantage point of an empowerment based on a white, American, and 'democratic' subject position.

Titanic feels very much like an English bourgeois heritage film set at sea, with the financial backing of a Hollywood corporation (20th Century Fox) to over-produce the awe and wonder of heritage spectacle, and to mix in Holly-wood stars with 'authentic' (heritage) British actors. As with the bourgeois heritage film[2] *Titanic* is predominately concerned with the lives and lived spaces of the upper classes. Much of the melodrama of the film takes place in the living quarters, decks, restaurants and smoking rooms of the first-class passengers, particularly around Rose, Cal, and Rose's mother Ruth. However, even when the action takes place in steerage, the steerage is so lovingly reproduced that it too becomes commodified, 'heritage-like' because of its sanitisation. Poverty and exclusion are heavily romanticised in the film: another positively valorised binary opposition to the brutal English whiteness found in first-class.

The film also works as a 'faithful adaptation', like so many heritage films. But here the 'translation' is not from some supposed great literary source but a translation from real history into historical 'authenticity'. A heritage cult of authenticity marks this film out through its painstaking, faithful reconstruction of the interior and exterior of the ship, to the very details of the clothes, to the retelling of supposedly true moments that did take place the night the ship sunk (like the story that the quintessentially English musicians played on until the very end). *Titanic* is part costume melodrama but also two parts postmodern pastiche. What is recaptured in the heritage-like setting of *Titanic* is not some authentic, accurate, informed sense of the past but the surface level reproduction of a commodity fetish.

The film works through or with an excessive spectacle display of 'authentic' settings so that it becomes a heritage-foregrounded narrative.[3] However, unlike a number of land-locked heritage films that return us again and again to the country house, the recurring motif of this film is the awesome sight of the ship and the grandiose interior that leads to the restaurant (twisting balcony, colossal chandeliers, and the antique Grandfather clock that keeps time so accurately—Rose herself returns us to this interior in the final death/dream sequence at the end of the film). When the camera roams in the film, which it frequently does, through Rose's point of view, and omnipresently, it captures oak and marble and glass, china crockery, all manner of finery, silver cutlery, and the fetishised lines and curves of the graceful ship as it soars through the waves.

When Jack lifts Rose up and forward in that now iconic moment from the film, so that they both appear to hover over the front of the ship as it cuts through the water, the camera arcs the vessel and the two young lovers, admiring and capturing in equal significance this richly-charged romance and the 'ship of dreams'. In these moments the narrative pauses, so that the breathtaking special effects and heritage settings can be admired, consumed. This particular sequence, partly because of the anthemic soundtrack, is reminiscent, in the camera's emphasis on *mise-en-scène* and choreography, of a number in a Classical Hollywood musical.

In terms of narrative and characterisation, the film works through the heritage dilemma of class and gender conflict.[4] From the very beginning we are asked to see Cal and Rose's mother Ruth as cold and heartless: we find out very quickly that Cal is only looking for a trophy wife and that there is no love in him (only economic greed), and only death in the mother. The conversations, pastimes, pomposity and arrogance of the English in the film is explicitly ridiculed (the oft repeated claim that the ship is unsinkable as it speeds to its demise is a case in point), and challenged not least by the main protagonist Jack (the Irish-American artist). When the English men go to the smoking room to talk politics and state affairs, Jack dances the jig and the night away in steerage with Rose beside herself with pleasure.

Rose, classically, is being 'suffocated' by all this (we literally see her trying to catch her breath as the panic of what she may become—like her mother—overtakes her). She is repressed by this ossifying class position and is desperately looking for a way out of this 'slave ship', and a slave marriage of convenience. Impressionist Art is one way she consoles herself, but it is the daring, and social levelling antics of Jack which offer her something 'Other' to this bourgeois Englishness. Just as Lucy rejects the excessively bourgeois Cecil for the bohemian Clive in *A Room With A View* (1985), in *Titanic* Rose rejects Cal for Jack. In both films a liberal critique of class privilege, excessive morality codes, and trophy wives is played out. *Titanic*, of course, does it through an American ideological framework of contrasting the United States and Europe: it is 'Old England' which is class-bound and patriarchal, which puts minorities and the working class into steerage, which built the class-bound, death ship, and which nurtured an exclusive type of whiteness. By contrast it is 'New America' (which Jack personifies and Rose desires), which the ship is sailing towards, which transgresses and equalises class positions. It is of course also in America that the film *Titanic* has been produced (and created the personality cult of Cameron); and an American expedition team photographed the wreck Titanic. Near the end of the film, having been saved from drowning, we see Rose standing in the pouring rain beneath the Statue of Liberty—we know now, under this mythic sign, she will lead a new life of opportunity.

But if *Titanic* is a pastiche of the English bourgeois heritage picture, then its heritage is not only understood by reference to national identity, or social class, or sexuality, or gender, but also through its associations with whiteness:

> . . . bourgeois whiteness came to provide the category's hegemonic meaning, symbolising a wide, and highly aspirational, set of social ideals; a synonym for a healthy and vigorous civilisation and also, by extension, for ambitious and expansionist capitalism.[5]

What both binds and distinguishes all the people on Titanic is their white, whitish skin (there is not one black person on board). Those with the bluest of blood occupy first-class (coincidentally, the lighting of Rose has often an expressionist blue hue). The exceptions to this are the positively connoted 'white

trash' Margaret 'Molly' Brown, the embodiment of a classless America and of
a philosophy of social mobility that underpins this film, and, ironically, Cal's
dark physical appearance works to support the film's ideological framework by
continuing a popular American cinematic history of evil upper-class 'English'
men being equated with darkness. By contrast, those of a different ethnic
appearance take position in steerage, and those who stoke the fires that fuel
the ship, are the darkest of all. Thus ethnic appearance (and the symbolic
reproduction of high and low spatial metaphors through steerage and first
class), codes the accommodation, and sets the privileges of class. Culturally
common black and white binaries are being simultaneously inverted and
maintained in the film: Cal is signified as dark and evil; Diaspora Jack is signified as pure and good. So through two parallel representational tropes whiteness is being established and contested as an identity: Cal's whiteness is dark
and deadly, Jack's whiteness represents light and promise. What moreover
binds and distinguishes all the people on Titanic is how well they act out or
embody whiteness. As previously argued, Cal embodies a specifically bourgeois whiteness in every thing that he does and says. He arrives at the port in a
chauffeur-driven car, impeccably dressed, and says to the incredulous Rose
'God could not sink this ship, Rose'. Cal 'reads' the ship as the technological
embodiment of what white bourgeois capital and creativity can achieve. On
the ship Cal has access to all quarters, all areas, and surveys the ship as if it is
his own, using his manservant to be his prying eyes. This is a trait of white
imperialist power: the exercise of surveillance, of being at home at any point
on the globe. But surveillance comes at a price if it is exercised by those who
embody these mentalities. Cal's explicit colonial behaviour is like a poison,
and the constant need to survey, to define and mark out the borders of his
power becomes a narrative trigger revealing how these borders are unstable,
under threat, and pernicious.

  Jack, by contrast, opposes this form of white identity, transgressing the rules
of courtship with Rose, transgressing the rules of table manners at dinner,
transgressing the very living spaces that separate steerage from first class, from
luggage to the burning inferno of the engine room. Jack is clearly marked as
'Other' in a number of ways. Firstly, he is Irish American (he dances the jig,
has Irish companions, plays cards, drinks Guinness, and has a stereotypical free
and easy manner). It should be noted here that the Irish have often been
encoded as simian in appearance.[6] While Jack is certainly not simian (he is in
fact the star DiCaprio, heavenly white and blonde-ish in the film) the coding at
least works to put him outside of the bourgeois whiteness that dominates in
first-class. When we are first introduced to Jack at the beginning of the film,
playing cards in a harbour bar, he says 'when you've got nothing, you've nothing to lose'. This type of aphorism is also the type of phrase ascribed to down-
and-out-blacks in American sociological studies of the 1960s (black respondent:

'I've been down so long, that down don't bother me'). Later, Jack is told by his Irish friend in steerage that it took '15,000 Irish hands to build this ship'. Jack's connection to the racial Other is further supported because he more widely embraces those ethnic groupings that occupy steerage, notably his Italian friend.

Apart from his ethnic coding as 'Irish', the second manifestation of Jack's otherness is to be found in the narrative's insistence that he can only pretend to belong to the world of bourgeois whiteness. Jack has to dress up in formal wear to pass as a gentleman at dinner. At first Cal doesn't recognise Jack in this scene, and only when re-introduced by Rose does he say 'you could almost pass for a gentleman Jack'. The irony is lost on him, but not on the audience. Thirdly, Jack is constructed as a bohemian Other: a travelling artist whose interest lies in, and with, the 'low life' of the world, specifically those Parisian prostitutes he paints. The film explicitly details Jack as a character drawn to the Dark Continent, here constructed as the mystery and threat of the sexualised woman which Rose, in part, becomes.

Finally, Jack is 'other' because of the way he is perceived as a (sexual) threat that needs to be incarcerated by the figures of power in the film. When Jack saves Rose from suicide he is handcuffed; he is escorted off first-class when he is discovered as Other; and after Jack has made love to Rose he is accused and found guilty of stealing the diamond necklace and then handcuffed, incarcerated, beaten, and left to die—depicted as just punishment for transgressing the dominant hierarchies. Perceived as immigrant Irish Other, Jack, in the eyes of the upper-class males, has thus symbolically had inter-racial sex with Rose. The greatest hyper-white taboo has been broken. As Dyer writes:

Inter-racial heterosexuality threatens the power of whiteness because it breaks the legitimisation of whiteness with reference to the white body. For all the appeal to spirit, still, if white bodies are no longer indubitably white bodies, if they can no longer guarantee their own reproduction as white, then the natural basis of their dominion is no longer credible.[7]

Cal and Jack are binary opposites, or rather opposite embodiments of particular types of whiteness. What is at stake for both of them is Rose. Cal must have possession of the 'English Rose' to anchor his identity, to give it heterosexual, monogamous normality, and to ensure his/its lineage. For Cal, Rose must be the type of radiant white woman found at one end of the continuum in Edwin Long's painting *The Babylonian Marriage Market* (1875), a woman white in skin tone and virginal in behaviour.[8] Rose is the ultimate commodity fetish.

Jack, on the other hand, wants Rose to confirm and sustain his Otherness, and to reproduce or confirm the myth that the United States is the land of freedom, hope and opportunity for all people. If Jack liberates Rose he will do so in the name of Diaspora America, and in opposition to the rigidly defined

and static hierarchies embodied by Cal, Old England, and the heritage codes
of the ship. But if Rose connotes white purity, she clearly evolves into an independent 'new woman'.

The first time we see Rose's image in the film is when the salvage team have
recovered and cleaned the naked portrait of her. The importance of this, outside of the narrative enigma and potential narrative motor that the por-
trait/Rose will represent, is that the first time we see Rose it is as a sexualised
woman on display, a woman after-the-fall of idealised, feminine whiteness. As
Dyer suggests,

> The white woman on the other hand was not supposed to have such (sexual) drives in
> the first place. She might discover that she did and this is the stuff of a great deal of
> western narrative, but this was a fall from whiteness not constitutive of it . . . The
> model for white women is the Virgin Mary, a pure vessel for reproduction who is
> unsullied by the dark drives that reproduction entails.[9]

Rose's pose in the portrait, her body positioning, the way her hair is styled,
the serene facial expression, the Impressionist painting style all recall Edouard
Manet's *Olympia* (1863). In this painting the prostitute Olympia, fetishised and
on display, is either coded as bad, as less than white, due to her implied relationship with the black woman servant who hovers in the background, or else
embraces the Other in an act of (white and heterosexual) transgression.

We can in part read Rose's portrait in much the same way: we later learn
that Rose is both attracted to Jack's ability to paint (naked women), and in
images of the prostitutes themselves ('you see people' she says enigmatically).
Rose commissions Jack to paint her but Jack constructs the model, the pose, so
that he can paint her very like the prostitutes he has painted previously. In this
portrait while there is no black servant girl to produce the association with
darkness and sex, there is the blue diamond necklace to fetishise Rose. At the
end of the sitting Rose pays Jack for his work. The sitting itself has been a business deal, a commodity exchange, a transgressive act that undermines her
womanly behaviour.

Rose is a traveller, a risk taker, an adventurer empowered to do and be
these things partly because of her status as a middle class white woman. Rose
dances wildly in steerage, knocks back Guinness, pulls Jack into the back seat
of the car to make love to him, throws the punch at the orderly, rescues Jack
from near death, and near sacrifices herself for Jack (the Other). In these
actions, the film portrays her as a white woman who has the power to oscillate
between compass points on a (post-) colonial map that she can read and command. Rose then has as much power to survey and to map out her encounters
as Cal, and this she does with real narrative and ideological determination.
When we first see a silver-haired Rose in the present, in her respectable middle
class home, full of world travel trinkets, sitting at a potter's wheel, turning clay,

we imagine a white woman who has explored the universe. This is confirmed later in the film when we see her own sepia-tinted photographs, taken during her 'lifetime of opportunity' after the sinking of the Titanic. These photographs, of her bare-back horse riding in the surf (Jack's dream for her), astride an elephant in deepest Africa, catching a whale of a fish aboard a schooner, reference her as a mobile, privileged white woman.

While the film almost immediately establishes that Rose intends to reject the privileges that first-class travel and Cal offer her (Rose delivers the following lines in the present, 'it is the ship of dreams to everyone else, to me it is a slave ship taking me back to the US in chains', as she remembers and we see her board the ship in the past), Rose is nonetheless marked out and signified as belonging to quasi-aristocratic stock—fallen on hard times—and as being pure and virginal. Her often translucent blue-white skin, her name itself, the pre-Raphaelite hair, posture, and pose, her worldly knowledge of Impressionist art and Freud, her refusal to get close to Cal locate her firmly within the ideological parameters of whiteness.

What happens on Titanic is actually Rose's own rite of passage. Rose's narrative journey of self discovery allows her to explore the heterogeneity of whiteness more fully, so that she can finally survey herself, and the world around her with mastery. What Rose (finally) comes to embody in the film is a form of contemporary white-centred 'social emollient'[10], in which gender and sexual codes have shifted to take into account the changing role of white women in society. Rose comes after two successful waves of feminism but the feminism imagined in the film is safe, sanitised, liberal—a particularly white type of feminism—and one which helps to reproduce the myth that it is in America where such social and cultural levelling has taken place.

The last shot of the film, when Rose returns to the Titanic in a dream sequence, to meet again with Jack, has every social class, every shade of white skin, every key protagonist from the film toast their reunion—everyone that is, accept Cal, Rose's Mother, and the villain manservant. The ideological values they represent have been extinguished in the present.

What therefore happens to whiteness in the film is that rather than it being replaced or over-thrown as a determining subject position, it is repositioned, (along a continuum of whiteness), repositioned to a centre that has had to acknowledge feminism, and deny the excessive class privilege in a modern world that cannot tolerate its implications first-hand. *Titanic* is a liberal film, but its liberalism masks the fact that whiteness remains, right to the end of the film, the structuring link, setting the borders.

Notes

1 Richard Dyer, *White*, (London and New York, 1997).

2 Cf. Andrew Higson, *Waving the Flag: Constructing A National Cinema in Britain* (Oxford 1995); John Hill, *British Cinema in the 1980s* (Oxford, 1999).

3 Higson, *Waving The Flag*.

4 Clare Monk, ' Sexuality and the Heritage', in *Sight and Sound*, vol. 5, no. 10 (1995), pp. 32–34.

5 Alastair Bonnett, 'How the British Working Class became White: The Symbolic Reformation of Racialised Capitalism', in *Journal of Historical Sociology*, vol. 11, no. 3 (1988), p.321.

6 Cf. Noel Ignatiev, *How the Irish Became White* (London and New York, 1995); Dyer, *White*.

7 Dyer, *White*, p. 25.

8 Sander L. Gilman, 'Black Bodies, White Bodies: Toward an Iconography of Female Sexuality in late 19th Century Art, Medicine, and Literature', *Critical Inquiry*, vol. 12, n.1, Autumn 1985.

9 Dyer, *White*, pp.28–29.

10 Robert Hewison, *The Heritage Industry: Britain in a Climate of Decline* (London, 1987).

CHAPTER EIGHTEEN

Riverdancing as the Ship Goes Down

K. J. DONNELLY

ANYONE WATCHING James Cameron's *Titanic* (1997) might think the original nautical event Irish-dominated—judging by the film's characters, its party in steerage, and the musical score's Irish edge, yet Irish people only made up some 7–8 per cent of the ship's passengers.[1] The prominent position of Irish people and culture in *Titanic* is something more than an acknowledgement of historical fact; it is structural and symbolic, which is arguably one of the principal functions of packaged 'Irishness' in the international cultural arena. Irishness certainly should be central to *Titanic*. The ship was made in Belfast (see John Hill's contribution in this volume), last put in at Cobh (Queenstown as was) and Irish people made up a proportion of steerage passengers and the crew. But instead, the Irish in the film occupy a bizarre position: firstly they constitute a colourful background, and secondly they embody a charged symbolism in the film, where dramatic (and other) concerns have obliterated representational concerns. Cameron's film keys into the international commodification of Irish culture, and in particular music, here filtered through the mythological aura surrounding the event of the Titanic's sinking.

James Cameron's *Titanic*'s mixture of representing the event and Hollywood film readymades adds a further mythological dimension to an event already saturated with mythology to the point where a clear perspective on the original event is almost impossible.[2] The film primarily aims at US audiences, audiences who are more likely to identify and empathise with the 'proletarian' passengers than with the US-WASP 'aristocracy', the latter of which seem more like the English, more 'foreign'. According to Laurie Ouellette, the film codes 'the rigid hierarchies governing the ship as rooted in European aristocratic traditions . . . [as] the un-American attitude of snobbish elites'.[3] The film's archetypal proletarians are patently Irish.

'Irishness' is often sold as a commodity and codes a number of different ideas. It is used to code the mystical, often appearing as an atavistic, lost aspect of the civilized 'self'. Its connection with mysticism is underlined by *Titanic* very auspiciously using an Irish (Catholic) priest to give the ship the last rites as it upends before its final sinking. Closely related to this idea is the notion of the primitive, which Irish characters regularly code in both British and American films. They are constantly presented as being closer to nature, as life-loving and life-affirming, as un-cultured and un-civilised, but this is not necessarily a negative and impertinent image. In *Titanic*, the party in steerage sums up these aspects of Irishness as a symbolic, linguistic device. In the case of this sequence, it also underlines the structural similarity between Irish and black characters in mainstream cinema: both continue to represent this 'primitive' notion, which is manifested in their fervour for dancing and music.[4] This form of ethnicity, constructed as a commodity and with mystical overtones, produces a specific form of 'Irishness'. In *Beyond Ethnicity*, Werner Sollors declares that modern ethnicity is defined for ethnic groups through the wielding of cultural items and artefacts.[5] Yet we should constantly question who is in control of these cultural items. While the Irish themselves have been very adept at exploiting certain images and ideas about Ireland for tourist consumption, international business interests—not least Hollywood—arguably have dominion over this global industry. Irish culture has been subject to the same process of cultural 'carpet-bagging' which has taken place with the Titanic disaster.

In recent years, advertisements for Irish beer have played upon certain images of Ireland that have international currency—in fact, it is not stretching a point to note their similarities to those evident in *Titanic*. Most beer advertisements on television sell Irishness as a musicalised, emotional and celebratory (although drawing back from a stereotypical drunken) culture. In 1998–99, an advertisement for 'Caffrey's' showed a group of men out on the town, accompanied by the strains of Anglo-Asian group Cornershop's 'Brimful of Asha'.[6] In a bar, one man then sits at the piano and plays a Celtic-style tune, which appears to bond the friends together. Oddly, this tune is a piece of film music—the main theme to the Coen brothers' *Miller's Crossing* (1990), written by American composer Carter Burwell, although based on an old Irish tune 'The Coolin'. The 'Irishness' in the advertisement is however only skin deep. Caffrey's happens to be a Northern Irish brewer, yet its publicity foregoes any reference to Ulster culture in an appeal to internationalised notions of Irishness that can be sold as easily as their beer. Beer adverts and their close relation, Irish theme pubs, are indices of how far there is conformity to an international image of 'Irishness'. Music is essential to advertisements for Irish beer and to Irish theme pubs, and as might be expected, is no less essential to the representation of the Irish in *Titanic*.

Titanic has a musical geography. It has a number of distinct time-spaces, which not only provide zones for dramatic spaces but also furnish a stratification of the passengers of the ship. There is the upper-class ambient music of the upper decks, which comprises popular music of the time, played by the mini-orchestra of a string quartet and a piano.[7] This upper-class space transforms as disaster strikes. Irish character Tommy Ryan, upon seeing and hearing the musicians play as the ship is sinking, says 'Music to drown by. Now I know I'm in first-class'. Ultimately, the quartet performs the Protestant (stoic and Calvinist, perhaps) angst music as the ship sinks, playing the hymn 'Nearer My God to Thee'. This is doubled by the Sunday service sequence, where the passengers, rather too presciently I might add, sing 'For Those in Peril on the Sea'. Elsewhere, there is the below-decks space, which neglects to represent second class, and is embodied by the 'Irish' party in steerage.[8] This is in effect a Ceili, and this music spills out of its space into the underscore when Jack and Rose run away from Cal's English henchman Lovejoy and earlier when Jack and Fabrizio run to get the ship. A further musical soundscape is provided by *Titanic*'s ubiquitous Hollywood film score, which occupies an ephemeral, heavenly space that runs parallel with, and across, these other spaces.

A focus on the use of sound and music in films offers an oblique perspective on the material, providing different insights. It highlights the modes of filmic narration and their setting of ethnic and ethical borderlines. As Michel Chion points out, 'music enjoys the status of being a little freer of barriers of time and space than other sound and visual elements'.[9] Music in films often observes a process that is not shackled by the film, that does not slavishly follow the film's construction, but has other determinants. Irish culture is regularly dealt with as being 'musicalised', with Irish folk music providing an 'essential' shorthand for Ireland and its representation (as witnessed by Irish theme pubs, and *Titanic*'s theme pub—steerage). The music regularly works as a portal, allowing entry to the misty Celtic world of dreams and desires. This is a world articulated by music, much like the world of cinema itself.

Titanic's musical score was written by James Horner. He is one of the most successful Hollywood film composers at present, and usually has a fairly identifiable style. For this score he uses a large orchestra, featured instrumental soloists, electronics and voices. Horner is known for recycling music, often his own. He recycles a theme from Khachaturian's *Gayane* ballet, most prominently in *Patriot Games* (1992) and *Aliens* (1986); while some of *Titanic*'s action music is reminiscent of the action music in *Aliens*, and it also has *Sneakers*-like (1992) crashing piano and gentle *Spitfire Grill* (1996) strings.

Horner frequently has used a Celtic/Gaelic edge to his scores. The obvious case is *The Devil's Own* (1997), a film partially about Northern Ireland that includes a song sung in Irish. His score for *Legends of the Fall* (1994) contains Celtic elements, and even uses a melody that appears in *Titanic* (and came to a wider audience as part of the Celine Dion single 'My Heart Will Go On'). Horner's music for *Braveheart* (1995) includes a melody that appears in the score for *Titanic*. The former also makes copious use of the uilleann pipes, a characteristically Irish instrument that resonates oddly with the film's Scottish setting. Horner seems to utilise Irish instrumentation and musical style as a 'universal' symbol of emotion and sentiment, despite the distinct ethnic identities of Scots and the Irish. On the other hand, film music is a language that is used by musicians, and understood directly by audiences, precisely because it can speak with certain distinctive 'accents'.

The 'Irish' musical accent is readily identifiable. It usually consists of either a 'pastoral' sound—lush strings playing strong rustic and lyrical melodies in a slow and languid manner—or fast and rhythmic jigs and reels. Instrument-ation is central. The principal instrumental sounds used are the aforemen-tioned uilleann pipes (literally 'elbow' pipes, which have a bellows controlled by the elbow), tin whistles and bodhrans (a hand-held drum that means 'deaf-ener' in Irish).[10] According to *Titanic* director Cameron, Horner 'was hearing in his mind's ear a kind of soaring and transcendent sound using human voice, perhaps accompanied by synthesised vocal textures, combined with Celtic instruments like uilleann pipes and pennywhistle to create lyrical and haunting emotionalism. This would create a timeless quality, while avoiding the classic 'period movie' sound'.[11] This is certainly no period film score. While the Irish instruments may evoke the cliché of Celtic emotionalism, and have in materi-al terms an emotional and expressively lyrical quality, their 'timeless' aspect is more difficult to discern. The instruments' appearance is also, as I have already noted, highly ethnically specific.

Horner's score for *Titanic* uses a small number of themes that repeat across the film although they are not used in any systematic manner to associate with characters or ideas in the film, at least not in the manner evident in many scores from the age of the classical Hollywood cinema. Perhaps the most func-tional theme is an evocative piano figure that cues the elderly Rose's reminis-cences of her adventures on board the Titanic. Rose has a theme for herself, which sometimes seems associated with her love for Jack. This is the melody of Celine Dion's single, 'My Heart Will Go On', which appears in its entirety across the film's end titles after having appeared at fairly consistent intervals throughout the film itself. A 'lament' theme is played on the uilleann pipes or tin whistle. It inaugurates the Celine Dion single, and is lyrical, sounding as if it might be a song and has a distinctly Irish sound. There is also a celebrative tune, which appears at moments of happy spectacle, notably when the ship sails from Southampton. The first two bars of the tune are based on the Anglo-Irish folk song of emigration, 'The Leaving of Liverpool', which sings of being 'off to California'. This song was popularised by Irish group The Dubliners, and underlines Liverpool's status as an entrepot port, especially for the Irish. Closely related to the celebrative theme is a waltz. While this may suggest the stately upper-class passengers on board the ship, it is also reminiscent of some of the work of Irish singer and musician Enya, in particular her song 'Book of Days', from the album *Shepherd Moons* (1991). Indeed, Enya's form of Celtic ambient and soundtrack music would have fitted the film well, but she de-clined an invitation from Cameron to work on the film.[12] Her music apparently was used to 'temp' part of the film's rough cut, and was used on an early trailer for *Titanic*.[13] Although Enya supplied no music for the film, the second soundtrack CD, *Back to Titanic*, included her sister, Maire Brennan, singing the song 'Come Josephine, in my Flying Machine'. Norwegian singer Sissel Kyikjebo supplies the wordless singing on the score to *Titanic*. She sounds not unlike Enya, and has connections with Irish music, having sung on the soundtrack to a 1998 television documentary about Irish immigration, called *The Irish in America: a Long Journey Home*.

Cameron's *Titanic* has reformulated the musical repertoire associated with the event and its dramatisations. The first music associated with the ship would have been the music played as the ship was sinking by the Titanic's band, namely their alleged final statement: the rendition of the hymn 'Nearer My God to Thee'.[14] In the wake of the disaster, a massive industry of popular songs flowered. The first commercial song was copyrighted ten days after the disaster, and in 1912-13 over 200 songs were published about Titanic.[15] Although most of these emerged in the USA, the UK saw in 1912 the release of the song 'Be British', which articulated Captain Smith's supposed last words, absent from Cameron's *Titanic*.

Titanic was a musical event as well as being a cinematic event. In some ways, the film's processes even make it reminiscent of classical musical films.[16] Apart from a massive hit single, Celine Dion's 'My Heart Will Go On', two soundtrack CDs were released: *Music from the Titanic* and *Back to Titanic*, later packaged as a double CD. The first sold more than any other instrumental score ever.[17] However, the film's success and subject matter stimulated the record industry and there were at least a startling 24 CD albums made available tied in some way to the film. This makes *Titanic* the film music event of the last century.[18] While a handful of the CDs included pieces of Horner's film music, and there was little in the way of Irish music, many of the CDs comprised polite period pieces for palm court orchestras, the rights to which could be acquired reasonably cheaply.

Irish music and Irish-style music is now endemic. The proliferation of Irish folk music and 'Celtic' New Age CDs testify to the persistence and international popularity of 'musicalised' Gaelic culture. Irish identity and culture have become drawn into the maelstrom of international commodity culture.[19] The record label Nature Quest's late 1990s 'New Age' CDs such as *Celtic Renaissance* and *Celtic Quest*, for example, are firmly based on Irish musical styles, Irish imagery on the covers, and a notion of Irish mysticism marketable overseas, yet with a lack of currency in the music market in Ireland itself, and probably with little hold in the Irish diaspora. The musicians are not Irish, or even trained in the traditions of Irish musical culture. What these CDs demonstrate is the reduction of Irish music, from being a vibrant culture expressive of a people, to a musical genre or language fully uncoupled from any organic cultural life. Perhaps a comparison could be Renaissance choral music, sung by agnostic students in an American university, or Delta blues performed by northern Europeans.[20] Thus Irish music becomes defined merely by its *differences* from other musical styles. Global musical communication has reified Irish musical culture, rendering parts of it invisible when they are not internationally recognisable, while promoting those stylistic aspects that have a distinctive flavour to the rank of international cliché and the absolute definition of Irishness in music.

As I have already mentioned, in *Titanic* Irish traditional music enters the underscore twice—firstly when Jack and Fabrizio run to catch the ship, and secondly when Jack and Rose run away from Cal Hockley's henchman. The fact that Irish music is being heard in the film this early establishes a connection between music and the proletarian steerage passengers. On both occasions, the music adds energy to scenes of people running. It does not match action and simply could have been 'cut into' the film, meaning that the film was cut to the pre-existing music. The music's aesthetic use cements the similarities between kinetic Irish folk music and rock music, which is used regularly in films set in the contemporary period, as an energiser. Irish music thus appears as a period version of rock music.

Indeed, the party in steerage sequence emphasises the similarities between contemporary parties with music and those of the past.[21] The beat of the Irish traditional-style music in the sequence sounds suspiciously similar to the sort of beat often encountered in rock music. The musicians who perform are Gaelic Storm, a Californian-based band, only one of whom is from Ireland. The first two shots of the sequence, both close ups, establish the instruments. The first is of the uilleann pipe player and the second is of the bodhran player. These instantly establish the 'Irishness' of the music and its 'authenticity' as a live event, which is consistently underlined by the visual track's recourse to cutting back to show the musicians at regular intervals. The two featured instruments are the two that are most closely associated with Irish folk music, despite the fact that plenty of other, more international, instruments have been more prominent in its traditions. Furthermore, the depiction of these instruments in the film arguably is anachronistic. According to Ciaran Carson, the bodhran and the uilleann pipes were both ancient instruments that had long been only marginally important in Irish folk music. Both were popularised by folk group The Chieftains in the 1960s and 1970s.[22] Interestingly, the uilleann pipes had their present version standardised in Philadelphia, USA, in the late 19th Century.[23]

There is one brief shot in the steerage party sequence that confuses and intrigues me. It is where the Irish character Tommy Ryan, who has had some delineation through having talked momentarily with Jack, sits alone and laughs uproariously. There seems to be little reason for him to laugh and it

seems somewhat laboured. Perhaps he is laughing at the spectacle being presented as an 'authentic' Irish object for international audiences? IRA-man
turned cultural commentator Eoghan Harris writes of a '*Riverdance* Rite of
Passage' in *Titanic* and some films set in Ireland.[24] He proposes that this is a
trite device aimed at the American market, suggesting that 'freedom' can
come through affiliating with Irishness and physical (and emotional) activity
such as dancing. The success of *Riverdance* has fed, fairly directly I would suggest, into the party in steerage scene in *Titanic*. The show's international status
certainly has boosted the global standing and currency of Irish music.

Riverdance, the dance and music stage show, is probably the most insistent
example of the way that Irish culture has arrived as a force in the international market. It is based upon the characteristic Irish dancing of high kicking and
rigidity of body, but with the innovation of having large-scale lines of dancers
in unison, creating an impressive spectacle. *Riverdance* made its first appearance
during the intermission of the 1994 Eurovision song contest set in Dublin. It
was a seven-minute dance show, produced by Moya Doherty, with music by
Bill Whelan, and sung by Katie McMahon from the vocal group Anuna. Its
appeal was instant providing impetus to take it further, leading to a single
being released with a shortened version of Whelan's music. Simultaneously,
the seven-minute piece was built up into a full show, which made its debut at
the Point Depot theatre in Dublin in February of 1995. The show was originally publicised as 'Bill Whelan's *Riverdance*'.[25] Fairly rapidly, Whelan's name
was less associated with *Riverdance* than that of American-born principal chore-
ographer Michael Flatley. Unhappy with restrictions set by the company,
Flatley left *Riverdance* in October 1995, and his own *Lords of the Dance* opened at
the Point Depot in Dublin in June 1996. In the summer of 1996, such was the
success and demand for *Riverdance* that it split into two companies performing
the same show, which allowed touring to the point of world domination. The
connections between *Riverdance* as an agent of Irish music internationally, and
the steerage sequence in *Titanic* is evident. To cement the film's connections
with the show, it is surely no accident that the second soundtrack CD, *Back to
Titanic*, featured Eileen Ivers who had been lead violinist on *Riverdance*.

Riverdance seems nominally Irish, but it is international and promiscuously
mixes styles. Symbols now have a life of their own, having lost contact with
their point of origin—'Irish' culture as a commodity often has little organic
connection with Ireland, or even the Irish diaspora, and often is consumed
entirely outside both. According to Jonathan Rutherford, 'capital has fallen in
love with difference . . . From World Music to exotic holidays in Third-World
locations, ethnic TV-dinners to Peruvian knitted hats, cultural difference *sells*.
. . . In the commodification of language and culture, objects and images are
torn free of their original referents and their meanings become a spectacle
open to almost infinite translation. Difference ceases to threaten, or to signify

power relations'.[26] But, in this case, I have to disagree. Irishness can be sold as a packaged subaltern culture, as in *Titanic*.[27] Yet Celticism is offered as an 'alternative' heritage, especially in England but also internationally, having only an arguable threat to power relations, but definitely signifying power relations through making what it present as a vanquished and subaltern culture a fashionable consumer choice.[28]

Titanic's 'Irishness' works as a signifier of difference, and precisely as a signifier of power relations, enhanced by its mystical overtones. Dramatic concerns obliterate representational concerns. As John Wilson Foster notes, 'nowadays the reality of death and disaster . . . ceases to be reality and is merely a set of images (trite or frantically fresh) to be exhibited, bought and sold, history evacuated of its human content for material gain or the prurience of low-intensity imagination'.[29] The film's Irish-inspired music marks a spectral presence, one that charms the audience. The disaster is abhorrent and music acts as a talisman against the bane and terror.

Sometimes, in the combining and recombining and the purchase and re-purchase of these compound commodities that are contemporary mainstream films, we do not really notice or acknowledge what we are consuming. *Titanic* sells us the disaster and mass death of the original event, and among other things, sells us 'Irish culture' too. The musical aspect is crucial: like *Riverdance*'s 'dance of life', the talismanic music in the film helps us to forget, accept or perhaps even to fetishise death, allowing us to consume the product all the better.

Notes

1 Senan Molony, *The Irish Aboard the Titanic* (Belfast, 2000).

2 John Wilson Foster, *The Titanic Complex* (Vancouver, 1997), pp. 13–14.

3 Laurie Ouellette, 'Ship of Dreams: Cross-Class Romance and the Cultural Fantasy of *Titanic*', in Kevin S. Sandler and Gaylyn Studlar, eds., *Titanic: Anatomy of a Blockbuster* (New Brunswick and New Jersey, 1999), p. 175.

4 The equivalence of Irish and blacks in the eyes of racial 'superiors' is described in Noel Ignatiev, *How the Irish Became White* (London and New York 1995); also see Richard Ned Lebow, *White Britain and Black Ireland: The Influence of Stereotypes on Cultural Policy* (Philadelphia, 1976).

5 Werner Sollors, *Beyond Ethnicity: Consent and Descent in American Culture* (Oxford, 1986), p. 116.

6 A previous Caffrey's advertisement used the song 'Jump Around' by House of Pain, an American group who trade on an Irish image.

7 The quintet is played in the film by 'I Salonisti', although the ship also had the Café Parisien's trio, who fail to make an appearance in the film.

8 On the *Back to Titanic* CD, the musical cue is called 'An Irish Party in Third Class'.

9 Michel Chion, *Audio-Vision: Sound on Screen* (edited and translated by Claudia Gorbman) (New York, 1990), p. 81.

10 Ciaran Carson, *Irish Traditional Music* (Belfast, 1999), p. 37.

11 Quoted on *Back to Titanic* CD sleeve notes.

12 Paula Parisi, *Titanic and the Making of James Cameron: The Inside Story of the Three-Year Adventure that Rewrote Motion Picture History* (London, 1998), p. 164.

13 Jeff Smith, 'Selling My Heart: Music and Cross-Promotion in *Titanic*' in Sandler and Studlar, *Titanic*, p. 56; Parisi, *Titanic and the Making of James Cameron*, pp. 164–5.

14 Interestingly, there are strong claims that other pieces of music were the last to be played. Ian Whitcomb claims that 'Songe d'Automne', a waltz written by Archibald Joyce was the final number (*Titanic: Music as Heard on the Fateful Voyage* CD sleeve notes), while Gavin Bryars noted that survivors confusingly remembered it to be the tune 'Aughton' and the episcopal hymn 'Autumn' (*The Sinking of the Titanic* Obscure Records LP sleeve notes). Richard Howells notes that earlier film versions of the Titanic disaster used different musical versions of 'Nearer My God to Thee'. 'Atlantic Crossings: Nation, Class and Identity in *Titanic* (1953) and *A Night to Remember* (1958)', in *Historical Journal of Film, Radio and Television*, vol.19, no.4, October 1999, pp. 427–8.

15 Foster, *The Titanic Complex*, p.32.

16 Indeed there was a stage musical, *Titanic—The Musical* (1997), and earlier there was a musical film, *The Unsinkable Molly Brown* (1964).

17 Smith, 'Selling My Heart' p. 47.

18 Apart from the two official soundtrack LPs already noted, there were: *The Ultimate Titanic Experience, My Heart Will Go On*, Ronan Magill's *Titanic, 10–15 April 1912: Five Pieces for Solo Piano*, (a 1998 re-recording of a 1988 piece), *Music Inspired By the Titanic and Other Hits of the Time, Titanic—Melodies from the White Star Music Book*, Ian Whitcomb and the White Star Line Orchestra's *Titanic: Music as Heard on the Fateful Voyage, Music Aboard the Titanic, Titanic Serenade: Music from an Age of Elegance, Celtic Love Collection: Songs Inspired by Titanic* (by the Countdown Orchestra), *Titanic: Music From the Era, The Ultimate Collection* (Themes from the film and the stage musical), Steve Cameron's *Titanic Suite* (written in 1988), *Spirit of the Titanic, Volume 1; Spirit of the Titanic, Volume 2, A Romantic Tribute to the Titanic* (by the New Millennium Chorus and Symphony), *Titanic & Other Movie Hits* (by the American Film Orchestra), *Joan Plays...Themes from Titanic* (by pianist Joan Matey Mallory), *Titanic Tunes: A Sing-A-Long in Steerage* (old music hall songs performed by Ian Whitcomb), *Titanic—My Heart Will Go On: Music From Titanic, Titanic Ship of Dreams, Titanic: Epic Songs of the Sea, Great Titanic* (by the Transatlantic Orchestra & Singers), and finally *Titanic* (by the Movie Sounds Unlimited Orchestra).

19 The plethora of New Age CDs playing upon 'Celticism' include albums such as *Celtic Twilight* and *Celtic Twilight 2* on Hearts of Space records, and the titles *Celtic Echoes, Celtic Spirit, Celtic Renaissance, Celtic Journey* and *Celtic Abbey* on Global Journey records in 1999.

20 To underline this, the uilleann pipes on the film's soundtrack were played by piper of international renown Eric Rigler, an American who once lived for a period in Scotland.

21 Particularly in comparison with *A Night to Remember*'s (1958) sedate Irish songs in steerage.

22 Carson, *Irish Traditional Music*, pp. 17, 37.

23 Carson, *Irish Traditional Music*, p. 13.

24 Eoghan Harris, 'Why Truth has been on the Ropes', in *The Sunday Times*, Section 11 ('Culture'), 1 February 1998, p. 3.

25 Whelan, the composer of the show's music, has also has written film music, including *Some Mother's Son* (1996) and *Dancing at Lughnasa* (1998).

26 Jonathan Rutherford, 'A Place Called Home: Identity and the Cultural Politics of Difference', in Jonathan Rutherford, ed., *Identity: Community. Culture, Difference* (London, 1990), p. 11.

27 Similarly, black culture regularly is packaged in this way for consumption, usually by and for middle-class whites.

28 Amy Hale and Philip Payton note the Celtic can represent a 'moral other'. 'Introduction', in Amy Hale and Philip Payton, eds., *New Directions in Celtic Studies* (Exeter, 2000), p. 6.

29 Foster, *The Titanic Complex*, pp. 13–14.

CHAPTER NINETEEN

The Technical Challenge of Emotional Realism and James Cameron's *Titanic*

MARK J. P. WOLF

TRADITIONALLY, discussions of emotional realism in motion pictures have focused mainly on acting and story, as well as such things as lighting and music and their influence on mood. Yet ever since the 'Kuleshov effect' was discovered, it has been clear that emotional realism is dependent on many factors. The emotional content of a scene, or what is perceived to be the content, then, depends on acting but also lighting, sound, editing, and so on.

Today, in the age of big-budget digital filmmaking, emotional realism is being enhanced and even produced through technical means, and James Cameron's film *Titanic* (1997) is an excellent example. Rising budgets and special effects technology have given directors even greater control over their images and have advanced what is possible in filmmaking. In a growing number of films, special effects play a large role in creating emotional realism, particularly in the area of *invisible effects*. While the use of special effects is obvious in films like *Star Wars* (1977) or *Jurassic Park* (1993), they are used in a less conspicuous manner in films like *Citizen Kane* (1941), *The Sweet Hereafter* (1997), or *Kundun* (1997). Instead of representing fantastic or unrealistic objects and events, special effects in these films are used to enhance the realism of the film, by allowing images to depict things that could actually happen (or have happened) but are too expensive, too difficult, or too dangerous to recreate completely. These effects are known as *invisible effects*, and often the goal of the effects artist is to integrate them so smoothly into the scene that the audience will not even be aware that effects work is present. Through the computer, physical or practical effects can be seamlessly interwoven with digital effects. *Titanic* uses physical and digital effects invisibly as a means of heightening and bolstering the emotional realism of the film, a technical challenge as well as an artistic one.

Overall, various technical factors contribute to *Titanic*'s emotional realism during preproduction, production, and postproduction, as well as in the discourse surrounding the film. First, there is the script; while the presence of stars like DiCaprio and Winslet certainly helped, much of *Titanic*'s huge popularity and success can be attributed to the overall experience it created for its viewers. The script, which attempts to be historically accurate and to thread the structure of its unfolding action over the short four-day period of the ship's voyage, is something of a technical challenge in itself. Critics have decried the lack of depth in some of the characterisations, but often without noting the three rounds of cuts before the film was given the go-ahead by the studio, and several rounds of cuts afterwards during which Cameron had to cut 'roughly eighty digital effects shots' and 'about thirty scenes or pieces of scenes' from the script for budgetary reasons.[1] Many of these scenes developed the characters further, including minor characters such as Fabrizio and his girlfriend. Yet despite these deletions, and dialogue that is occasionally corny, the film had a great emotional impact on audiences, due in large part to its visual effects, perhaps more so than the acting of the film's leads.

In many films, special effects detract from emotional realism. Poor quality effects render serious scenes laughable, reminding viewers of the artificiality of what they are seeing. Or, in films like *Jumanji* (1995) or *Independence Day* (1996), effects become so central that the film is little more than a showcase for them. *Titanic*, however, places special effects in service to the story, and to the recreation of historical events. If the ship was merely fictional, there would be no link to a real-life tragedy, and less emotional reaction. One technical challenge, then, is the construction of a story giving the audience the best access to the events and experience of the ship's sinking, integrating and accommodating the many well-known facts within it. The script, written by Cameron, is structured around the historical events surrounding the *Titanic*, and in many ways the ship is itself the main character, a historically real, tragic character whose story becomes a cautionary tale (even within the film, the ship is often personified). Like *Gandhi* (1982), *Amadeus* (1984), and other historical, biographical epics, the story begins after the title character's death, and the character's life is told in flashback. On board the Keldysh, the elderly Rose is shown a computer simulation of Titanic's sinking, giving the audience the technical overview of the sinking and getting it out of the way before the emotional one is recounted in depth. Having the ship as a central character, then, means emotional realism will require technical expertise and direction.

In *Titanic*, the usual roles of foreground and background story are reversed; Cameron wanted first and foremost to do a story about the ship and its sinking, writing in his early notes for the film, 'Needs a mystery or driving plot element woven through with this as background'.[2] The ship's few days at sea and its sinking—historical events which normally provide the background are here the main story of the film; while the story about Jack and Rose, ostensibly the foreground story, is only a fictionalised entry point for the audience to enter into the larger story of the ship. The Jack/Rose story is woven through the known events of the sinking of the ship so as to include all the points of action as they happen, as well as other experiences of both classes of the journey; we follow Jack and Rose through a first-class dinner *and* a steerage dance, Rose is present when one of the iceberg warnings arrives, both are on deck when the iceberg hits, and they manage to stay just a little ahead of the water as it rises deck by deck through the ship. Jack and Rose are out on the top deck along with the first-class passengers *and* are locked below in steerage; Rose both leaves on a lifeboat *and* stays on the ship as it goes underwater; and she is later left behind in the water by the lifeboats *and* is saved by them. The overall effect is to tie the audience into the lengthy sinking sequence, the technical and emotional grand finale of the film. In some ways then, the more typical and less idiosyncratic Jack and Rose are of the classes they represent, the better they fit into the background story (though the foreground story suffers). The story also goes out of its way to introduce many minor characters from first-class, third class, and the ship's crew, bringing the background story of the sinking ship and its historical personages to the fore.

The film's script, special effects, and Cameron's deep dives to the actual Titanic wreck, all had to be aimed at finding ways to attain the emotional realism that was needed. The film's framing story, about a treasure-hunter who comes to realise the enormity of what happened to Titanic's passengers, summarises Cameron's own story and the effect he wanted the film to achieve in its audience. According to Cameron's dive diary, one night after a deep dive, 'I just sat there, and I just started to cry, thinking about the dive and everything I'd seen and experienced. That's the moment my technical guard got let down and I got kind of overwhelmed by it. Then I made myself the promise to always take the time to be there emotionally'.[3] The tone of the whole project changed: 'At that point, I realized I was approaching it wrong, and that the important thing, maybe even more important than getting the footage, was capturing the emotional significance of the ship and what happened to it, and what happened to the people on it'.[4] Whereas other Cameron films like *Aliens* (1986) and *Terminator 2* (1991) had been big, science fiction summer releases, he sensed this film was not a summer release, even though 20th Century Fox had initially wanted it to be. And so the director who had typically made technologically complex films on technical subjects set out to make a period romance, a costume drama in which technology would have to aid emotion rather than replace it, although the story's main character -the ship—was still a technological entity.

Pre-production also includes advance consideration of the publicity and marketing a film will receive. When a film of this magnitude or technical complexity is made, it is not uncommon during its early stages to begin documenting the making of the film for 'Making of' books and television programmes. The technical challenge of emotional realism, then, becomes apparent in the marketing of the film and the discourse surrounding the film. Reports of the no-expense-spared historical accuracy, elaborate physical and digital special effects work, and several books and television programmes on the making of the *Titanic* all combined to give an added dimension to viewers who might not otherwise be aware of the efforts toward accuracy and realism. Reports of cost overruns as *Titanic*'s budget went over $200 million gave a certain aura to the film, implying that the effective telling of *Titanic*'s story depended heavily on the accurate recreation of the ship and the events surrounding it. And many people no doubt went just to see what a $200 million film looked like.

Two themes dominated the discourse surrounding the making of *Titanic*: the attempt at historical accuracy, and the elaborate special effects work. Despite the fictional Jack/Rose story, the film is about an event that actually took place. Would the same exact film been as successful or powerful if the story was entirely fictional and the real Titanic never existed? The great degree to which the Titanic and the events that occurred on board were documented gave the filmmakers much of what they needed for the recreation of the voyage, and this is emphasised in reports of the film's sets and props. The book *James Cameron's Titanic* with text by Ed W. Marsh released shortly before the film's opening is rife with comparisons between the set and historical photographs, showing details of wood-carved panels and plaster mouldings in halls and staterooms, as well as furniture and such things as silverware, tea cups, candlesticks, clothes hangers, and so on. Since some these details might easily be missed by an audience watching the film, the book highlights them ahead of time, allowing the audience to remember their presence while viewing the film. Some of the historical accuracy was due to necessity in the building of the sets. For example, when it came to the wall paneling, 'it was only marginally more expensive to work with real oak than to paint plywood or plaster to look like wood'.[5] Also, for the ship's lighting fixtures:

. . . economics dictated that the ceiling sconces be molded plastic, but the high-wattage bulbs required for the photography caused them to melt and they had to be remade in glass. When a decision had to be made about the chandeliers, Cameron had [*production designer*] Lamont skip the Lucite and go directly to crystal, so they would   tinkle and tilt just so during the ship's demise.[6]

Such small details subtly nuance the look, sound, and overall emotional feel of many scenes in the film. Ironically, though, for a few viewers the attention to historical accuracy reduced emotional involvement in one of the scenes; at the film's test screening in Minneapolis, some audience members thought it was 'unrealistic' that the band continued to play on deck while the ship sank, even though it actually happened.[7]

The other theme in the discourse surrounding the film is the elaborate special effects work. Articles in *American Cinematographer*, *Digital Magic*, *Post*, as well as newspaper reports gave the film an aura of high-tech illusions and empha-sised the attention to detail within the production. Reports of accomplish-ments, predictions as to whether the effects would work, rising costs, and chaotic sets led many to question the success of the film. Curiosity alone may have attracted some viewers. The storyline of *Titanic*, like Cameron's *Termin-ator 2*, is at once a cautionary tale about an over-reliance on technology while the film itself is a marvel of technical virtuosity and often reported as such.

The production of the film was largely determined by what could be done with physical and digital effects, and at what cost. The film's title character, the ship, would be the product of partially-built life-sized sets, models of vari-ous sizes, and digital effects work. The 775-foot set of the ship had a hull only on its starboard side and was immobile, but had to be seen from all angles, sailing out of port, traversing the open sea, and sinking. In the first half of the film, the audience would have to be convinced not only of the ship's elegance and grandeur, but also the completeness of the on-screen ship as a narrative space. Thus we are given various scenes of the ship's interior; first-class, third class, various decks, dining rooms, and even scenes of the engine room, fur-naces, the wireless room, and the bridge. Elaborate fly-overs show the entire ship, displaying its length and breadth in single, unbroken shots. One such shot, involving over 200 optical or digital elements, begins with a close-up of Jack and Fabrizio standing at the end of the ship's bow and pulling back and upward as the entire ship passes through the shot, and sails into the distance, tying the small scale of the actors' faces into the large scale of the ship. The shot design, camera moves, and storyline all conspire to solidify the ship's real-ity and completeness for the viewers, to create an immersive experience for the audience.

Having established the luxury and geography of the ship, the demise of the ship in the sinking sequence is made more powerful, since the audience 'knows' the ship just as one might 'know' and feel sympathetic towards a human char-acter. The sinking sequence also contains many shots without the main (human) characters and not from their points of view, in which the ship is the central character; for example, when the iceberg cuts a gash in the ship's side, we see the jets of water shooting in. We see dishes falling from shelves, empty corridors flooding and walls splintering, tables and plates floating in the water, the watertight doors closing, and so on. Quite often we leave the Jack/Rose story momentarily and experience the destruction of the ship in various loca-tions, as if to empathise with the ship itself. In the deep dives of the framing story as well, the audience is often alone with the ship.

Just as match-dissolves are used as visual transitions between the elderly and young Rose, there are several match-dissolve transitions from the deep-ocean wreck of the ship to the new ship of 1912. The first scene in which the new ship appears opens with one of these dissolves. The same devices are used for both human characters and the ship. At the end of the film, after Rose throws the diamond into the water, the audience is once again alone with the shift, drifting through the water towards the wreck and tracking along it. And just as the denouement at the top of the staircase reunites the two main human characters, it features all the others who died, and, naturally, the ship itself restored to its former grandeur. It might also be noted that the advertising and poster for the film depicts the three main characters as well; Jack, Rose, and shown more predominantly than either of them, the ship; and even the film's clumsy tag line 'Collide with Destiny' seems better suited to the ship than the human characters.

Apart from bringing the ship to life as a central character, special effects add to other performances in the film, helping generate emotional realism by surrounding, enhancing, and even creating the performances of the actors in the film. First, physical effects often surround performances in the film. To simulate the ship's sinking, many of the interior sets were built on a system of hydraulic risers designed to lower them into a five million gallon tank of water. The actors performed as the sets filled with water, in the midst of a giant physical effect providing a moving stage for the scene's action. Temporally, shots of the live-action footage on the life-size sets are intercut with effects shots of models, bringing large and small scales together. And in many of the shots, digital effects are composited in around live-action elements. For example, in the long tracking shot of the entire ship mentioned above, a live-action element of Jack and Fabrizio was combined with a camera move over a 45-foot scale model of the ship. The camera move itself had to be done in several sections instead of a single take:

Photographed over four days under the supervision of visual effects director of photography Erik Nash, the complex move required that the one shot be divided into six separate motion-control passes. Each pass recorded a specific section of the overall shot with a small amount of overlap. Digital Domain's Carey Villegas, a compositing supervisor on Titanic, aligned the six separate passes together by hand using Inferno, compensating for any shift in the motion-control rig.

'It was the scope of the camera move', explains Nash, 'that forced us into shooting this shot in pieces. For example, the lighting required for the shot at the bow was inappropriate for the end of the shot. Hence, there are several different lighting set-ups at work throughout the shot, each one filmed with enough overlap between surrounding set-ups to allow for long and, hopefully, invisible dissolves as transitions'.[8]

After the shot was constructed, water around the ship was computer-generated, and many other computer-generated details were added separately; seagulls in the air, smoke from the smokestacks, and people walking around on the deck of the ship.

Not only were ship models used in the film, but some interiors were also models. In one scene, shortly after he learns the ship is sinking, Thomas Andrews, the ship's designer, walks through the first-class lounge where the band is playing, and is offered a drink. The walls of the set are all part of a scale model, composited in behind the live action. One does not expect a simple interior set to be a model, and so the effect remains largely invisible.

In the examples above, special effects literally surround the action, providing a stage, but special effects can be used to enhance the actors' performances as well. Besides effects makeup giving floating actors iced hair and a pale and frosted appearance, Cameron outlined the stages of hypothermia for the cast, hoping to increase the accuracy of their reactions.[9] Occasionally, the attempt to get an accurate performance can go too far; for scenes in which Rose wades through chest-deep water in the lower decks of the ship, Kate Winslet requested that cold water be used for the scene for realism's sake. Apparently it was too much, and shooting stopped until the water was heated again.[10]

For the end scenes in the freezing water, Cameron had considered refrigerating the set, but that turned out to be impractical. Growing up in Canada, Cameron knew that for a scene to appear convincingly cold, you had to see condensing breath when people spoke or breathed, an effect many films set in winter lack. Since *Titanic*'s sets were outdoors in Mexico, or indoors in stages too large to refrigerate, Cameron enhanced the actors' performances by adding clouds of cold breath digitally in postproduction into over 100 shots.[11]

Special effects enhance the image of the actor, and can help to motivate performances. Hydraulically-controlled moving sets flooding with water provided a challenge for cast and crew. An occasional mishap revealed the real dangers involved:

At first, everyone was nervous to be working with the strange gravitational dynamic of the moving set, 1.3 million pounds of heaving wood and steel. But after working there for a few hours, people were beginning to get comfortable. Then, suddenly, the set let out a heaving groan and, for no apparent reason, plunged five feet. 'Pieces started falling off the ceiling and water started rushing in, and man, I'll tell you, it got *real!*' recalls Cameron, 'from then on, everyone understood the set could sink and we could really be on the *Titanic*', said Cameron, noting, 'Nobody ever dozed through the safety briefings again'.[12]

In many flooding scenes, where actors panic and try to evade the rushing waters or are swept up by them, there was a fine line between 'acting' and simply trying to keep out of harm's way. With hundreds of lights and electrical cables, electrocution was also a very possible danger. Likewise, in scenes with tumbling lifeboats and actors clinging to tilting decks and stunt people falling off, the film's elaborate on-set physical effects helped generate performances reflecting real fears.

Special effects also help create performances in another way. In many long shots where actors are jumping or falling off the ship, running down its deck, or even walking along it in the sunlight, computer-generated people were used. Human beings are the greatest challenge to animate believably, so this was done only in long shot, where individual characters could not be scrutinised in close-up. Since the complexity of the movement of the computer-generated characters differed from scene to scene, different methods were used to animate them. Some computer-generated characters were animated by hand using a combination of photographic reference material and motion-capture data. Motion-capture is a process in which actors perform movements while wearing markers on various parts of their body such as joints and extremities. The positions of the markers are detected and recorded by a computer, providing a three-dimensional record of the movement captured. This data is then used to animate computer-generated characters, and because the motions captured are recorded in three dimensions, the computer-generated character can be depicted from any angle.

Although used extensively in the sinking sequence, motion-capture data was especially important for the scenes in which CG (computer graphics) people were walking around on the ship's decks in daylight. As digital effects supervisor Mark Lasoff explained, 'It's harder to convince somebody that a CG character looks right when they are just walking, because your eye knows what's right and what's wrong. That's different from viewing someone who is clinging onto a rail and tumbling to their death'.[13] Another difficulty with shots of characters in daylight was that they had period clothing that moved as they walked. According to Steven A. Simak:

Capturing the clothing required the use of approximately 60 markers per character, as opposed to the 24 to 30 markers used in typical motion-capture sessions. 'It was very hard work,' recalls House of Moves president Tom Tolles, 'because in regular motion capture you have a tight-fitting body suit on somebody. With clothing, you have so many markers—on, let's say, the hem of a dress—and they came become temporarily covered, or they can swish around a lot. It's more difficult to track and clean up that data'.[14]

The ability to populate *Titanic*'s decks with passengers increases the realism of the scenes, and gives the audience human characters to add to the vicarious experience. The sinking sequence is particularly made more effective when dozens of people can seen moving about the deck of the ship as it breaks in half.

Motion-capture represents one of the more recent divisions of an actor's performance into its component parts. Actors' voices are commonly used for characters in animated films, or one actor's voice might even be used with another actor's live-action body (for example, Darth Vader or Darth Maul, who are voiced by other actors). Today, the actor's performance is divided into still more component parts. Motion capture records the physical movements of a performance, and applies it to an animated figure, separating image and action. For films like *Titanic* and *Virtuosity* (1995), actors' faces are scanned, their images texture-mapped onto computer-generated heads, separating an actor's image from the rest of his or her performance. A number of films like *Lost in Space* (1998) and *Stargate* (1994) employ digital costumes, and *Titanic* has shown even a character's breath can be made and added separately.

The division of the actor's performance into component parts means that emotional realism depends on how well the various components of the performance are recorded or made and how seamlessly and believably they are combined together. Typically, performances made from component parts were found mainly in animated films and special effects films—but as digital special effects spread into all genres and simulate a wider range of things, performances assembled from component have become more common. Actors are often called upon to act without the scene's other characters or scenery around them, as well as have their image, motion, voice, and other elements manipulated or exchanged, emotional realism becomes more of a technical challenge, and a difficult one not always met successfully. In some ways, we might see this as the Kuleshov effect—emotion produced through context rather than merely content—on a much larger scale.

Unfortunately, it is easy for technical considerations to take precedence over the emotional experience of the audience, resulting in slick, beautiful imagery lacking a sense of purpose and emotional depth. Digital effects only recently have begun to simulate organic forms like animals and water instead of just mechanical things like robots and spaceships. Many filmmakers and studios tend to showcase the latest advances in digital effects in their films, rather than care about emotional involvement. In the end, the emotional connection made with the audience—with or without special effects—determines much of a film's success and popularity, and emotional realism will always be a challenge for cast and crew, whether a technical one or otherwise.

Notes

1 Paula Parisi, *Titanic and the Making of James Cameron* (New York, 1998). On the initial three rounds of cuts, see p. 131; on the cutting of digital effects, see p. 93; on the over thirty scenes or parts of scenes cut from the script, see p. 2.

2 Parisi, *Titanic and the Making of James Cameron*, p. 8.

3 Parisi, *Titanic and the Making of James Cameron*, p. 68.

4 Parisi, *Titanic and the Making of James Cameron*, p. 68.

5 Parisi, *Titanic and the Making of James Cameron*, p. 128.

6 Parisi, *Titanic and the Making of James Cameron*, p. 127.

7 Parisi, *Titanic and the Making of James Cameron*, pp. 190–1.

8 Steven A. Simak, 'Masters of Illusion' in *Digital Magic*, February 1998, p. 26.

9 Ed W. Marsh, *James Cameron's Titanic*, foreword by James Cameron, photographs by Douglas Kirkland (New York, 1997), p. 168.

10 Parisi, *Titanic and the Making of James Cameron*, p. 162.

11 Simak, 'Masters of Illusion', p. 28.

12 Parisi *Titanic and the Making of James Cameron*, pp. 144–5.

13 Quoted in Simak, 'Masters of Illusion', p. 31.

14 Simak, 'Masters of Illusion', pp. 27–8.

CHAPTER TWENTY

Expanded Narrative Space: *Titanic* and CGI Technology

AYLISH WOOD

THE STORY of the sinking of R.M.S. Titanic has become a part of the cultural history of the 20th century, pieced together in scientific, historical and fictional narratives, sometimes all at once. One of the strands of this story has explored both the extraordinary nature of the ship, its size and speed and sumptuous accommodations (at least for first class), and also the misplaced trust in its technological supremacy as a ship which could not sink. *Titanic* (1997), written and directed by James Cameron, picks up the story of this strand of the great icon of early twentieth century maritime engineering, and re-threads it with the romance of the two fictional characters Rose and Jack.

Several years after the release of the film, it may seem obvious to say that *Titanic* is as much about the romance of the ship, as it is about the romance of the central characters Rose and Jack. But the very obviousness of this statement requires more explanation. What is it about *Titanic* that enables viewers, or at least some of us, to see the ship as more than the vehicle for the tragedies of the human individuals who died or survived the events of the night of 14 April 1912? Stephen Keane addresses this point in his discussion of *Titanic*:

[I]t could be argued . . . that the main 'character'—or at least element—introduced and developed through the film's overall production values is the ship itself. This is to say that in the first two hours of the film we are given a lot more insight into the workings and majesty of the object of the disaster than any other plane, ship, or building before . . . From launch to disaster we are on a journey with the ship itself, by turns a lavish set and a convincing, hazy computer-generated illusion carried along by the perceived context of movement.[1]

But how exactly is this insight achieved? To answer this question, in addition to looking at the design and model work, I focus on the digital effects. The argument I present here is that the CGI technology used in making *Titanic* expands the narrative space available to the filmmakers. In part, this expansion occurs from the intermingling of images of human story and the technological story. As is usual in the construction of a narrative in a popular film, events lead from one to another, and action frequently develops through parallel editing of different parts of the plot, allowing them to be interwoven with each other. In *Titanic* this does not only occur around the characters (Rose and Jack, Jack and Fabrizio, Rose and Cal, Cal and Spicer Lovejoy, Bruce Ismay and Captain Smith, and so forth), but also between characters and technology. The parallel editing not only allows different human stories to emerge, but also that of R.M.S. Titanic. Parallelism is, of course, nothing new, but the distinctiveness of its use in *Titanic* lies in how the visual spaces of the parallel narratives finally converge on-screen. If space is taken to be the visual and aural dimensions inhabited by characters and objects used in the plotting of a story, conventionally its composition is understood to function in the telling of a single dimension of a narrative. In *Titanic* there are moments when the parallel stories of technology and human co-exist on the screen, especially in the final section where the images of human and technological destruction come together in an expanded narrative space.

One effect of *Titanic*'s structure of interwoven parallel narratives is that the story arises across a range of elements. My approach to *Titanic* is to think about the relationship between different narrative elements and how they can be organised. Theorists in fields as diverse as history, science studies and philosophy, have discussed the ways in which narratives that appear to operate through identifiable linearities, rely instead on the organisation of elements contingent on a network of influences, some of which seem to bear little obvious linkage to each other.[2] I want to take up a particular version of this kind of perspective articulated by Andrew Gibson.[3] Although he is not especially interested in popular texts, Gibson's ideas are a useful starting point in thinking about *Titanic*. He conceives of narrative as expanding outwards in various directions, directions that are not under the control of the resolution. Events or elements remain important, but their relationship to the resolution is loosened, they can have narratives of their own, opening up alternative narrative spaces within the text. As Gibson says: 'Narrative space is now plastic and manipulable. It has become heterogeneous, ambiguous, pluralised'.[4] Another way of articulating this position is that a narrative consists of sets of elements, and that their alignments need not take us towards the resolution, they can take us into other spaces.

In this reading of *Titanic*, I make use of the idea that narratives exist as a construction generated through linking sets of elements, but alter Gibson's trajectory. He is interested in moving away from narratives tied into a resolution. I want to argue that while the narrative of *Titanic* is constituted by a series of heterogeneous elements, they nevertheless cohere around a central core that controls the overall organisation of the meanings of these elements. However, this central core, though it may reduce the apparent ambiguity of meanings, does not provide a singular organisation since *Titanic* is a text of multiple narratives. There can be no doubt that *Titanic* does have a linear narrative—the ship does sail forth, hit an iceberg and sink; Rose's narrative of her romance with Jack also follows through in a sequence of events. But the elements that cohere around each other as they organise into linear narrative, or I should say narratives, cannot *all* be put into the same cause and effect sequence.

Take for instance, the narrative around the technology of the ship. Its constitutive elements emerge across a whole network of influences, some of which seem to bear little direct relationship to each other, but which nonetheless are important in the articulation of the overall story. Although many relevant elements arise from outside of the textual operations of *Titanic*—the diverse mythologies of R.M.S. Titanic, and also those surrounding the making of the film—I focus here on the operations inside the text. These include the mediating commentaries of the characters, both the contemporary and historical versions, the conventional *mise-en-scène* of the text and the digital sequences, all of which constitute a network of influences out of which the narrative on technology emerges.[5]

Beginning with the beginning, the opening of *Titanic* has unusual credits. To an instrumental version of the film's ballad, there are sepia-toned images of R.M.S. Titanic and crowds of waving people, which dissolve into deep blue images of sea. Apart from those of the production companies, only the name Titanic appears, and it is spread fully across the width of the ratio, white letters against ocean blue. In the absence of anything else, the ship is the star.[6] William MacQuitty, the producer of *A Night to Remember* (1958) commented in the context of a discussion about the difficulty of getting audiences in the USA to come to a film without a recognisable star, that 'the ship was the star'.[7] The opening sequence of *Titanic* suggests a willingness of the 1990s filmmakers to also take this position. Not only is the recreation of the ship's detail, like that of *A Night to Remember*, fulsome, but as I will argue below, it is expanded by virtue of the technological innovations available in the late 1990s.

The emphasis on technology is also more generally apparent in the opening segment of *Titanic* in that it invests heavily in a technological display. There are shots of the deep dive with robot cameras; Bodine's 'forensic' explanation and computer generated visualisation of the R.M.S. Titanic striking the iceberg and sinking; and cinematic technology is used to morph from the underwater wreck to the 1912 vessel beginning its maiden voyage at Southampton. This focus gives way to the mediating view of Rose, the single character whose experience of the events makes her the link between past and present, when she starts her reminiscences with details about the smell of paint, unused china and sheets. Her connection back to the 'ship of dreams' is strengthened in the transformation of the encrusted door panels of the wreckage back to the pristine state in which she originally encountered them, a transformation motivated as a flash of memory. While Rose's narrative serves to introduce the romance, there remain numerous occasions in the pre-iceberg section where the historical characters on the voyage discuss the ship as 'the largest moving object ever made by the hand of men in all of history'. Thomas Andrews, the ship's designer, speaks of how Bruce Ismay, the White Star Line owner, had dreamt of a vessel so great it was unsurpassable. The special-ness of R.M.S. Titanic is further re-iterated in the evocation of its splendour, something that is both spoken about and made visible in the *mise-en-scène* of the first class apartments. The luxuriousness of the decor, the apparently accurate reconstructions of the central staircase, the lounges and corridors, the details of the panelling, the chandeliers, the table-ware and of course the costumes of the characters, make *Titanic* a kind of 'heri-tech' film. The technological object is reconstructed in a nostalgic glow that remains undiminished by the jigs and reels of the multi-ethnic steerage passengers not allowed in those spaces until the final moments of the disaster, or the sweat of the men shovelling coal into the vast boilers that powered the ship.

These various elements dispersed across a range of scenes organise into the different narrative spaces where the story of Rose and Jack's romance begins, or where class snobberies are played out, as much as they also begin to tell the story about the technology of the ship. But these elements merely set the scene, for while the size of R.M.S. Titanic can be described by the various characters, the ship can only be fully shown through the use of digital imaging to create a reconstruction eliciting a viewer's appraisal of the technology. The first such image of the ship is at Southampton, using digital technology to show the height and length of the vessel against the mass of people on the dock; it also demonstrates the possibilities of digital technology. Although the technology is not new, Cameron already having vied for 'King of the Morph' status with *The Abyss* (1989) and *Terminator 2: Judgement Day* (1992), the morph from old to new provides a seamless shift between chronological periods, so that Titanic is literally brought back to life before our very eyes.

The star status continues as R.M.S. Titanic has romantic sunset shots all to itself: anchored off Cherbourg against a pink-blue sky, and steaming across the Atlantic, efficient engines leaving a trail of black smoke. In an ebullient sequence the special-ness of the ship, and the special-ness of the digital effects come together in a double articulation of technological prowess. Following the Southampton sequences, which have already shown off the height and length of the ship from the perspective of the quays, this one shows off its speed and power. Beginning with Captain Smith's order to go to full speed, there follows a series of images into and around the boiler room, the pistons driving the engines, the propeller speeding up, the score overlain with the sounds of each element as it increases in power. But this series of images is not simply about the mechanistic inner workings of the vessel since it initiates a moment where parallel narratives briefly come together. The images of the ship (and boiler room crew) at work are intercut with Jack and Fabrizio's celebration of their journey towards America. As they stand on the bow of the ship, their excite-ment about the future captured in their enthusiasm for the leaping dolphins and the sensation of standing into the wind, this sequence also conveys some-thing of the hope for the future of the ship as a piece of awesome technology. This enthusiasm carries over into the display of the digital images themselves, as the modern technology which enabled the old technology to re-appear is celebrated in a series of movements around the bow of the ship and onto the Bridge. As Jack, Fabrizio and the ship steam off to their future, they share the same structure of feeling. A similar effect is repeated in the more romantic echo of this bow sequence, in the scene where Rose goes to Jack. This bow scene is played out against the sunset, the wind and waves just audible above the Irish folkish theme of the score. And as Rose says she is flying, there is a rapid swooping movement across the bow of the ship, finally coming around which capture both the couple and the ship in the glow of the sunset as it ploughs through the ocean.

In addition to being the moment where two narratives converge, the ship-based effects of this sequence also demonstrate how digital work can expand the possibilities for a filmmaker, primarily through its ability to extend the time of the image of the ship on-screen. This extended time becomes more obvious by looking at the different screen-time spent on the detail of the R.M.S. Titanic in *A Night to Remember* and *Titanic*. The models and optical effects used in *A Night to Remember* are good examples of special effects work from the late fifties, but a comparison with those of *Titanic* indicates how digi-tal technology enables filmmakers to introduce different elements. In both films the effects supply an authentic air to the events, and in the same way as the models, sets and optical effects of the earlier film, the digital rendering of the vast ship creates the place for the various narrative events that will unfold. Both *A Night to Remember* and *Titanic* include various images of R.M.S. Titanic steaming across the Atlantic, and each has one which serves to demonstrate something of the proportion of the vessel at sea. In *A Night to Remember* there is a shot of the ship at night. Taken from a low angle, the image tracks across a scale model. The lit rows of portholes look like swathes of cabins running the length of the ship, whilst the illumination of the upper decks, bright white picked out above the black body of the lower decks creates the sense of a huge height. While this shot stands out as being far longer than any others of the ship in motion (approximately 15 seconds compared to 2–4 seconds), and gives an impression of the vast size of the vessel, it still only allows a half-view of the ship's length. The equivalent shot in *Titanic* is twice as long (around 35 sec-onds), and its digital construction allows not only for a full view of the ship, but also for a swooping movement covering its length. The shot begins at the bows and moves back in a diagonal, crossing the centre line above one of the four funnels, finally coming to rest behind the ship as it then rapidly moves away into the distance. This image is held as the dialogue from the next shot begins, allowing the wake to extend towards the increasingly small R.M.S. Titanic. David Lubin has written that the effects in *Titanic* serve the role of illusionism: 'Cinematic special effects . . . [such as] shots of the Titanic as it cuts through the sea or sinks into it, are meant to re-create reality but to do so with such an extravagance of detail as to stun the viewer with the excellence of the simulacrum'.[8] My argument is that the extravagant detail not only generates an impact through authenticity, but also in the sense of recreating the R.M.S. Titanic as an object in its own right. The digital shot, with its movement and scale, extends the possibilities of the model shot, allowing the viewer to see not only the detail of ship more closely, but to be also given the impression of it speeding away. As the image stays longer on the screen, it becomes more than the place where the actions will occur, and expands into another dimension in the story, one that places a particular emphasis on the story of the technological giant.

In the pre-iceberg section, *Titanic* is structured around a series of interconnecting elements that organise into network through which the narrative of the ship's technology emerges. These elements, which bear little apparent causal or linear relationship to each, link together to expand the narrative beyond the stories of Jack and Rose, the snobberies and the social injustices which are alluded to before the iceberg hits. Digital imaging takes this expansion further by providing extended images of the R.M.S. Titanic which visually secure the narrative elements around technology. In addition, through the combination of digital effects and live-action, parallel narrative elements can converge in the same visual space, allowing them to share in the same structure of feeling; pre-iceberg, this feeling is one of celebration.

The presence of interconnecting elements continues post-collision, when the feeling of celebration comes to an abrupt end once the iceberg is sighted from the crow's nest. And each of the different elements is reconfigured through the subsequent developments of the plot: dreams are shattered, lives ended, pride turns to cowardice, and so on. When seen from a perspective of R.M.S. Titanic as the height of technological grandeur, the post-iceberg imagery retrospectively weights the celebratory sequence towards being a eulogy for the ship. But this eulogy is unusual in that it is followed by a demonstration of its object's destruction, one that is paralleled by the deaths of many of the passengers who had been a part of the voyage. The turning point from celebration to tragedy begins in the moments between the sighting of the iceberg and before the ship hits the iceberg. This is captured by the progression of images depicting the desperation of the crew (the officers, the helmsman, the entire engine room crew) as they try to make the vast ship turn away from the iceberg. Coming after the celebration of the ship (and so soon after the consummation of the lovers' affair), when it became a part of the hope for the future, this sequence feels as though it holds the narrative still, paused on the edge of the tragedy to come. Part of this sensation of holding still before the chaos is contingent on what we as viewers have already accumulated across the network of elements from both inside and outside of *Titanic*. We know from Bodine's early demonstration to the elderly Rose exactly what is about to happen, how the ship will hit the iceberg and how it will sink. We also know the life-story of the ship, how it went from a dream of supremacy to the drawing board, gradually taking shape in Belfast with flaws in the bulkhead design and a rudder too small to turn the giant vessel with any speed. We know too the configuration of elements on the night of the disaster—the stillness of the ocean, the ice warnings, the mistaken belief in Titanic's unsinkablity, the speed of the ship, and the overwhelming desire to prove the Titanic in action rather than in words. In the midst of all these different influences, the efforts of the crew form the first action sequence of *Titanic*. Following 'iceberg dead ahead', the beat of the music steps up, the camera whips across the image as everything possible is done to prevent the collision. There are images of frenetic activity: running men, matched rotations of the helm, valve controllers and propellers, the thuds of a serial closure of dampers, all intercut with the slowing mechanism of the pistons. But this action sequence is far from the kind that unleashes a series of events in which our heroes will ultimately transcend the obstacles before them. In that brief instant when everything stills, when the pistons and propellers are caught in the momentary inertia of a perfect balance between forward and backward motion, there is nothing hopeful. For this is an action sequence whose outcome we already know, its point is that despite all the actions taken, the ship would never turn in time—the rudder is too small and no matter how fast those reversing engines kick in, the disaster is set in motion.

For the next 80 minutes or so of the film R.M.S. Titanic's end is played out. As Andrews says in response to Ismay's assertion that the ship cannot sink: 'Titanic will founder . . . it is a mathematical certainty'. This certainty is brought to its closure in an expanded narrative space, as the digital imaging brings together the narrative elements about human loss with the encroaching devastation of the vessel. Stephen Keane comments 'In its combination of action, peril and attempts at survival, the climax of *Titanic* is certainly one of the most sustained of all disaster sequences'.[9] This extended disaster sequence is constructed around set-based action sequences and special effects work. People flee their compartments with the water quietly following; they panic trying to break through the barriers holding them back, while more forceful water destroys everything that had been so carefully put in place for us—the dining rooms, the staterooms, the Captain and his Bridge. In the final moments, where each shriek and cry is accompanied by the shudder and groan of the ship, and a precipitous fall accentuates the extreme angles of the ship in water, the human tragedy and the technological tragedy are inseparable.

The combination of model shots, compositing, and digital effects maintain the shared space of the above-deck narrative elements. Similar in many ways to *A Night to Remember* in using tilting sets and a mass of struggling bodies to convey the attempts of people to survive, the filmmakers of *Titanic* also have available to them modern digital technology. The later digital images are distinct from the earlier ones that lingered on the size and speed of R.M.S. Titanic. In the final sequences, full of destruction and desperation, the fully digital images of the vessel are interspersed with digitally assisted shots of model and action-based effects. Although the intercutting of these sequences gives them less single shot screen-time, it extends their presence as they co-exist with reaction shots, and counter shots from different angles that include human figures. This is true of both the moment when the vessel splits and when the aft sinks. The rupturing vessel is directly shown digitally and also through reaction shots of human figures as they fall through the widening gap. Similarly, the overhead shots of the aft falling back and bouncing on the surface of the ocean is interwoven with the reaction of Rose, Jack and other passengers. The importance of movement in sustaining the effectiveness of the digital imagery is evident in the 'bobbing aft' sequence as water runs from the propeller down the length of the section, and the trajectory of tumbling bodies matching the vertical angles.

Of the final sequences of the aft slipping down into the water, Peter Krämer comments that 'the protagonists are placed not so much as participants in the action, but as spectators, much like the film's viewers in the movie theatre'.[10] This view, however, depends on the protagonists existing in a separate space from that of the sinking vessel. And while Rose and Jack are indeed unable to act at this moment, they are not apart from the action since they exist within the same narrative space, and are going down with the ship. The shared experience of human figures and technology can be seen in the intercutting between Rose and Jack's point of view of the digitally created mass of struggling bodies and rushing water, with profile and a high angle images of the final descent of the vessel into the water. The narrative space only becomes separate when the two kick up to the surface, leaving Titanic to recede into the gloom of the deep water.

It is only then that *Titanic* turns fully to the human stories, firstly with the frozen deaths of the people left in the water, and then in the return to Rose's story as she throws the Heart of the Ocean into the Atlantic. Even though Rose's story has been an explicit device throughout the film, a counterpoint to Bodine's 'forensic' description of the sinking of R.M.S. Titanic, the impact of *Titanic* resides not simply in Rose's story, but in the whole range of elements from which the narrative is constructed. As well as the histories and myths that surround R.M.S. Titanic, this in part relies on the ways in which the digital effects introduce parallel and expanded spaces, recreating the technology of the ship as a special object.

Notes

1 Stephen Keane, *Disaster Movies: The Cinema of Catastrophe* (London, 2001), p. 117.

2 This approach, informed by contingencies and networks, is evident in the writings of Hayden White on history, John Law's heterogeneous elements in technological systems, and Deleuze and Guattari's ideas about assemblages and territorialisations. See John Law, 'Technology and Heterogeneous Engineering: The Case of Portuguese Expansion' in W. E. Bijker, T. P. Hughes and T. Pinch (eds.), *The Social Construction of Technological Systems: New Directions in the Sociology and History of Technology* (Cambridge, Mass, 1987); Hayden White, *The Content of Form: Narrative Discourse and Historical Representation* (Baltimore, 1987) and Gilles Deleuze and Felix Guattari *A Thousand Plateaus: Capitalism and Schizophrenia* (London, 1987).

3 Andrew Gibson, *Towards a postmodern theory of narrative* (Edinburgh, 1996).

4 Gibson, *Towards a postmodern theory of narrative*, p. 12.

5 Geoff King comments that *Titanic* treats R.M.S. Titanic as a technological wonder. See Geoff King, *Spectacular Narratives: Hollywood in the Age of the Blockbuster* (London, 2000).

6 This is not to say that the stars of the film did not matter as the publicity around Leonardo DiCaprio and Kate Winslett clearly indicates otherwise. Given this, it is perhaps even more unusual that their names are absent from the opening credits.

7 William MacQuitty discussing his role as producer in *The Making of A Night to Remember*, a documentary included on the 1998 Carlton Home Entertainment DVD release of *A Night to Remember*.

8 David M. Lubin, *Titanic* (London, 1999), p. 33.

9 Keane, *Disaster Movies*, p. 118.

10 Peter Krämer, 'Women First: Titanic, Action-Adventure Films, and Hollywood's Female Audience,' in Kevin S. Sandler and Gaylyn Studlar (eds.), *Titanic: Anatomy of a Blockbuster* (New Brunswick, New Jersey, London, 1999), p. 115.

Index of Titles

Titles, unless otherwise stated, are film titles

Index of Names and Subjects